Preventing Alcohol Problems

Philip Tether and David Robinson

Preventing Alcohol Problems

A Guide to Local Action

A Richm
Halifax
March 1987

Tavistock Publications

First published in 1986 by
Tavistock Publications Ltd
11 New Fetter Lane, London EC4P 4EE

This publication is based on research funded by the Department of Health and Social
Security. However, the views expressed are those of the authors and not necessarily those
of the DHSS.

Typeset by AKM Associates (UK) Ltd, Southall, London
Printed in Great Britain by
Richard Clay (The Chaucer Press) Ltd,
Bungay, Suffolk

British Library Cataloguing in Publication Data

Tether, Philip
    Preventing alcohol problems: a guide to local action.
    1. Alcoholism—Great Britain—Prevention
    I. Title   II. Robinson, David, *1941–* 362. 2′9286   HB 5446

    ISBN 0-422-60510-7
    ISBN 0-422-60520-4 Pbk

Contents

Acknowledgements

We gratefully acknowledge:

- the assistance of Maggie Wicks who worked on the DHSS-funded project which led to the report upon which this guide is based.
- the help and encouragement from our colleagues in the University of Hull; Rob Baggott, Tony Gurevitch, Larry Harrison, Adrian James, Yvonne Keeley Robinson, Stephen Marshall, Vivienne Parker, Barry Pashley, Heather Roughton, and Vicki Silver.
- the support of the DHSS Addictions and Homelessness Research Liaison Group, in particular Jim Orford, the associated client team, especially the late Chris Ralph and Ron Wawman, and the Office of the Chief Scientist, in particular Phoebe Hall, Vince Keddie and Anne Kauder. However, the views expressed are those of the authors and are not necessarily those of the DHSS.
- and the day-to-day expertise of Tricia Daly, Karen Edwards, and Val Hurst which is so inadequately summed up in the phrase secretarial asssistance.

In addition we record our grateful thanks to the very many other people who so generously helped us by providing information and materials, replying to our 'trawling' letters, being willing to be interviewed, commenting on our ideas and draft report and, most important of all, taking seriously our concern with the question of how to *prevent alcohol problems at the local level*.

Philip Tether and David Robinson
University of Hull
October 1985

Preface

'It is . . . essential that there should be as wide an understanding as possible of what are the facts and what are the possibilities for improvement.' (*Drinking Sensibly*, HMSO 1981: 9)

Over the past twenty years alcohol consumption in Britain has doubled and every indicator of alcohol-related harm has shown a substantial increase. There has also been an increase in professional and public awareness of alcohol problems and of the need to prevent them. This guide is concerned with the prevention of alcohol problems *at the local level*.

The guide is divided into ten chapters. Chapters 1 and 2 are general, while the remaining eight each examine prevention possibilities in relation to a specific area of local activity. Any organization or group ✓ which is identified as having a prevention role is encouraged to promote and develop the prevention options which are described and to establish contacts with others in the same subject area to devise common prevention activities.

Strictly speaking, this guide applies only to England and Wales. It was sponsored by the DHSS which does not have any responsibilities for Scotland and Northern Ireland. But although some of the legal and organizational details contained in the guide may not apply exactly in Scotland and Northern Ireland, we believe that all those who have some role to play in relation to prevention of alcohol problems will find in the guide some useful information and ideas.

The guide is a long document, because it is a detailed document. For this we make no apology. For if it is to be more than just one more report which merely exhorts, it must provide some concrete guides to ✓

action – and that requires details of organizations, materials, resources, and activities.

However, the guide is not a definitive account of every organization in every locality, their activities and their prevention potential. The guide is, we hope, a living document. In any locality the chapters need to be translated into local terms because, of course, no two localities are exactly the same. A local Council on Alcoholism in one locality is an Alcohol Counselling Service in another and a Problem Drinkers' Advice Centre in a third. Some localities have an alcohol treatment unit or a community alcohol team, while others have neither. At the end of each chapter are blank pages for adding further useful information; addresses, details of events, extracts from materials, examples of good practice, and so on.

Given limitless time, money, and personnel, most of us could propose and mount exciting and far-reaching plans for preventing or responding to alcohol problems. The emphasis of this guide, however, is on the small scale, the practicable, the inexpensive, and the immediately possible. Nothing that is proposed requires massive government expenditure, changes in the law, re-jigging of the economy or complicated organizational restructuring. And when prevention possibilities are inexpensive in terms of time, effort, and money is there any excuse for doing nothing?

Preventing Alcohol Problems

CHAPTER 1

Preventing alcohol problems: an introduction to the guide

1

Useful national organizations
Alcohol Concern; Action on Alcohol Abuse; Institute of Alcohol Studies; Health Education Council

Further reading 20

CHAPTER 1

Preventing alcohol problems: an introduction to the guide

'To control growth in alcohol misuse and in the harm it causes
requires preventive action in which central government, local
government, the health professions and institutions, the business
sector and trade unions, voluntary bodies, and the people of the
United Kindom as individuals can all recognize and play their
separate parts.' (*Drinking Sensibly*, HMSO 1981: 65)

Each chapter in this guide examines a particular area of local activity
and identifies a related set of local prevention resources. Readers with
specific tasks or responsibilities may find some helpful suggestions in
one particular chapter. But, we hope, most readers will find something
of interest and value in every chapter.

Prevention

This guide has been produced against a background of changing ideas
and activities. In this section some of the key features of this
background are briefly set out: wider recognition of the alcohol problem
and increasing emphasis on prevention; competing models of prevention and current prevention debates; and the concentration on national,
as opposed to local, prevention.

Alcohol, alcohol problems, and the need for prevention

Since 1950 there has been an increase of approximately 50 per cent in

3

world-wide alcohol consumption. The three main features of this increase are:

- The largest increase has been in the previously lowest consumption countries;
- There has been a decrease in the difference between countries' general drinking patterns – in predominantly beer-drinking countries there has been a rapid increase in wine and spirit consumption, while in predominantly wine-drinking countries the biggest increase has been in spirits and beer;
- Finally, within countries, the biggest increase has been in those sections of the population who were previously the lowest consumers – women and young people.

These processes within the world-wide alcohol market have been mirrored in the UK market where, since 1950, overall alcohol consumption has doubled; accounted for by a 60 per cent increase in beer consumption, a 350 per cent increase in spirits, and a 600 per cent increase in the consumption of wine.

The well-recognized benefits of drinking alcohol in moderate amounts are that it stimulates the digestive juices, loosens the tongue a little and encourages a sense of general well-being. These are all significant benefits, particularly in today's world with its fast and often indigestible foods, its demands on us to be socially competent in a wide range of situations and fleeting relationships, and its stresses and strains which increase our need to be able to relax. So we should not be surprised that the majority of people in most countries like to have a drink, whether it is a glass of beer, or wine, or distilled spirit.

If everyone drank moderately then alcohol would cease to be one of the chief causes of contemporary health and social problems. Clearly, not everyone does drink moderately. In fact, alcohol consumption above a moderate level has been found to be a significant contributory factor in almost every situation in which harm is done by people to themselves or to each other, whether this is in relation to physical and mental health, family and social relationships, work, or the law.

Given the ubiquity of alcohol and the contribution of alcohol to so many contemporary health and social problems it has become widely recognized that there is no such thing as 'the alcohol problem'. There are many alcohol problems and there are many problems in which alcohol consumption is a component. This guide is based on the assumption that in every major area of contemporary life there are people getting into difficulties to a greater or lesser extent because of their alcohol consumption. It follows from this that there is in every area of contemporary life a *potential for prevention*. This guide is about identifying those opportunities for prevention *at the local level*.

Models of prevention and prevention 'debates'

Partly as a result of the many and varied calls for prevention from government departments, expert committees, involved professions and concerned individuals there is now a measure of agreement that 'something must be done'. Unfortunately it is not quite so easy to find ✓ agreement on what is the best preventive approach, or even what the focus of prevention should be.

Three levels of prevention Much prevention literature, irrespective of the particular problem to be prevented, attempts to structure the discussion by making distinctions between primary, secondary, and tertiary prevention. When we began working on this guide we attempted to structure our discussion of local resources and organizations according to whether they were concerned with preventing alcohol problems from starting – primary prevention; spotting the problem early and preventing it from developing – secondary prevention; or responding to the problem once it has developed and preventing the further consequences of it – tertiary prevention.

This way of dividing up the prevention world is very tidy in the literature. Unfortunately, the real world is rather more complex. To begin with, few workers in organizations which have a part to play in a local prevention strategy are aware of the three-level prevention model. As a result it does not inform their work, their view of their place in relation to alcohol problems, or their relationship with other organizations. But more important is the fact that most organizations have the potential to respond at all three prevention levels and, quite often, they do. The distinction then, between primary, secondary, and tertiary prevention is unhelpful.

Three foci of prevention Another possible way of categorizing the local prevention field relates to three common conceptions of the 'real' nature of the problem. For some it is problem drinkers who are the main focus of attention. For others the major emphasis is on contemporary society, its drinking patterns and attitudes. For yet others, the concern is with alcohol itself. Each of these concerns leads to a different prevention emphasis.

Those who see problem drinkers as the real problem emphasize the need to prevent people who are particularly at 'at risk' from developing their condition. The preventive aim is to devise ways of getting people to recognize the early signs of alcohol problems in themselves and in others and to educate them to know what action to take and where to go for help and support.

Those who see the root of the alcohol problem in the way that alcohol is used in our society focus their attention on unhealthy drinking practices and attitudes. The notion of unhealthy drinking covers such things as drinking for effect, to be tough, to solve problems, or to make bearable otherwise difficult relationships or situations. Unhealthy drinking attitudes include the belief that all social occasions must be drinking occasions, that intoxication is something to be tolerated or even encouraged, or that drunkenness is an excuse for otherwise inexcusable behaviour. The preventive aim is to increase knowledge of alcohol and its effects and through positive health education to encourage moderate drinking and responsible hosting.

Those who focus on alcohol itself draw attention to the links between levels of overall consumption and the rates of alcohol problems of various kinds. As *Drinking Sensibly* puts it:

> 'The recent sharp *increase* in misuse as measured by a variety of indicators, seems clearly to be linked with the equally marked rise in overall consumption of alcohol that has occurred in the United Kingdom in recent years and the changes in people's drinking habits which underlie it.' (HMSO 1981: 64)

The preventive aim is to regulate, through taxation, licensing, and other controls, the availability of alcohol in the community since, runs the argument, the less alcohol there is the less alcohol problems there will be.

As with the three-level model of prevention, the categorization of preventive approaches based on these views on the central nature of the alcohol problem – problem drinkers, drinking habits, and the alcohol itself – is fine in the literature but unhelpful in real life. Although one particular perspective may predominate, the activities of most organizations and groups of workers are informed by elements from each perspective. For instance, liquor licensing falls squarely within the third perspective in that it is clearly concerned with controlling the availability of alcohol. However, in addition, the licensing process itself (see chapter 5) provides opportunities for promoting education about alcohol, for shaping the drinking environment and discouraging immoderate drinking, and for fostering the development of alcohol and work policies for a particular, high-risk occupational group – the licensed trade.

So although various models and categories of prevention are helpful for clarifying thought, the guide is not structured to reflect them.

The endless list of debates Just as there are various models and categories so there are several important contemporary prevention debates. Some are concerned with alcohol prevention policy in general, others with specific aspects of it. It is almost impossible to consider any alcohol issue without running up against at least one of them. For example:

- 'Will a relaxation of liquor licensing controls lead to an increase in consumption or to the development of more moderate drinking patterns?'
- 'Does an increase in alcohol advertising and promotion increase consumption?'
- 'In a democratic society how far can the majority be controlled in order to protect the minority from itself?'
- 'Would the introduction of random breath-tests be a long-overdue public health and safety measure or an intolerable infringement of personal freedom?'
- 'Can health education ever really compete with the promoters of alcohol for the attention of the general public – and if not, is health education anything more than a sop to our conscience?'

The list of debates and unsolved issues is endless. And a great deal of attention and research time is focused on them. This guide does not, however, review this literature, although the 'Further reading' at the end of each chapter will indicate where much of it can be found. Nor does the guide come down on one side or the other of most of these debates. In particular chapters we indicate briefly the nature of the debate and then identify the 'prevention options' which it generates.

The local perspective

Many recent reports have laid out the extent of the alcohol problem, exhorted governments to 'do something' and stressed that prevention is everybody's business (see 'Further reading'). The types of prevention activities that are called for, however, tend to reflect a view of 'everybody' as being on the receiving end of *national* action: being 'done to' rather than 'doing'. Much play is made of the need for major national initiatives, such as stricter controls over – or the banning of – drink advertising; massive expenditure on health education; tax changes to prevent alcohol getting any cheaper than it is now; reform of the drink-driving laws; and so on.

National prevention policies are certainly essential. But concentration on action at the national level to the exclusion of anything else is mistaken. It implies, unhelpfully, that any worthwhile response to some set of contemporary health and social problems is primarily a matter for central government. This diverts attention from the wealth of *local prevention resources* which are so often unrecognized and, therefore, untapped.

No purely local 'prevention strategy' will, of course, be able to change such things as liquor licensing law, retailing law, or the Chancellor of the Exchequer's taxation policy. Nevertheless, a wide range of sensible and effective things can be done at the local level without the backing of legislation, massive funding, or direct central government involvement.

Scope for action at the local level

> 'The size and nature of the problem of alcohol misuse is such that the health and social services available can cope with only part of it.'
> (*Drinking Sensibly*, HMSO 1981: 31)

Given the extent of alcohol, drinking, and associated problems, prevention really is everybody's business. As a result, every local prevention resource must be brought into play. But what are these resources? And what is local? This section discusses these two issues, calls for the identification and mobilization of all local resources and, finally, stresses the importance of every locality being in a position to monitor alcohol problems, prevention, and progress.

Local resources and good practices

What are resources? Clearly, they include all the obvious services and obvious groups of people – counselling agencies, community health and social workers, treatment teams, day centres, and health education units. But in addition to these 'obvious' services, local resources include a very wide range of less obvious institutions, groups, policies, organizations, regulations, activities, and opportunities. If recognized and mobilized, they could contribute to an overall local prevention strategy in relation to a vast range of local alcohol-related issues and situations.

These 'issues and situations' include, for example: occupational safety; magistrates' training; driving licences and disabilities; home and water safety; environmental health; insurance; domestic accidents; advertising and codes of practice; alcohol and sports sponsorship; professional education and in-service training; alcohol and work policies; local media and the presentation of alcohol; drink-driving and pedestrian drunkenness; school health education; drink trade activities; liquor licensing; road safety and driving education; consumers' rights; etc. The list is extensive. This guide is concerned with making suggestions about action which can be taken in relation to all these issues and situations and more besides.

What is local?   All resources of whatever kind will have associated with them some definition of 'local'. These will not be coterminous. The police department's boundaries will be different from the district health authority's boundaries and both will be different from the local boundaries of the Institute of Environmental Health Officers, the Institute of Personnel Management, and the local BBC radio station.

In each chapter specific organizations will be identified. The precise definition of 'local' in relation to these organizations will be a matter for discovery in each locality. Any group or organization which wants to take an overall rather than a partial or sectoral view of the local prevention of alcohol problems may well decide that the most useful definition of local is the boundary agreed for purposes of joint funding between the district health authority and the local authority social services department. These 'localities' are large enough and have enough structural identity to support detailed local action.

Good practices This guide seeks to raise awareness of alcohol problems and to stimulate a re-evaluation of everyday work among a wide range of organizations and groups at the local level. It seeks to overcome the belief that there is little that can be done locally to prevent alcohol problems. The guide is not, however, just a series of exhortations. Each chapter is designed to present clear information about the particular area of activity under discussion and to present, as illustration, some instances of good practice.

The examples of 'good practice' that are presented have been collected in a variety of ways from a variety of organizations in various parts of the country. They have been added to by our own suggestions about how everyday practice can be improved. The ideas presented in this guide are not intended to be ideal models. They are presented to demonstrate a range of possible prevention activities and to stimulate debate on whether they could be useful in any specific locality and how they could be adapted to meet specific local priorities, local circumstances, or local problems.

Monitoring problems, prevention, and progress

Any local prevention activity should be carefully monitored. However, before any monitoring can be done the organizations and groups of workers mentioned in this guide will need to be in a position to assess the scale and nature of the alcohol problems which they face or the alcohol-related activities that they are engaged in.

Every locality will be able to draw on some official statistics relating to the size and impact of alcohol problems. There will be figures for pedestrian drunkenness offences, drink-driving offences, offences against liquor licensing regulations, and admissions with a primary or secondary diagnosis of alcoholism or alcoholic psychosis to mental hospitals, mental treatment units, and other services, and deaths from cirrhosis of the liver. Few other facts and figures will be available.

The great majority of those resources which are identified in this guide will have no record whatsoever of the alcohol component of their work. Record forms, questionnaires, case-notes, interview forms, or admission sheets which ask specific questions about drinking and associated problems will be hard to find. Ensuring that organizational record systems routinely note alcohol-related information is a high priority, therefore, for every locality (see chapter 8).

Once some idea is gained of the scale and nature of the overall local alcohol problem based on routine recording systems, then the question arises of how to monitor prevention activities. Monitoring questions can be asked in relation to individuals. For example, are patients taking advantage of the leaflets and notices which are available in general practitioners' waiting rooms? Are those members of the work force who come forward under a company's alcohol and work policy profiting from the help that is being arranged for them and are they then resuming their previous work standards? Are those clients who joined a probation service alcohol counselling group modifying their drinking behaviour and attitudes?

Monitoring is not easy   Monitoring an individual's rehabilitation is not easy, but it is easier than monitoring the impact of a prevention strategy on a community. Monitoring is extremely difficult when the criterion of 'success' is a reduction in some community-wide indicator. For example, who is to say whether a fall in the level of public drunkenness convictions is due to a new drunk cautioning scheme, a change in the local liquor licensing policy, the introduction of some new local controls over advertising, or a local public health education campaign which has alcohol as its prime focus?

The difficulty of monitoring the impact of specific policies on the overall level of problems will increase as more organizations and groups initiate local prevention activities. The more initiatives there are the greater the likelihood of a cumulative impact, but the more difficult it becomes to tease out the role played by any particular initiative.

This guide stresses the importance of monitoring. The first stage in developing a community-wide system is to ensure that as many relevant organizations as possible have basic recording systems which enable numbers of problems, prevention activities, and individual and organizational progress to be monitored. Chapter 8 contains a section on 'doing research' and some basic books on research and evaluation are listed in 'Further reading'.

Toward a local strategy

'There are at present many groups and interests involved in this field which sometimes duplicate effort and at times even appear to be in competition.' (*Drinking Sensibly*, HMSO 1981: 66)

The effectiveness of any local prevention strategy depends on the cumulative impact of a wide range of prevention activities involving many different organizations and groups. Any integrated strategy should include a range of activities which covers each of the three basic prevention foci which were identified earlier – problem drinkers, drinking habits, and alcohol itself. Any strategy which emphasizes one particular component – such as control over the availability of alcohol –

to the exclusion of the other two would be unbalanced and would not draw on the full range of local prevention resources.

Compatible activities and ideas

At the most simple level 'compatible' means ensuring that agencies recognize each other's existence and understand the contribution they can each make to a rounded and coherent local prevention strategy. Part of the task of this guide, therefore, is to describe briefly the powers, the organizational structures, and the aims of many of the local agencies which have a prevention contribution to make.

But an integrated strategy will involve more than a recognition and understanding of the various agencies and their prevention potential and activities. It will involve, ideally, the projection of common or at least consistent messages. If educators and trainers and those working with patients, clients and members of the 'public' are saying different things about alcohol or are using widely different vocabularies and giving widely differing pieces of advice then the impact of any strategy will be reduced. Chapter 2 discusses this issue further and highlights a small number of core messages which any local strategy could incorporate.

At heart, the message is contained in *Drinking Sensibly*:

> 'Alcohol gives harmless pleasure to many, and most people drink sensibly. But a significant minority drink in such a way to cause harm to themselves and others – that it to say, they misuse alcohol. The aim . . . is not to stop people drinking but to encourage sensible attitudes towards the use of alcohol.' (HMSO 1981: 7)

For maximum impact a local prevention strategy needs maximum participation. It is hoped that a wide variety of people in many localities will take up and develop at least some of the ideas that are outlined in this guide. The spread of any local strategy can, to some extent, be promoted by the participants in one organization lobbying associated organizations and groups of workers and drawing attention to the prevention activities which relate to them. For instance, personnel officers could draw the attention of health and safety at work officers to the alcohol and work material while liquor licensing justices could discuss with the local police force, the social services department, the probation service, and others and contributions which they might make in relation to liquor licensing.

Promoting prevention

The development of the strategy and its spread would be encouraged if each locality had a group which was clearly seen to be responsible for disseminating knowledge about the prevention of alcohol problems, which lobbied local organizations to develop their prevention potential and which was the repository of ideas about good practice and a clearing house for materials and knowledge of prevention developments.

Whether this focus of local prevention activity is a local Council on Alcoholism, a Joint Care Planning Team, an associated liaison committee, or an *ad hoc* local alcohol group set up specifically for the purpose, it will need to know not only about the prevention contribution which all local organizations and groups of workers can make but also about the structure of these organizations, how to gain access and who to approach. Each chapter in the guide contains, where appropriate, information of this kind so that the local action group – whatever its organizational form and membership – can make the contacts necessary to instigate, maintain, and develop an integrated local prevention strategy.

It may be that the local action group will not just stimulate and encourage but may take responsibility itself for various local prevention activities. There may be the need to organize multi-disciplinary alcohol education, multi-professional in-service training, a public education campaign, or a range of lobbying activities in relation to national organizations which it would be inappropriate or inconvenient for any other local organization to undertake.

Similarly, it may be that the local action group is the *only* organization which can, with help from a local university or other institution, draw together and disseminate basic information which could be used for assessing the extent of alcohol problems or for monitoring the impact of prevention activities. Yet again, the local action group may develop teaching skills, become a repository for alcohol education materials, and even undertake prevention 'consultancies' with local organizations. In some localities there will be very few people with any interest in or experience of working in the area of alcohol problems. The formal establishment of a group to bring together the few people that there are could be a vital first step towards local action.

The question of funding

In any area of general health and social problems, the question arises of who is going to pay for any worthwhile new scheme or activity. The history of the funding of local Councils on Alcoholism has shown how difficult it is to build on the pump priming of central government for anything other than the provision of services. Those councils which can demonstrate to any local joint funders or other interested parties that they are providing a service in the sense of counselling or advice are much more likely to get support than those who say that they are primarily concerned with education or the prevention of alcohol problems.

Guides to funding   The following body:

National Council of Voluntary Organizations
26 Bedford Square
London WC1V 3HU
(Tel: 01–636–4066)

has recently updated its advice on sources of statutory money, *Government Grants – a Guide for Voluntary Organizations*. This provides a concise description of the grant-giving policies of government bodies and also includes details of EEC Funds. NCVO have produced three other reports which will also be of use to any local action group looking for funds to support its activities. *Grants from Europe: How to Get Money and Influence Policy*, written by Ann Davison, tells how the EEC works, what funds it has available for voluntary organizations, what decisions it makes and how to influence them. The issue of *Finding and Running Premises* is dealt with in the guide produced by Judith Unell and Anne Weyman. They review ways in which to find premises, forms of tenure, grants for renovating and developing properties, and the kind of technical expertise needed and how to use it. Finally, *The Charity Trustees Guide* by Adrian Longley, Martin Dockray, and Jacqueline Sallon provides a useful source of reference for trustee and charity managers. It also deals with the issue of charitable status, incorporation, the charity commissioners, and taxation.

The 2p rate   At a local level there is always the '2p rate'. This is the power which all local authorities have under Section 137 of the Local Government Act 1972, which empowers them to spend the equivalent of a free twopenny rate each year on any activities which are likely to benefit the inhabitants of the locality. The kinds of activities which a local action group concerned with preventing alcohol problems may well want to stimulate could be appropriate for this money.

Useful national organizations

The exploitation of local resources and the systematic exploration of the opportunities they provide to prevent alcohol-related problems in no way reduces the need for action at the *national* level. So all local action groups should be aware of and liaise closely with four national organizations: Alcohol Concern, Action on Alcohol Abuse, the Institute of Alcohol Studies, and the Health Education Council.

Alcohol Concern   This was established in 1984 on DHSS funds as the successor organization to a number of national bodies concerned with alcohol education, prevention, and services. Its regional network reaches into every locality and one of its aims is to stimulate, co-ordinate, and develop prevention activities. Its address is:

Alcohol Concern
305 Gray's Inn Road
London WCIX 8QF
(Tel: 01–833–3471)

Action on Alcohol Abuse   'Triple A' is not supported by government money and is primarily a ginger group to raise national issues of policy particularly in the prevention area. Any local group should be aware of Triple A's views and activities. Its address is:

Action on Alcohol Abuse
Livingstone House
11 Carteret Street
London SW1H 9DL
(Tel: 01–222–3454/5)

The Institute of Alcohol Studies   This was established in 1984 by the United Kingdom Temperance Alliance to provide information to the public, government, researchers, professional workers, and others and to provide education and training programmes concerned with the identification, management, and prevention of alcohol misuse. The IAS address is:

Institute of Alcohol Studies
Alliance House
12 Caxton Street
London SW1H OGS
(Tel: 01–222–4001/5880)

The Health Education Council   This is concerned with the planning and promotion of health education at national level in England and Wales. It is an independent, non-departmental public body supported in the main by the DHSS. Alcohol is the focus of one of the council's main programmes of activity which includes training, publications, research, mass media campaigns, and the development of alcohol education syllabuses and materials. The address of the HEC is:

Health Education Council
78 New Oxford Street
London WC1A 1AH
(Tel: 01–631–0930)

But although there is some action at the national level, the point of this guide is to stress that those engaged in the identification, management, and prevention of alcohol problems should *not* be waiting for national initiatives. They should be creating policies at the periphery where the problems and so many of the, as yet untapped, resources are located and where, moreover, innovative developments can serve as models for national policy-makers. For good practice at the local level today is often, as any political analyst knows, tomorrow's central policy.

This is intended to be a *living* 'guide to action'. Therefore, it needs to be revised and added to in the light of local needs and local experience.

The following two pages are for jotting down examples of good practice, and addresses relevant to the issues covered by this chapter.

We hope to update the guide, and would be delighted to receive any advice about corrections, new material or any other information which should go into the next edition. Please send all suggestions, before 31 December, 1987, to:

> Philip Tether and David Robinson
> Addiction Research Centre
> University of Hull
> Hull HU6 7RX

Examples of Good Practice

Useful Addresses and Telephone Numbers

Further reading

Official reports

Prevention and Health: Everybody's Business – A Reassessment of Public and Personal Health, HMSO, London, 1976

Prevention, report by the Advisory Committee on Alcoholism, DHSS, 1977.

The Pattern and Range of Services for Problem Drinkers, report by the Advisory Committee on Alcoholism, DHSS, 1978

Education and Training, report by the Advisory Committee on Alcoholism, DHSS, 1979

Moser, J., *Prevention of Alcohol-Related Problems*, an international review of preventive measures, policies, and programmes, compiled by the Division of Mental Health, WHO, Geneva, Addiction Research Foundation, Toronto, 1980

Wilson, P., *Drinking in England and Wales*, an enquiry carried out by OPCS on behalf of the DHSS, HMSO, London, 1980

Drinking Sensibly, a DHSS discussion document, HMSO, London, 1981

Journals

Alcohol and Alcoholism, the journal of the Medical Council on Alcoholism, six issues per year, Pergamon Press, Oxford. Editor: Allan D. Thompson.

British Journal of Addiction, the journal of the Society for the Study of Addiction, six issues per year, Carfax Publications, Oxford. Editor: Griffith Edwards

General

Alcohol Problems, collected articles from the *British Medical Journal*, London, 1982

Camberwell Council on Alcoholism, *Women and Alcohol*, Tavistock, London, 1980

Davies, I. and Raistrick, D., *Dealing with Drink*, BBC Publications, London, 1981

Heather, N. and Robertson, I., *Controlled Drinking*, Methuen, London, 1983

Krasner, N., Madden, J. S., and Walker, R. J. (eds), *Alcohol-Related Problems: Room for Manoeuvre*, Wiley, Chichester, 1984

Office of Health Economics, *Alcohol, Reducing the Harm*, OHE, London, 1981

Orford. J. and Harwin, J (eds), *Alcohol and the Family*, Croom Helm, London, 1982

Plant, M. (ed.), *Drinking and Problem Drinking*, Junction Books, London, 1982

Plant, M and Ritson, B., *Alcohol: The Prevention Debate*, Croom Helm, London, 1983

Prys Williams, G. and Thompson Brake, G., *Drink in Great Britain, 1900–1979*, B. Edsall, London, 1980

Robinson, D., *From Drinking to Alcoholism*, Wiley, Chichester, 1976

Robinson, D., *Alcohol Problems: Reviews, Research and Recommendations*, Macmillan, London, 1979

Royal College of Psychiatrists, *Alcohol and Alcoholism*, Tavistock, London, 1979

Shaw, S., Cartwright, A., Spratley, T., and Harwin, J., *Responding to Drinking Problems*, Croom Helm, London, 1978

CHAPTER 2

Educating about alcohol

23

CHAPTER 2

Educating about alcohol

'Where social controls on alcohol use are strong and where drunkenness is frowned upon alcohol is taken moderately and in appropriate circumstances, and the amount of problem drinkers tend to be low. Health education, in this context, is about the strengthening of social controls.' (*Drinking Sensibly*, HMSO 1981: 31)

Uncertainty is widespread about alcohol, its effects, how to handle it, how to recognize problems in oneself and other people, and how to respond to such problems. This uncertainty is due not simply to lack of knowledge. Our society has ambiguous and equivocal attitudes toward alcohol which make it difficult for us to appraise objectively our own drinking habits and those of other people.

All recent government reports and those from professional and other bodies have stressed that alcohol education must be a central component of any national prevention strategy. This is true also for any *local* prevention strategy.

Basic information on aspects of the *content* of alcohol education is outlined in this chapter, together with an indication of the range of *materials* for learning and teaching about alcohol and, finally, some suggestions on how best to *promote* alcohol education for the 'general public'. This does not, however, exhaust the discussion of the 'education dimension' of the strategy. In addition, each chapter in the guide examines certain alcohol education issues – such as specific training structures, educational opportunities, and educational materials.

Many groups and organizations appear to think that they have 'done' alcohol education once they have run a 'workshop', a couple of seminars, or a short course of lectures. But to change attitudes and practices and to overcome organizational inertia requires more than token nods toward alcohol education. To have any worthwhile impact, a programme of alcohol education must have the commitment of trainers and educators, and be firmly embedded in routine training activities at all levels.

Since alcohol problems are so widespread, education about alcohol and alcohol problems will be relevant to several components of any organization's training programme. This, though, can be a weakness if it is seen to be no one's particular responsibility. On the other hand, if the situation is recognized and capitalized on it can constitute a strength. By being fully integrated into a training programme alcohol education can provide a common thread linking together different parts of the training process.

Messages about alcohol

Many people are ignorant about alcohol and the nature, range, and extent of alcohol-related problems. Unhelpful beliefs and attitudes abound, ranging from the belief that the ability to drink large amounts of alcohol is 'manly' to the conviction that alcohol is an indispensable adjunct to every festive and social occasion. Unhelpful behaviour in relation to alcohol includes drinking to excess, regular solitary drinking, drinking on inappropriate occasions, drinking to bolster confidence, and encouraging someone else to drink inappropriately. Alcohol education should aim to erode these unhelpful attitudes, promote healthier and safer ones and, in short, encourage sensible drinking.

The need for consistent messages

One of the weaknesses of much alcohol education is that it fails to identify the attitudes and behaviour which it hopes to promote. Often, the material is entirely negative – it is clear what it is *against* but not what it is *for*. To overcome this deficiency, it would be helpful if alcohol educators in any locality could agree a set of simple and straightforward 'messages' about alcohol, to made explicit the changes they are working toward and to provide a framework for learning.

Four core messages

There are many 'core messages' which alcohol educators might try to promote whatever the teaching occasion. These could usefully relate to, among other things:

- The myth of the two populations;
- Drinking guidelines;
- Alcohol as an excuse;
- Alcohol the indispensable.

The myth of the two populations Many workers are inhibited in their response to problem drinking issues by the stereotype of the 'alcoholic'. The 'alcohol problem' is often equated with a minority of drinkers who are very visible, grossly damaged, and dependent. Many sections of the general public also identify the alcohol problem with 'alcoholics' and this unhelpful association is often reinforced by the media. Concentration on the 'alcoholic' encourages the notion that there are two populations of drinkers – the small, vulnerable minority who misuse alcohol and the great majority who can use and enjoy it safely and sensibly.

However, the increasingly recognized links between overall consumption levels and levels of harm suggest that there is only one population, not two. As *Drinking Sensibly* puts it:

> 'The experience in other countries tends to confirm the link between total alcohol consumption and harm. What this implies is that, when total consumption increases, the increase is distributed, to some extent at least, in increased consumption at every level of drinking, with some who had a previously high, but tolerable, level of drinking becoming problem drinkers.' (HMSO 1981: 29)

These links between overall consumption levels and levels of harm emphasize the crucial fact that prevention really is 'everybody's business'. The recognition that there is only one drinking population means that *everyone* must examine their own drinking habits and attitudes. For educators and helpers this must be done before others can be taught, guided, or helped. It also means a shift from an exclusive preoccupation with the dependent drinker toward concern with the full range of alcohol-related problems which can be experienced by *anyone* who drinks unwisely, intemperately, or inappropriately.

Drinking guidelines   Health education about smoking aims to encourage people to stop. Health education about alcohol aims to educate people to 'drink sensibly'. The notion of 'sensible drinking' might include some level of alcohol consumption which is considered to be 'safe' or 'normal'. However, the attempt to define a 'safe' limit is fraught with difficulties.

First, differences in physique and metabolism mean that any 'safe' limits for women would be lower than for men. In fact, individual metabolisms vary so much that it would be almost impossible to fix a limit which is applicable even to all men or to all women. Second, 'safe' says nothing about the appropriateness of drinking. Drinkers can stay well within any set of limits but, for example, have their driving skills impaired or their work efficiency reduced because they consume a 'safe' level of alcohol at an inappropriate time. Third, there is the basic question of whether or not it is wise to talk about 'safe' limits at all.

Setting a 'limit' might, it is often argued, encourage people to drink *up to* this level in the belief that they have been given an official assurance that to do so is acceptable and 'safe'. Those who fear that safe limits encourage individuals to drink more than they might otherwise do, would prefer to emphasize that there is no particular consumption level at which drinkers suddenly begin to experience adverse consequences. Instead of publicizing 'safe limits' they believe that alcohol educators should be promoting the simple 'message' that 'the more you drink the more problems you will experience'.

Given these problems and objections, authorities have been exceedingly cautious about committing themselves to any 'safe limits'. But several have done so in recent years. In 1979 the Royal College of Psychiatrists in their report *Alcohol and Alcoholism* suggested that an intake of 'four pints of beer a day, four doubles of spirits or one standard-sized bottle of wine' constitute an upper limit of drinking, although the College stressed that it is 'unwise to make a habit of drinking even at these levels, and anyone driving a vehicle should not drink at all before driving' (p.140).

Even with these caveats the Royal College of Psychiatrists' upper limits were considered by many to be excessive and in 1984 the Health Education Council (HEC) began publicizing considerably lower 'safe limits': two or three pints, or their equivalent, two or three times a week for men and, for women, two or three units of drink two or three times a week. A unit equals a measure of spirits, a glass of wine, or half a pint of lager or beer.

Also in 1984, the Consumer Association magazine *Which* said that a man who drinks eight or more units a day – or fifty units a week – or a woman who drinks more than five a day – or thirty-five units a week – is substantially increasing the risk of developing some alcohol-related condition.

The final argument against defining 'safe limits' is based on the obvious difficulty caused by several authorities each producing its own set of limits. Nothing is more calculated to devalue a health promotion exercise in the eyes of the public than 'experts' offering competing or contradictory advice.

But although there are considerable difficulties with the whole concept of 'safe limits', alcohol educators are very often faced with the demand for advice about 'safe' and 'normal' drinking. People, under-standably and rightly, do want a reference point, something by which to judge their own and other people's drinking. So given that alcohol educators will be pushed into defining safe drinking, it would be particularly helpful if local alcohol educators all use the same set of 'safe limits' when faced with this kind of demand. But which set?

The Health Education Council is well known and the amounts it recommends are easy to remember. However, the term 'drinking guidelines' could usefully be substituted for 'safe limits'. This might go some way toward reducing the possibility that 'safe limits' are seen as an officially sanctioned consumption level. A guideline emphasizes that in the end, it is the individual's responsibility to drink sensibly. Blame cannot be put on a 'safe' limit for mishaps which result from drinking at or below that level.

The guidelines approach is particularly relevant where the most well-known of all the alcohol 'limits' is concerned; the drinking and driving 'legal limit' currently enshrined in law as a blood alcohol content (BAC) of 80 milligrammes of alcohol in 100 millilitres of blood (80 mg/100 ml); 35 microgrammes of alcohol in 100 millilitres of breath (35 ug/100 ml); or 107 milligrammes of alcohol in 100 millilitres of urine (107 mg/100 ml).

The limits were set at this level because it was considered that this is the point at which driving skills deteriorate very rapidly and the risk of accidents sharply increases. However, *any* alcohol diminishes driving skills and consequently increases the risk of accidents and prosecution. The 'legal limit' is merely the level at which a prosecution will be automatic. A prosecution for driving when unfit through drink can be made at *any* blood alcohol level. So as far as driving is concerned the only guideline is 'don't drink and drive'.

Alcohol as an excuse　Alcohol is valued in our society as an aid to conviviality, relaxation, and social intercourse. Our ideas about alcohol include the notion that it 'takes the lid off' our inhibitions and enables us to be more truly 'ourselves'. For many people this view is reinforced by the mistaken idea that alcohol is a 'stimulant'. Although it does loosen inhibitions alcohol is a depressant because it depresses certain functions of the central nervous system and reduces – 'depresses' – control over our speech and actions. Given that we value the release afforded by this loosening of control it is hardly surprising that we often find a lack of control in others to be entertaining and amusing. The drunk has been a stock figure of fun from the writings of ancient Greece, through intervening literature and drama, to contemporary films and the comedian's repertoire.

One task of alcohol education is to undermine the link between alcohol and acceptable irresponsiblity. Health education in all its forms is concerned to increase the scope for informed choice. Alcohol educators should emphasize that we are all responsible for our own drinking behaviour and that behaviour which would not be acceptable if we were sober cannot be excused because we are drunk. The link between drunkenness and irresponsibility can and should be weakened not only by emphasizing that we choose whether or not to *become* drunk but also that how we behave *when* drunk is as much socially as physiologically determined.

Alcohol the indispensable　'Going out for a drink' is the most popular recreational activity. There is scarcely any social event at which the provision of alcohol would be considered inappropriate. In fact, the organizers of most events will almost invariably make sure that at least some alcoholic drinks are provided. The fourth core alcohol education 'message' is that alcohol is not, necessarily, an indispensable adjunct to every social occasion.

Individuals should have an opportunity to *choose* not to drink alcohol. This choice is often denied. Just as the previous 'message' asserted that individuals are responsible for their own drinking behaviour, so this 'message' too is about responsibility but about responsibility for other people's drinking behaviour. A court in the USA has recently held that a host who allowed a party-goer to become drunk was 'responsible' for the drunken-driving accident which subsequently occurred. Acceptance of responsibility for our own drinking behaviour must be supplemented by a recognition that we are partly responsible for and can influence the behaviour of others.

Alcohol education: materials and information

There is a large and rapidly growing body of books, films, videos, teaching packs, leaflets, and games designed to educate about alcohol and alcohol-related problems. A comprehensive list would be impossible to compile and even if compiled would become rapidly out of date.

Each chapter in this guide identifies – either in the text or in 'Further reading' – alcohol education material and information which seems especially useful in terms of its information content, clarity of presentation or its relevance to a particular group of workers.

Although there is a substantial degree of overlap, alcohol education materials and information can be divided into three basic types: *general*, of use to anyone who wants to learn more about alcohol; *for trainers*, to help to identify training needs and develop suitable programmes; and *for helpers and self-helpers* including simple drinking diaries and other self-help material which anyone can be encouraged to use.

General materials and information

Many of the reports, pamphlets, books, and 'packs' which are identified in the various chapters of this guide can be classed as 'general'. Chapter 1 lists some books for further reading which are introductory and general while chapters 3–10 identify general materials geared toward a particular problem area and of interest to particular groups and organizations. However, there is some additional 'general materials and information' which will be of interest to anyone concerned with the promotion and development of alcohol education. Much of it is produced by or can be obtained from the following six organizations.

The Health Education Council   This regularly produces a catalogue containing a wide range of alcohol education materials. The HEC's address is:

Health Education Council
78 New Oxford Street
London WC1A 1AH
(Tel: 01–631–0930)

The Teachers' Advisory Council on Alcohol and Drug Education

(TACADE).   TACADE is a national, voluntary body working in health and social education, with particular interest and expertise in alcohol and drug education. To date, it has not worked with the public at large, but has sought to provide support and guidance to the teaching, health, and related caring professions. This support is provided through in-service training courses, a wide range of publications, a Manchester-based resources centre, a mail order library scheme, extensive committee work, a consultancy service, and innovative research. Information about all these materials and activities, together with TACADE's quarterly magazine 'Monitor' is available from:

TACADE
Head Office
(Training North and Midlands, consultancy, resources centre, publications department)
2 Mount Street
Manchester M2 5NG
(Tel: 061–834–7210)

TACADE
Southern Office
(Training South)
202 Holdenhurst Road
Bournemouth BH8 8AS
(Tel: 0202–295874)

Scriptographic Publications Ltd   This produces an excellent range of alcohol education posters. These are ideal for workplaces, waiting rooms, schools, offices and public buildings and can be obtained from:

Scriptographic Publications Ltd
92/104 Carnworth Road
London SW6 3HW

Alcohol Concern   This produces a bi-monthly journal, *Alcohol Concern*, which is free to individuals or organizational subscribers. Alcohol Concern is also in the process of building up a collection of books and other resources which alcohol educators will be able to draw upon. Membership of Alcohol Concern will enable any individual or organization concerned about or involved with responding to alcohol-related problems to participate directly in national debate and action. The address is:

Alcohol Concern
305 Gray's Inn Road
London WC1X 8QF
(Tel: 01–833–3471)

Action on Alcohol Abuse This produces a bi-monthly *Triple A Review* which is free to individual or organizational subscribers. The *Review* contains news items culled from the press, parliamentary reports, and news of the work of the organization Out of Court which seeks to divert individuals with drinking problems from the judicial and penal systems. It also contains news about, and comment upon, current alcohol issues. Membership of Triple A is important for anyone seriously interested in alcohol issues. The address is:

Action on Alcohol Abuse
Livingstone House
11 Carteret Street
London SW1H 9DL
(Tel: 01–222–3454/5)

The Institute of Alcohol Studies This offers a current awareness service, comprising published data, information on publications, coming events, and significant developments in the field. The Institute also has an 'Alcohol Study Pack' covering such issues as 'alcohol and you', 'alcohol myths', 'alcohol and the law', and 'alcohol and young people'. The United Kingdom Temperance Alliance, which established the IAS, publishes the quarterly journal *Alliance News* which contains a wealth of statistical data, comment, and informative material on alcohol issues. Details of the IAS and *Alliance News* can be obtained from:

Institute of Alcohol Studies
Alliance House
12 Caxton Street
London SW1H 0QS
(Tel: 01–222–4001/5880)

Materials for trainers

The HEC has promoted the development of the *Drinking Choices Manual* (*DCM*) which is designed to provide alcohol education training for statutory and voluntary workers. The manual, written by Ina

Simnett, Linda Wright, and Martin Evans, aims to inculcate the knowledge, attitudes, and skills necessary for workers to educate others, either within their own discipline or on a multi-disciplinary basis, who then educate their own patients and clients through courses, in groups, or on a one-to-one basis in their everyday work. The knowledge, attitudes, and skills which are developed by *DCM* are appropriate both for general educative and preventive work and for helping people who already have drinking problems.

The *DCM* was developed by HEC and TACADE in the course of the North East alcohol education programme which revealed the low level of alcohol education skills among many of the workers who have a role to play in identifying and responding to alcohol-related problems. The *DCM* is being disseminated through 'key tutors' who attend a short 'Drinking Choices' course and take away their knowledge and skills to promote the development of alcohol education in their locality.

Key tutors are drawn from a variety of backgrounds so that they can appreciate each other's roles and lay the basis for future local, multi-disciplinary training and collaboration. *DCM*-trained workers include doctors, directors of local Councils on Alcoholism, psychologists, probation officers, social workers, and health education officers. Many of the statutory and voluntary workers identified in this guide would benefit from participation in the *DCM* dissemination courses and could become important key tutors inside their own organizations and for their own localities. Anyone interested in becoming a key tutor or in the availability of a local 'Drinking Choices' course should write to the HEC.

Another guide to developing alcohol education, entitled *Teaching about Alcohol Problems*, is designed for use on training courses for social workers, probation officers, health visitors, medical students, and other helping professions (see chapter 8). It contains a collection of ideas, materials and perspectives on problems which should help trainers seeking to include a module on alcohol problems in their particular curriculum. The development of this guide, by Terry Lawrence, was sponsored by the DHSS. More details about it can be obtained from Alcohol Concern.

Material and information for helpers and self-helpers

The Health Education Council has published a brief and readable guide to sensible drinking entitled *That's the Limit* which contains a diary to enable people to record their own drinking patterns and consumption and to identify any problems. This pamphlet suggests 'safe limits' for men and women and can be obtained from any local NHS health education unit or from the HEC.

Many people can be helped to help themselves. A useful self-help manual entitled *So You Want to Cut Down on Your Drinking?* has been written by Ian Robertson and Nick Heather. It was published in 1985 and can be obtained from the Scottish Health Education Group. The address is:

Scottish Health Education Group
Woodburn House
Canaan Lane
Edinburgh EH10 4SG
(Tel: 031–447–8044)

This manual is clear, and full of interesting material. It provides information on the way alcohol affects people, encourages them to think about why they are drinking, and offers a range of methods for cutting down. These include keeping a daily drinking diary, deciding on personal drinking rules, and fixing a daily cut-off point for drinking. It also discusses alternatives to drinking as a response to the various problems and pressures which people may encounter.

Breathalyzers These can be used for diagnostic and educational purposes in a variety of settings. Coin-operated breathalyzers can be installed in public houses. GPs can use them in their surgeries and a number of workplaces have experimented with the introduction of breathalyzers on a self-monitoring basis. Two companies in the UK produce a variety of machines to suit most purposes:

Lion Laboratories
Ty Verlon Industrial Estate
Barry
Wales
(Tel: 0446–744244)

Camic Ltd
35 Upper Camden Street
North Shields
Tyne and Wear
(Tel: 0632–596821)

Questionnaires   Several questionnaires have been developed to help identify problem drinking. Most have been developed in structured, clinical situations where a reasonable degree of compliance can be expected. Their utility for the general population is untested but a wide variety of groups and organizations might find them helpful. Two well-known questionnaires are the ten-question brief Michigan Alcoholism Screening Test (MAST) and the four-question CAGE questionnaire – CAGE is an acronym formed from the key words in each of the four questions. Sources for the brief MAST and CAGE questionnaires are given in the 'Further reading' at the end of this chapter.

Counselling   Everyday counselling in the sense of making time, listening, and displaying a concerned interest does not require special training and yet it can be of enormous help to someone with a problem. However, specialist counselling skills may be needed to help some people with their alcohol problems (see chapter 8). General information about counselling can be obtained from the British Association for Counselling (BAC) which brings together counsellors and those who use counselling skills in their work. It disseminates information and seeks to identify and promote standards. The address is:

British Association for Counselling
37 Sheep Street
Rugby
(Tel: 0788–78328)

The BAC produces a quarterly newsletter for members only and a quarterly journal entitled *Counselling*. Both these publications are free to members but nearly four hundred non-members subscribe to the journal. The BAC has approximately 2000 individual members and 160 organizational members. It acts as a co-ordinating body for six autonomous specialist divisions. Approximately three-quarters of all BAC's members belong to one of these divisions:

- Association of Pastoral Care and Counselling;
- Association of Student Counselling;
- Counselling in Education;
- Counselling in Medical Settings;
- Counselling at Work;
- Personal, Sexual, Marital, and Family Division.

The BAC operates locally through fourteen branches in England and Wales which bring together counsellors of all kinds. The branches are listed in the BAC's annual report. BAC also has links with the Scottish Association for Counselling and the Northern Ireland Association for Counselling.

Educating the general public

The majority of the general public will be unlikely to be in contact with any specific alcohol education and may be untouched by many of the other prevention activities outlined in this guide. Any local prevention strategy must, therefore, include education aimed at 'the general public'.

All participants in the local prevention strategy should know something of the issues and techniques surrounding public health education so that, if called upon, they can play an effective part. Of course, it is open to any group or organization to undertake public education on its own and, in some cases, this may be particularly appropriate. The fire service may want to publicize the relation of alcohol to fire accidents and the local Home Safety Committee may want to alert the general public to the links between alcohol and home accidents (see chapter 4). But whatever the focus of public education, those who take part in it should clearly understand that there are many opportunities for public education and should also know how to use the media.

Opportunities for public education

There are many opportunities in any locality for promoting educational messages. Although they may be less glamorous than appearing on TV they can be very effective. The Manchester Regional Committee for Cancer Education, for example, used a panel of speakers over an extended period of time to give talks to a large number of small groups. This contact and re-contact with a large number of people was found to be more effective for this task than traditional mass media approaches.

In any locality there are many societies and groups which are always on the look-out for speakers. Local alcohol educators could publicize the fact that they are available to give talks and to lead discussion groups. Local political parties, for example, usually have a programme of meetings with invited speakers. Alcohol educators could make a very useful start toward influencing the local political system by talking at these events.

This guide identifies many groups of workers who need to know more about the nature, range, and extent of alcohol-related problems and how they can contribute to their prevention. Usually, these groups have their own organization outside the workplace and alcohol educators could well give a talk to local personnel officers or health and safety at work officers (see chapter 6), or to the local branch of the BMA or a Royal College of Nursing local centre (see chapter 8).

Local public education programmes should also be particularly alert to any under-exploited opportunities for promoting messages in their locality. For instance, the sides of local ambulances have been used in Scotland to project health education messages. This example raises other possibilities. Could space be provided for alcohol education messages on the local buses or taxis?

Using the mass media

Although there are many educational opportunities and many ways of reaching sections of the general public, the mass media remain particularly important since they can, in their various forms, reach almost everyone. It is vital for local prevention workers to be able to use these media with knowledge, skill, and confidence.

Local newspapers   These are an important medium for health education messages and information. However, the local press will not be interested in dry 'facts' or unattractive information. Material for the local press must be interesting and stimulating. Curious and unexpected facts often make the best basis for a story. Where possible the material ought to be given a 'human interest' angle.

Participants in the local prevention strategy should go out of their way to make contact with local journalists and especially, if the paper has one, with the health correspondent. Material is more likely to be used by the local press if the contributors are known and the paper understands something of the local prevention strategy, how its various components fit together, and what the various participants in it are trying to do. Similarly, it is important for participants to learn something of the journalists' requirements and what will constitute a useful and interesting story.

One important issue which must be dealt with concerns language and approach. A great deal of press reporting on alcohol issues – precisely because it has to be easily readable, interesting, and eye-catching – is less helpful than it might otherwise be because of the concentration on 'alcoholics' or because of a laboured jokiness. If the participants in a local prevention strategy could get the local press to emphasize the variety of alcohol-related problems and to report them seriously a great deal of progress will have been made. As least one local Council on Alcoholism holds regular half-day seminars for local journalists to explain the range of alcohol problems they deal with and to discuss what constitutes helpful press reporting. This very useful idea is clearly worth adopting.

Radio This is another major resource for health educators and one which is rather underrated and under-used. Radio can be listened to at work, in the car and in the home. However, every local station is different and sees its responsibility in a different way. Alcohol educators should know how to take advantage of the opportunities that are there or know how to create them.

Both BBC and Independent Local Radio (ILR) have a responsibility to serve the community, though this is couched in rather vague terms. BBC stations are expected to give 'a new means of expression to a [community's] particular interests and aspirations, serving to reinforce its distinctive character and sense of identity' (*Broadcasting White Paper*, 1966, Cmnd 3169, para. 35). ILR station programmes should 'contain a suitable proportion of matter calculated to appeal specifically to tastes and outlook of persons served by the station' (*Broadcasting Act*, 1973, section 4(1) (d)).

In addition to personal contact there are 'constitutional' channels for influencing local radio stations. The BBC is linked to its local radio stations through a Controller of Local Radio at Local Radio Head-quarters in London. The station manager of each BBC station must follow any policies that are passed down, but enjoys a great deal of autonomy. Programme policies are the responsibility of each station's programme organizer.

The station manager and programme organizer have a local Radio Advisory Council (RAC) to advise on programme policy. The Council should reflect the range of tastes, interests, and concerns of people in the area served. Members, approximately sixteen in number, are appointed by the BBC's Board of Governors on the basis of nominations by listeners, local organizations, and the station manager and most councils meet every two months or so. It is open to any participant in the local prevention strategy to obtain a place on their local RAC.

In addition to the station manager, the programme organizer and the local RAC, local BBC radio stations may have an education producer and most will have a community affairs producer. These producers may be assisted by relatively informal panels, committees, or groups on a station-by-station basis.

The position of Independent Local Radio is rather different. The Independent Broadcasting Association (IBA), based in London, is responsible for both Independent Television and ILR. It does not make its own programmes or own any stations. When the Home Secretary has decided that a particular area can have an ILR station, the IBA chooses one of the companies bidding for the contract or 'franchise'.

Each ILR station is run by a limited company, with shareholders, a board of directors, and a managing director. A wide range of commercial interests arc represented among shareholders, from multi-nationals to local small businesses and newspapers. Directors oversee advertising, sales promotion, and staffing as well as programmes. But much of the programme policy is left to the programme controller who has much more authority than the approximate BBC equivalent – the programme organizer.

A Local Advisory Committee (LAC) is appointed by the IBA office dealing with the region in which the radio station is situated. Before an ILR station comes on the air, the regional office places advertisements in local newspapers inviting applications from anyone who is interested in serving on the LAC. The IBA officers then select what they regard as a cross-section of community interests: including local government representatives, the Church, youth, business, education, and ethnic minorities. Local alcohol educators could see that their interests are adequately represented on their local LAC either at a station's inception or as vacancies occur in the existing membership.

Although most ILR companies are commercial enterprises there are two exceptions – Cardiff Broadcasting Company and Moray Firth Community Radio, Inverness, which are known as 'community-based ILRs'. These companies have reserved half the seats on their boards for elected representatives drawn from local community organizations. In these areas, therefore, it may be easier for community and voluntary organizations to influence programme policy.

Community Cable Radio   There is more to local radio than just BBC stations and ILR. There are also a small number of Community Cable

Radio (CCR) stations in new-towns and housing developments. Programmes are transmitted via cable and the services vary in size from the whole of Milton Keynes – over thirty thousand population – to a single tower block in Birmingham with approximately four hundred residents.

CCRs usually transmit for a few hours a day from very modest studios staffed by one or two professional trainer-co-ordinators and volunteers from the community. Such developments pose some problems of finance and public accountability, but they provide another set of alcohol education opportunities. More information can be obtained from:

Association of Community Broadcasting Stations (ACBS)
WSM Community Radio
215 Willowfield
Woodside
Telford
Shropshire TF7 5WT
(Tel: 0952–583520)

Hospital Radio　There are now over 150 stations serving hospitals and groups of hospitals around the country. These stations provide music interspersed with short news and information items. They are an important 'radio resource' for local alcohol educators bearing in mind the extent of alcohol-related problems among hosptial patients of all categories (see chapter 8). Hospital radio stations belong to:

National Association of Hospital Broadcasting Associations
3 Waltham Close
Abbey Park
West Bridgford
Nottingham
(Tel: 0602–624300)

Campus Radio　A number of university campuses have their own radio service. Concern has been expressed over student drinking problems (see chapter 7) and, like hospital patients, students are a group which could benefit from informative, well-presented, and interesting alcohol education. There is a National Association of Student Broadcasting (NASB) which has over twenty member stations. The address is:

National Association of Student Broadcasting
Holywell Cottage
Ashby Road
Loughborough
Leicestershire LE11 3QU
(Tel: 0509–216236)

Local Radio Kit   Finally, understanding the structure of local radio and the opportunities it presents is only a beginning. Alcohol educators will, we hope, be asked to take part in 'phone-ins', to be interviewed, and to discuss a wide variety of alcohol issues. Learning to communicate effectively via what can be an intimidating medium might seem a daunting task. But, fortunately, good advice is available. The National Extension College (NEC) has produced 'The Local Radio Kit' by Keith Yeomans and John Callaghan. The kit consists of:

- A *booklet* which explains how local radio works, how to use it, and how other people have successfully used it, and gives addresses of local radio stations and organizations which may be able to advise and support would-be broadcasters.
- A *flow chart* which takes users through the stages of planning a project for local radio. It advises on how to contact the right people and make the right decisions at the right time.
- A *cassette* which explains how to be interviewed and how to take part in a phone-in programme, and which gives some tips on technicalities which could make a performance more polished.

This kit is indispensable for any local alcohol educator who wishes to use local radio to reach the 'general public' or any specific 'target group'. The address is:

The National Extension College
18 Brooklands Avenue
Cambridge CB2 2HN

Local television   This is the third major media resource for all those who want to influence and educate the local general public about alcohol problems and related issues. Both independent television and BBC have responsibilities to serve the community and there are many opportunities to work with the companies at the local level. These opportunities relate to, among other things:

- Public service announcements;

- News items;
- Discussion programmes and documentaries;
- Alcohol and work policies for the television companies themselves.

Any group can approach the local BBC and independent television stations and propose that it should be the subject of public service announcements. These announcements are short thirty-second slots in which an organization can 'announce' its existence, its purpose, and how those who wish to get in touch with it can do so. Clearly, a local Council on Alcoholism, a local counselling service, or any other local organization with a particular part to play in the local prevention strategy may wish to announce its existence in this way. The television company will give production assistance, but the local group or organization must be absolutely clear about what the purpose and point of the service announcement is. Similarly, they must be ready to deal with any phone calls or other responses to the announcement and have materials available to distribute to people with more information. There must also be a counselling or other service available if the public service announcement encourages those with problems to 'get in touch'.

Local groups can provide news items to local television companies in much the same way as they provide press releases. These must be news-worthy and might be about any local activity related to the prevention of alcohol problems, such as the publication of the annual report from the chief constable to the licensing committee or the production of a report from the local Council on Alcoholism or a change in legislation which has some impact on the alcohol world or the meeting of the local licensing forum (see Chapter 5).

Another way of dealing with topics of social concern is via local discussion programmes and documentaries. Members of any local alcohol group could offer themselves as resources and sources of advice for such programmes. One important reason for close collaboration between a local group and local television companies is to prevent coverage slipping into the trap of dealing only with the problems of severely dependent people – 'alcoholics'. Local groups can propose topics for documentaries and discussion programmes related to some of the wide range of alochol prevention issues. Alcohol and work problems, alcohol and safety, the issue of local liquor licensing practice, new developments in alcohol education, and alcohol and young people are just some of the specific topics which could be suggested. If these could be particularly focused on local developments, local problems, and the particular needs of a local situation they may well be much more interesting than programmes which merely repeat the fact that there is an alcohol problem, often unspecified, and that there is a need for 'someone' to do 'something' – again often unspecified.

One of the spin-offs from co-operating with local television companies to develop public service announcements or documentary and discussion programmes is that members of the companies themselves may come to recognize that either they or their colleagues may be developing an alcohol problem. The experience of one local Council on Alcoholism has been that after every programme on which they have collaborated there has been some member of the TV staff who has come forward to the Council because of a worry over either their own or a colleague's drinking. A television company should be treated in exactly the same way as any other company; that is, along the lines set out in chapter 6.

Being authoritative   The task for any local prevention group is to be an authoritative voice on prevention and alcohol matters. The aim should be for local radio, press, and television companies automatically to come to the group whenever there is a need for advice about or comment on some national or local alcohol issue. One way of developing this relationship with local media personnel is for the local Council on Alcoholism or other appropriate group to organize meetings, conferences, and seminars. Such events are of mutual benefit, enabling the media to explain their requirements and opportunities to participants in the local prevention strategy and allowing the prevention group to explain to the media the range of problems that exist, the range of local facilities that are available, and the range of major issues that lie behind the broad heading of 'the prevention of alcohol problems'.

This is intended to be a *living* 'guide to action'. Therefore, it needs to be revised and added to in the light of local needs and local experience.

The following two pages are for jotting down examples of good practice, and addresses relevant to the issues covered by this chapter.

We hope to update the guide, and would be delighted to receive any advice about corrections, new material or any other information which should go into the next edition. Please send all suggestions, before 31 December, 1987, to:

> Philip Tether and David Robinson
> Addiction Research Centre
> University of Hull
> Hull HU6 7RX

Examples of Good Practice

Useful Addresses and Telephone Numbers

Further reading

Consumer Association, 'Alcohol and Your Health', *Which*, 445–49, October 1984

Finn, P. and O'Gorman, P. A., *Teaching about Alcohol: Concepts, Methods and Classroom Activities*, Allyn and Bacon, Boston, 1981

Grant, M., *Same Again: A Guide to Safer Drinking*, Penguin Books, Harmondsworth, 1984

Gwinner, P. and Grant, M., *What's Your Poison?*, BBC Publications, London, 1979

Health Education Council, *Alcohol Education: Publications and Teaching Aids: A Source List*, Health Education Council, London, 1982

Hudson, C. S. and Jeremy, D, J., *A Survey of Alcohol Education in the United Kingdom*, Christian Economic and Social Research Foundation, Ilford, 1985

Leather, D. S., Hastings, G. B., and Davies, J. K. (eds), *Health Education and the Media*, Pergamon Press, Oxford, 1981

Mayfield, D., McLeod, G., and Hall, P., 'The CAGE Questionnaire: Validation of a New Alcoholism Screening Instrument', *Am. J. Psychiat.*, 131, 1121–123, 1974

Milgram, G. G. (ed.), *Alcohol Education Materials: an Annotated Bibliography*, Rutgers Center of Alcohol Studies, New Brunswick, New Jersey, 1980

Miller, W. R. and Munoz, R. F., *How to Control Your Drinking*, Prentice-Hall, Englewood Cliffs, New Jersey, 1976, re-issued by Sheldon Press, London

Mills, C. M., Neal, E. M., and Peed-Neal, I., *Handbook for Alcohol Education: The Community Approach*, Ballinger Publishing Co., Massachusetts, 1983

Pokorny, A. D., Miller, B. A., and Koplan, H. B., 'The Brief MAST: A Shortened Version of the Michegan Alcoholism Screening Test', *Am. J. Psychiat.*, 129, 342–5, 1972.

Sutherland, I. (ed.), *Health Education: Perspectives and Choices*, Allen and Unwin, London, 1979

Wallack, L., 'Assessing Effects of Mass Media Campaigns: An Alternative Perspective', *Alcohol, Health and Research World*, 5, 1, 17–27, 1980

Appendix 2.A

List of ITV Companies
Anglia Television (East of England)
Anglia House
Norwich NR1 3JG
(Tel: 0603–615151)

Border Television (The Borders)
Television Centre
Carlisle CA1 3NT
(Tel: 0228–25101)

Central Independent Television (East and West Midlands)

East Midlands
East Midlands Television Centre
Lenton Lane
Nottingham NG7 2NA
(Tel: 0602–863322)

West Midlands
Central House
Broad Street
Birmingham B1 2JP
(Tel: 021–643–9898)

Channel Four Television
Channel Four Television Company Ltd
60 Charlotte Street
London W1P 2AX
(Tel: 01–631–4444)

Granada Television (North-West England)
Granada TV Centre
Manchester M60 9EA
(Tel: 061–832–7211)

HTV (Wales and West of England)

HTV Wales
Television Centre
Culverhouse Cross
Cardiff CR5 6XJ
(Tel: 0222–590590)

HTV West
Television Centre
Bath Road
Bristol BS4 3HG
(Tel: 0272–778366)

Independent Television News
ITN House
48 Wells Street
London W1P 4DE
(Tel: 01–637–2424)

London Weekend Television (London weekends)
South Bank Television centre
Kent House
Upper Ground
London SE1 9LT
(Tel: 01–261–3434)

Thames Television (London weekdays)
Thames Television House
306–316 Euston Road
London NW1 3BB
(Tel: 01–387–9494)

Television South West (South-West England)
TSW House
18–24 Westbourne Grove
London W2 5RH
(Tel: 01–727–8080)

TV-Am (Breakfast Television)
Breakfast Television Centre
Hawley Crescent
London NW1 8EF
(Tel: 01–267–4300 and 01–267–4377)

Television South (South and South-East England)
Television Centre
Southampton SO9 5HZ
(Tel: 0703–34211)

Tyne Tees Television (North-East England)
The Television Centre
City Road
Newcastle upon Tyne NE1 2AL
(Tel: 0632–610181)

Yorkshire Television (Yorkshire)
The Television Centre
Leeds LS3 1JS
(Tel: 0532–438283)

CHAPTER 3

Alcohol advertising, promotion, and presentation in the media

CHAPTER 3

Alcohol advertising, promotion, and presentation in the media

'It has . . . been argued that whether or not the volume of advertising leads to increased drinking, the contents of advertising may result in harmful patterns of consumption.' (p. 37)

'It would not be surprising if the depiction of drinking during TV and radio programmes, in plays, in books and in films were a stronger influence on people's behaviour than commercial advertising sponsored by obviously interested parties.' (p. 38)

(*Drinking Sensibly*, HMSO: 1981)

Alcohol is big business. In 1983/84 the tax revenue accruing to the Treasury from the sale of alcohol totalled £5,964 million. These sales are promoted with the aid of advertising of all kinds. It is generally assumed that advertising stimulates sales. The trade, on the other hand, argues that alcohol advertising has no effect on total consumption but is aimed, rather, at securing brand loyalty and hence a larger *share* of the market. Debates about the role of advertising in general and in relation to particular markets such as alcohol are technical and inconclusive.

Although the relationship of advertising to consumption is disputed it is widely agreed that the *content* of alcohol advertising is important. While any unhelpful ideas, images, and 'messages' may be rejected by the majority, they can be absorbed by certain 'vulnerable groups', such as the young, and can promote or reinforce harmful patterns of consumption.

As a result of concern about media impact self-regulatory controls of advertising content have been developed. Anyone concerned about the prevention of alcohol problems at the local level should know about

55

these controls, how to make sure they are observed, and how they might make them more effective. This chapter deals, in turn, with advertising in the non-broadcast media, advertising in the broadcast media, the promotion of alcohol through sports sponsorship, and the presentation of alcohol in the media.

Advertising in the non-broadcast media

The British Code of Advertising Practice (BCAP) regulates advertising in the non-broadcast media. It is self-regulatory; developed by the advertising industry and implemented by the Advertising Standards Authority (ASA). The BCAP is sometimes referred to as the 'ASA Code'.

The British Code of Advertising Practice

The BCAP applies to most non-broadcast advertising although there are exceptions such as advertisements for medicines aimed specifically at the medical and allied professions, and packaging except when promotional schemes are involved. In addition, the ASA has no influence over magazine publishers who are not members of the Periodical Publishers Association, such as the publishers of 'soft-porn' magazines, many of which have a circulation in excess of a quarter of a million. A considerable proportion of advertising in these magazines is devoted to alcoholic drinks. The February 1984 edition of *Playboy*, for example, had 30 per cent of its total advertising space devoted to alcohol.

The basic principles of the code are that advertising should be 'legal, decent, honest, and truthful'. In these essentials the code has changed little over the years from its origins in the guidelines first drawn up in 1924 by the National Vigilance Committee and then by its successor, the Advertising Association, in 1926.

No one is obliged to accept and publish an advertisement even when it conforms in every particular to the BCAP Code. 'Media privilege' confers the right to reject any advertisement or to require additional changes.

The ASA   This body investigates complaints about advertisements and is assisted in this task by case officers whose reports go to the ASA's council. The results of the council's adjudications are published as case reports. The ASA council does not refer to previous cases in its decisions but the 1979 annual report makes it clear that it does consider itself to be bound by past precedent. Nevertheless, there is no formal body of 'case law' for consumers to refer to. The system depends upon the trade accepting the spirit of the regulations rather than upon a legalistic, adversarial approach. Consumers are not able to argue their case before the council and there is no appeal against the council's decision.

In 1983, 7,500 complaints were received by the ASA. The proportion of complaints that are investigated fluctuates from year to year. In 1981 it was 30 per cent, in 1982 it was 40.5 per cent and in 1983 it was 38.5 per cent. Some related to broadcast advertisements and were referred on to the IBA. Many had already been investigated. Some fell outside the ASA remit in that they were unrelated to advertisement content. In many cases inadequate details were given by the complainant and further details were requested by the ASA. One of the commonest reasons for rejection is that there is 'no case to investigate; no apparent breach of the Code'.

In 1974 an investigation of the work of the ASA conducted by the Consumer Association found that, in their opinion, 14 per cent of advertisements in the British national press appeared to be in breach of the BCAP. The Office of Fair Trading, in 1978, arrived at the very similar figure of 13 per cent for press advertisements. Although the ASA did not agree with the way in which the Office of Fair Trading had interpreted the Code, they were persuaded to begin their own systematic monitoring of publications.

The BCAP and alcohol advertising

When the BCAP was first introduced in 1962 there was no specific reference to alcohol advertising. However, alcohol was covered by the Code's general provisions. It was not until 1975 that the Code was extended by the addition of two appendices dealing specifically with cigarettes and alcohol. The current regulations can be found in Appendix J of the BCAP which is reproduced as Appendix 3.A to this chapter.

Appendix J of the BCAP lays down a number of conditions for alcohol advertisers. These include not showing anyone drinking who appears to be under the age of twenty-one and not implying that drinking is necessary for social, sexual, or business success. It is reproduced in a leaflet entitled *How the British Code of Advertising Practice Affects Alcohol Advertising* which is available free from:

Advertising Standards Authority
Brook House
2–16 Torrington Place
London WC1E 7HN
(Tel: 01–580–5555)

In addition to alcohol advertising being covered by the general provisions of the Code and by Appendix J, section 2.1–3 and 2.2–3 of Appendix A refer to advertisements for breath testing devices whilst section 2.4 of the same appendix relates to products which purport to mask the effects of alcohol.

According to the ASA, complaints about alcohol advertising are rare. Excluding complaints about mail order delays, between May 1983 and May 1984 the ASA investigated 1,264 complaints. Only twelve concerned alcoholic drinks and nine of these were complaints over the unfairness of free offers, promotions, and competitions. When Appendix J was adopted in 1975 brewers, distillers, and wine merchants were advised to submit their advertising copy to the ASA Secretariat for pre-publication advice. Many do, so a large number of alcohol advertisements are checked before publication. The monthly case reports do not indicate the total number of complaints about alcohol advertising which are rejected because the ASA does not consider that there has been any breach of the Code.

Local action

Self-regulatory codes of advertising practice have been criticized. The European Consumers' Consultative Committee has argued that codes drawn up by, or whose content is substantially controlled by, the trade are inherently weak and uphold trade interests. This feeling is widely shared.

An article entitled 'Behind the Ads' in the July 1977 edition of *Which* claimed that many alcohol advertisements break the Code. In the *Which* article Sir Bernard Braine, MP, referring specifically to vodka advertising, said that: 'what is now the fastest growing sector in the drink industry uses methods which come very near in my view to a violation of the public code of advertising practice on liquor advertising'. Some corroboration for this view can be found in the *Morning Advertiser* for 27 July, 1984, which reported that Smirnoff would be spending £1.5 million between August and December 1984 on a campaign 'aimed at the young drinker'. Appendix J of the BCAP says that 'advertisements should not be directed at young people'.

Because of these apparent weaknesses, *awareness* and *action* are important in promoting and maintaining a strict interpretation of all the BCAP's provisions relating to alcohol advertising. Pressure for a stricter application of the provisions can be generated by all participants in a local prevention strategy, who should be prepared to complain if they consider that an advertisement breaches the provisions of the Code. This would signal prevention workers' concern about non-broadcast alcohol advertising and about the interpretation and possible shortcomings of Appendix J.

Participants in a local prevention strategy might find that local consumer groups and organizations could be persuaded to take an interest in alcohol advertising and to give their support to any complaints which are made. There are approximately sixty local Consumers' Association groups. Many publish their own magazine. Each group is a source of independent consumer information. The addresses of local groups can be obtained from:

The National Federation of Consumer Groups
12 Mosley Street
Newcastle upon Tyne, NE1 1DE

Metropolitan districts, county councils and London boroughs also have consumer protection responsibilities. Consumer Protection Committees oversee the work of Consumer Protection Departments which have responsibilities in relation to food and drugs, trade descriptions, and weights and measures. Among other things, Consumer Protection Departments will seek to ensure that certain labelling requirements, such as a statement of alcohol content of wine, are observed and will analyze samples of beer from licensed premises to ensure that specified standards are maintained. At least one Consumer Protection Department takes a rather wider view of its responsibilities and is acting jointly with its local Council on Alcoholism and district health authority to monitor drink advertising in its area. Consumer Protection Departments act in an advisory and educative capacity to both traders and the general public regarding consumer affairs and they might be willing to help with a local publicity campaign designed to encourage awareness of the BCAP, its provisions, and its shortcomings, and how to complain effectively.

Organizations participating in the local prevention strategy itself could subscribe to the ASA monthly case reports to monitor trends and individual judgements which might be helpful in framing complaints. The monthly case reports are free.

Many complaints will involve questions of interpretation, particularly those arising from section 3.5 of Appendix J which forbids the depiction of drinking as essential to social, business, or sexual success. Since many advertisements involve attractive people in attractive settings, it can be argued that the impression is conveyed that drinking alcohol is part of being a successful person. On one level, the 'Tetley Bittermen' emphasize the 'pleasures of companionship and social communication associated with the consumption of alcoholic drinks' which is not forbidden by the Code. However, another interpretation might be that the advertisement clearly links alcohol with what is evidently meant to be an attractive masculinity. This link and any effect it might have upon impressionable adolescents are both forbidden by the Code if taken at face value.

A weakness of the Code's application to alcohol advertising concerns the role of 'humour'. The argument that if an advertisement is meant to be 'humorous' it could not possibly be taken seriously is viewed favourably by the ASA. As a result advertisers circumvent many of the Code's restrictions. It is difficult to understand the weight which is given to the humour argument, since humour is just as likely as anything else to contribute to the body of tacit, taken-for-granted ideas about the world in general and alcohol and drinking in particular. Indeed, it may be a more potent influence than other more 'serious' representations. Many would argue that jokes about race, far from being 'harmless' and 'not taken seriously by anyone' are an important means of reinforcing prejudices and perpetuating stereotypes. Complainants might specifically address this issue in their complaints and point out why, in their opinion, 'humour' does not constitute an adequate defence for an otherwise unacceptable advertisement.

Any complaints which tackle the interpretation of the Code's provisions run a high risk of being 'screened out' by the ASA and not being investigated. However, the range and status of complainants and the volume of complaints may encourage the ASA to redefine and reassess its position.

The participants in a local prevention strategy might also consider complaining about unhelpful advertisements which are *not* covered by the Code. This might help to set the agenda for future revision. For example, Appendix J lays down that 'advertisements should not associate drink with driving or dangerous machinery'. However, there is no mention of drinking and water safety. Advertisements frequently depict people drinking by the side of swimming pools, on exotic beaches, on yachts, or even in the bath. This is particularly unhelpful since alcohol is implicated in approximately 20 per cent of all drownings in the UK (see chapter 4).

Another omission in Appendix J is any mention of the depiction of solitary drinking which is specifically identified as unacceptable by, among others, the IBA Code of Advertising Standards and Practice.

Participants in a local prevention strategy could press for certain changes in the way the ASA presents its information. The annual reports provide information on the total number of complaints received and the total number of complaints 'screened out' because there was no apparent breach of the Code. The overall number of 'investigated complaints' is broken down into the major 'complaint categories' such as holidays, travel, and property. It would be helpful if 'screened out' advertisements were also categorized according to product. Any major 'gaps' between properly framed 'complaints registered' and 'complaints investigated' would then be evidence that the Code, or the ASA's interpretation of the Code, was not in step with significant and concerned opinion.

There are a number of simple points to remember when complaining about alcohol advertisements. Many complaints are rejected or delayed because they are not properly framed or because of inadequate information.

- All complaints must be made in writing. Oral complaints will not be accepted.
- If possible, attach a cutting of the advertisement. If this is not possible, as in the case of a poster, send a photograph or describe the content carefully and give details of its location.
- Specify the precise section(s) of the Code which the advertisement has breached and lay out the reason for complaining clearly and carefully

All complaints whether from an individual or an organization should be addressed to:

The Advertising Standards Authority
Brook House
2–16 Torrington Place
London WC1E 7HN
(Tel: 01–580–5555)

Two special cases – newspapers and public posters

Two specific forms of advertising, in newspapers and on public poster sites, provide opportunities for local action over and above complaining to the ASA to ensure the strict implementation of the existing BCAP and, possibly, its improvement.

Newspapers   The council of the Newspaper Society recommends that its members – which include most, but not all, local and regional provincial newspapers – publish their support of the BCAP by making space available at 'frequent intervals' in their classified advertising columns for the following notice:

> 'The Bigtown Bugle has taken considerable trouble to ensure that all advertisements in this issue are truthful, legal, decent and honest, complying with the British Code of Advertising Practice overseen by the Advertising Standards Authority, Brook House, 2–16 Torrington Place, London WC1E 7HN (Tel: 01–580–5555).'

In addition, the Newspaper Society publishes its own guide for all those who have responsibility for accepting newspaper advertisements. The guide, entitled *Advertisement Points to Watch*, supplements the BCAP. It also provides guidance on advertising legislation and contains a sub-section on alcohol advertisements. A copy of this guide can be obtained from:

The Newspaper Society
Whitefriars House
Carmelite Street
London EC4Y OBC

The Newspaper Society endorses the standard conditions of acceptance for the transaction of business between newspapers and advertisers which have been agreed between the Newspaper Society and the Institute of Practitioners in Advertising. The conditions include the following:

'Advertisement copy should be legal, decent, honest and truthful; should comply with the British Code of Advertising Practice and all other Codes under the general supervision of the Advertising Standards Authority; and shall comply with the requirements of current legislation.'

Any newspaper can include, in addition to the standard conditions of acceptance, any special conditions of its own.

A local newspaper can be an important prevention resource through its advertising policy and its coverage of alcohol issues. This is part of the 'education of the public' (see chapter 2). There are a number of questions which participants in a local prevention strategy could ask. Is the local newspaper a member of the Newspaper Society, and does the newspaper regularly publish the Newspaper Society's recommended notice? If the newspaper is not a member could it, even so, be encouraged to publish the notice? In either case, what is sufficiently 'regular', and could the notice be displayed more prominently and amended to include specific reference to alcohol advertising and Appendix J of the BCAP?

Do the local newspaper's conditions of acceptance conform to the recommendations agreed by the Newspaper Society and the Institute of Practitioners in Advertising? Since the newspaper is free to add to these recommendations can it be persuaded to insert a specific reference to the BCAP's Appendix J? Can local prevention workers and the local newspaper agree the wording of a clause which would indicate the newspaper's intention to refuse to publish the kind of lifestyle-orientated drink advertisements which many feel breach the spirit if not the current interpretation of the letter of the BCAP?

Public posters Poster advertising is a highly visible form of mass communication. Posters on hoardings – which have become such a significant feature of the urban environment – are known in the trade as 'pure' advertising because they are not just part of a newspaper or a magazine nor an interlude between television programmes.

Poster contractors erect the poster panels and put up the posters. The majority of poster contractors belong to the Outdoor Advertising Association of Great Britain. Some poster panels are in permanent positions at the roadside, in shopping areas, and on gable ends. But many are on temporary sites, such as land awaiting redevelopment.

Some sites are owned freehold by the poster contractors themselves but most are held under rights acquired from site owners who range from local authorities and property companies to private householders and the owners of corner shops. The great majority of poster sites are owned by local authorities.

Poster panels occupy land on the basis of a licence or a lease. The most usual is a 'licence', which is essentially a 'permission to do' without implying any legal rights whatsoever. It is not a specific form of legal document. It will usually be a simple proforma letter containing agreed terms and conditions. A 'lease', on the other hand gives the lessee rights, which make it difficult to move them off the site at short notice.

Both licences and leases could be used by any local individual or organization owning poster sites to control alcohol advertising. 'Control' could mean a complete ban on posters advertising alcohol. For multiple site owners it could mean limiting alcohol advertisements to particular areas or limiting their overall number. It could mean securing the removal of a particular advertisement, or series of advertisements. One northern Metropolitan District Council banned the advertising of certain products which it considered 'undesirable'. This Council has negotiated a lease which contains the following standard 'control' clauses:

- The tenant shall obtain all such approvals or consent that may be necessary.
- Upon the request of the landlord the tenant will remove forthwith any advertisement which is of religious or political significance and which is in the opinion of the landlord unsuitable, inappropriate or objectionable or is likely to subject the landlord or tenant to prosecution.

These clauses are supplemented by a verbal agreement that there will be no posters advertising cigarettes or South African products. A local authority in the South Midlands is considering, in conjunction with the district health authority and alcohol agencies, banning poster alcohol advertisements on its sites.

The particular department responsible for agreements with poster contractors varies from authority to authority. However, the key committee will usually be a Land and Property Committee or its equivalent which oversees the work of an Estates Department. Local poster advertising generates income for local authorities. The Association of District Councils does not have any overall figures nor does the Chartered Institute of Public Finance and Accountancy. The amount will vary widely from authority to authority. It may total £3,000–£4,000 in a semi-rural authority and considerably more in a large urban one.

Since precise figures are often 'lost' in the annual accounts under such items as 'revenue from land holdings' it may be difficult to establish how much revenue accrues to an authority from poster sites.

Clearly, local authorities are extremely important. But the participants in a local prevention strategy should not forget that there are other major site owners – such as British Rail, the Churches, and development companies – which may be prepared to co-operate in controlling poster alcohol advertising.

Any local group or agency concerned with alcohol-related problems could – instead of seeking the total abolition of alcohol advertising – press for any partial controls which are appropriate *and* for a portion of alcohol poster revenue accruing to the local authority to be devoted to the support of local alcohol prevention activities.

Advertising in the broadcast media

The code of practice which controls alcohol advertising in the broadcast media is the Independent Broadcasting Authority (IBA) Code of Advertising Standards and Practice. Unlike the BCAP it has some legal status. The IBA has a statutory responsibility for the content of all broadcasting on independent radio and television. It is required by Act of Parliament to maintain a Code of Advertising Standards and to ensure that broadcasters comply with it. Changes in the IBA Code must be approved by the Home Secretary.

The IBA Code of Advertising Standards and Practice

The preamble to the IBA Code notes that the general principle which must govern all broadcast advertising is that it should be 'legal, decent, honest and truthful'. Its many provisions deal with such things as programme independence, 'subliminal' advertising, good taste, and price claims.

The IBA administers the Code with the aid of the Independent Television Companies Association (ITCA) (which is the commercial television companies' trade association) and the Association of Independent Radio Contractors (AIRC). Scripts and tapes for television and independent radio advertisements are submitted to the ITCA/AIRC Copy Committee which approves advertisements before they are broadcast. If changes are necessary, agencies may not proceed with production until the revised advertisements have received approval. If an advertisement for independent radio transmission is to be broadcast by one station only, scripts are not sent to ITCA/AIRC but direct to the station concerned. However, this does not apply to medical and financial advertisements, pilot and test campaigns, or advertisements for alcoholic drink. In these cases the script must be sent to the ITCA/AIRC even if only one station is involved. In this way, all TV and independent radio advertisements are 'pre-screened'. Despite this 'pre-screening' it is possible to complain about broadcast advertisements and, indeed, the IBA has drawn attention to this fact.

The responsibility for implementing, interpreting and developing the IBA Code of Advertising Standards and Practice is shared between:

- The Independent Broadcasting Authority;
- The IBA's Advertising Advisory Committee, which contains representatives of consumers and advertisers;
- The Medical Advisory Panel, composed of doctors who advise on advertisements which have medical implications;
- The ITCA/AIRC Copy Committee.

The IBA Code and alcohol advertising

At about the same time as the BCAP was revised to include Appendix J, the IBA also responded to pressure for better control of liquor advertising. Rules relating to the broadcast advertising of alcoholic drink came into force in October 1978 and are contained in section 33 of the IBA Code of Advertising Standards and Practice. Section 33 is reproduced as Appendix 3.B to this chapter. Like the BCAP it lays down a number of conditions for alcohol advertisers. These include not showing anyone younger than 'about 25' in an alcohol advertisement, and not linking drinking with driving or potentially dangerous machinery.

In addition to the rules laid out in section 33, other parts of the IBA Code cover alcohol-relevant issues, such as advertisements for breath-testing devices, products which purport to mask the effects of alcohol (section 17a), and products for the treatment of alcoholism (Appendix 3–2(c)).

The Broadcasting Act 1981 empowers programme companies to impose stricter standards than those laid out in the Code. Like all advertisers they have a recognized right to reject any advertisement they wish.

The IBA Code is supplemented by 'notes of guidance' on a variety of topics. Notes of guidance for television advertising are issued by ITCA and for independent radio and Oracle teletext by the IBA itself. These notes of guidance are 'case-law' and are regarded by the IBA as an integral part of the Code and not, in any sense, optional. Alcohol is dealt with in Notes of Guidance No. 7 *The Advertising of Food and Drink*. This contains provisions which are not spelt out in the main Code. For instance the notes say that care should be taken that treatments featuring sportsmen being refreshed after activity do not give any impression that their performance is enhanced by alcoholic drink, and that sporting and other personalities likely to inspire loyalty, admiration, or emulation in young people are not acceptable in drink advertisements. In particular, professional footballers and pop stars should be avoided, even when fictitious and played by actors. Thus recent poster campaigns associating breweries and their beers with particular football teams would not be permitted in television advertisements unless the advertisement was agreed to be 'humorous'.

Local action

The participants in a local prevention strategy should be just as prepared to complain about broadcast alcohol advertisements as non-broadcast ones. The aim, as with non-broadcast advertisements (see above), would be to encourage stricter interpretation and implementation of the IBA Code and to push for its improvement.

When it was introduced the IBA Code was welcomed by consumer groups because its tighter provisions seemed an improvement on the BCAP. However, like the BCAP, the IBA Code is self-regulatory. A number of advertisements do appear to be aimed specifically at young people – especially young males. There is nothing to prevent sporting and other personalities appearing in 'humorous' advertisements which, like non-broadcast alcohol advertisements, can be interpreted as projecting messages which would otherwise breach the Code. They may influence vulnerable groups despite the claims that they are 'not meant to be taken seriously'. The Code forbids the depiction of *regular* solitary drinking but it is difficult to know how 'regularity' might be shown in a broadcast alcohol advertisement. Should the Code be revised to forbid the depiction of any solitary drinking?

All complaints should clearly identify the advertisements being complained about and should specify which parts of the IBA Code or the notes of guidance are being breached. Since all broadcast alcohol advertisements have been 'pre-screened' and, therefore, judged to be in conformity with the Code's provisions, it will be necessary to spell out in full detail why an advertisement is felt to be unacceptable.

As with the BCAP, the purpose of complaining is not only to clarify ambiguity and to sharpen the implementation of the IBA Code but to help remedy its omissions. Complaints could, therefore, be made about advertisements which associate drinking and water sports or bathing or those in which sportsmen and other personalities appear even though the advertisements may be 'humorous'. Complainants should urge the up-dating of the IBA Code to incorporate the provisions in the notes of guidance dealing with *The Advertising of Food and Drink*. It is unhelpful that the various provisions regulating to the broadcast advertising of alcohol are divided up in this way.

Complainants should write to the IBA but it might be useful to send a copy also to the Advisory Committee. On occasions, it may be appropriate to send a copy to the Medical Advisory Panel and the ITCA/AIRC Copy Committee. The address of the IBA is:

The Independent Broadcasting Authority
70 Brompton Road
London SW3 1EY
(Tel: 01–584–7011)

The Advertising Advisory Committee and the Medical Advisory Panel are located at the same address. Any copy of a complaint sent to the ITCA/AIRC should be addressed to:

The ITCA/AIRC
52–66 Mortimer Street
London W1N
(Tel: 01–363–6866)

The promotion of alcohol through sports sponsorship

Neither the BCAP nor the IBA Code make any specific mention of alcohol and sport. However, both codes have provisions forbidding the association of alcohol with 'physical performance'. In addition, the notes of guidance on alcohol advertising, which supplement and extend the IBA Code, make it clear that the use of sporting and other personalities – even when portrayed by actors – should not be used in drink advertisements. The failure of the codes to make a specific reference to sport has given rise to criticism. However, the association between alcohol and sport is much more common and 'visible' in the area of sport sponsorship – a growing form of indirect advertising.

Sports sponsorship – a two way deal

'Sponsorship' is direct financial or other assistance provided to sports organizations, clubs, or individuals involved in sport. It includes providing money for a specific event or series of events in return for advertising and publicity. The title of the event or organization may or may not include the name of the sponsor or one of the sponsor's products. If sponsorship is fully integrated into a marketing plan a sponsor has a number of opportunities to exploit the investment in areas such as television, press, and public relations.

Both the Sports Council which seeks to promote sport and the Central Council of Physical Recreation (CCPR), the umbrella organization for over 240 sporting bodies, actively encourage sports organizations in the UK to seek financial and other promotional support from sponsors. In 1982 the Sports Council and the CCPR launched a Sports Sponsorship Advisory Service, the aim of which is to increase commercial involvement in sport. The Service offers free advice on sponsorship to governing bodies of sport and to potential sponsors. At the launch of the Sports Sponsorship Advisory Service the director said:

> 'Sports sponsorship offers a financial lifeline for many sports, and for every company involved there are another two hundred who are not. This new service can help tap these resources to the benefit of both sport and business.'

The mutual benefits for sporting organizations and companies have led to a dramatic increase in sponsorship. The 'Howell' Committee of Enquiry estimated that in 1971 £2.5m was spent by companies on sports sponsorship. By 1983 this had grown to approximately £30m – the equivalent of £100.2m at 1971 prices. Total money spent on sponsorship is probably much greater than these figures indicate because of the 'hidden costs' that are involved. In evidence to an enquiry in New Zealand it was claimed that for every dollar spent on sponsorship, three more are spent by sponsors on promoting the fact of their sponsorship.

Television and sponsored sports

Television coverage is an important factor in sponsorship of an event. In 1982, the top thirty-five sponsored sporting events attracted 647 hours of television time. Tobacco companies dominated this coverage with 247 hours. Insurance companies came second with 228 hours, whilst in third place came drink companies with 61 hours of coverage. However, of the 700 or so companies which were then involved in sports sponsorship, well over 500 of them sponsored sports which were not shown on television. It is not necessary to have sponsored events televised in order to achieve successful product promotion or publicity.

Both the BBC and IBA have certain guidelines governing the televising of sponsored sporting events in order to place some limits on the transmission of 'free advertising'.

The BBC acknowledges that there is a demand to see major, sponsored events on television and that it has an obligation to the public, from whom it derives its licence fee income, to meet it. At the same time its charter forbids commercial intrusion into its programmes.

In 1982 an internal committee examined the whole question of advertising and the BBC. Its 'committee' conclusions were contained in a report entitled *The BBC and Advertising – Guidelines*. These guidelines have been distilled and are available to BBC staff to help them make consistent and informed judgements. They are for internal use and are not generally available to 'outsiders'. Their interpretation and application may vary from case to case. When, despite the guidelines, a doubtful situation arises, BBC staff are expected to 'refer upwards' to their superiors for an authoritative decision.

The section of the guidelines which relates to the coverage of sponsored events stresses that the BBC has no obligation to sponsors. Its relationship is with the promoters or governing bodies organizing the events. The guidelines deal with the detailed considerations which should be kept in mind when broadcasting a sponsored event. They include the following provisions:

- Placards carrying the name of the sponsor must not be unduly prominent and must not come between the viewer and the action.
- Two banner-type signs which, at the BBC's discretion, may show the name of the sponsor or the registered title of the sponsoring organization, can be within range of the main camera position.
- Not more than two verbal credits should be made in a programme and no brand or product names are permitted unless the BBC has

agreed, in advance, that in popular usage such a name has become indistinguishable from that of a manufacturer.

The IBA's *Television Programme Guidelines* include advice to the television companies on the televising of sponsored events. The guidelines are generally available and, indeed, in his foreword to the February 1984 edition, the Director General says:

'The existence of written Guidelines should help to maintain good practice, not only between the IBA and the companies, but also between the companies *and outside bodies and individuals.*' (emphasis added)

The section of the IBA guidelines devoted to sponsorship and indirect advertising makes it clear that 'sponsored programmes' – in the American sense – are not allowed on ITV. When a programme contains an acknowledgement to a funder no advertisement incorporating the funder's name is allowed within or around that programme.

Detailed guidance on sponsorship and indirect advertising is found in an appendix to the IBA guidelines which reproduces the conclusions of a 1976 working party on indirect advertising. These conclusions were distributed not only to television companies but also to the organizers of major sporting events and potential sponsors of such events. The large number of provisions contained in the appendix include:

- Two sponsor's signs may appear on the course or on the arena. The siting of such signs must not, in the opinion of the producer at the time of the survey, obtrude either on the television pictures or on the action of the event.
- There may be two verbal credits relating the sponsor to the event during the transmission of the programme.
- The name of the competition may appear on the scoreboard of the event.

The report of the 'Howell' Committee of Enquiry into Sports Sponsorship noted in chapter 13, section 21, that abuses of sponsorship exist; and that many of them are linked with television coverage and attempts to get sponsors' advertising onto the small screen. These attempts include the painting of advertisements on the surface of boxing rings, cycle tracks, motor tracks and similar arenas and the sudden appearance of unauthorized banners among crowds at sporting events. In addition, journalists told the committee that they were often pressurized to mention the names of sponsors in their articles.

Alcohol and sponsorship

Alcohol companies currently spend £18m a year on sports sponsorship, about 9 per cent of their £200m advertising expenditure Over twenty different football league teams receive alcohol company sponsorship. First Division Tottenham Hotspur has signed a £425,000 deal with lager makers Holstein. The brand name will be displayed around the ground, on programmes, and on the players' sports gear, despite recent legislation to restrict alcohol sales at football grounds.

Drinks companies sponsor many different kinds of sports. A Sports Sponsorship Advisory Service publication, *UK Companies, Products and the Sports They Sponsor, 1980–81* identifies 102 alcohol brand names linked to sports as diverse as greyhound racing, angling, and badminton.

Brewing companies are prominent. In June 1982 the Brewers' Society issued a questionnaire on sports sponsorship to all its seventy-eight full member companies – which produce about 99.5 per cent of all beer brewed in the UK. It was found that fifty-seven of them sponsored sports. Some spent as little as £500 while four spent over £250,000. The range of sponsorship expenditure closely paralleled the size of the brewers in terms of barrels produced per annum. Brewers sponsored amateur and professional sport, well-known and minority games, individual leagues, events, and specific matches. They presented trophies and prizes, helped create specific competitions, and sponsored sport at local, county, regional, national, and international levels.

The strong local associations of many breweries and their products mean that the sponsorship of local sports is particularly important. Forty-nine brewers sponsored *only* local sports.

One of the aims of sponsorship is to increase the public's perception of the sponsoring company as a benefactor of the community. In addition, its product may also be seen to be associated with the 'healthy lifestyle' which sport implies. The major question from a public health point of view is: what does the association of healthy sporting activities with products such as tobacco and alcohol have on participants and spectators? Can sponsorship by tobacco and alcohol companies be reconciled with public health goals? The sports-minded young may be particularly vulnerable to this form of indirect advertising. As the author of *The Game Companies Play* put it:

'The young are a specific target group for the promotion of sport. The promotion of sports has built around the promotion of heroes. They are inseparable. Spectators go to a match to see figures that are larger than life, who are out on their own and possessing skills which they could never match. Such philosophy is pitched at youth.' (*Australian Business*, 24 September, 1981)

The association of sport and tobacco has attracted considerable attention. Since 1977 the sponsorship of sport in the UK by tobacco companies has been regulated by a code of practice agreed by the Tobacco Advisory Council, the DHSS, and the Department of the Environment. Its current provisions include:

- Spending on sponsorship cannot rise above 1976 levels, except for increases in line with inflation.
- Health warnings have to be included on advertisements for sponsored events and on promotional signs at the events.
- The companies must consult with the minister if they intend to sponsor a new sport.

There have been no similar moves to regulate the sponsorship of sport by alcohol companies. The main sporting organizations are firmly opposed to such a move. The CCPR argues that sport and pubs have been connected for over four centuries and that some sports owe most of their popularity to the active participation of amateur enthusiasts who play the games in pubs and that other sports such as angling and cricket owe much to their pub and brewery connections.

The council of the Brewers' Society has recommended that members should apply the principles of the BCAP and the IBA Code when arranging sponsorship and the Central Council of Physical Recreation has noted that this recommendation means that any suggestions that alcohol enhances physical performance are not permitted. The CCPR also notes that the principles of the two advertising codes preclude the use of 'heroes of the young' in sponsorship.

If, as has been suggested, much sport pivots around 'heroes' who are particularly attractive to the sports-minded young, it is difficult to see how breweries which accept their own council's recommendations can justify sponsorship involving, for instance, the local football team.

The council of the Brewers' Society has also recommended that its members should not sponsor motor sport. It is considered that any connection between drinking and driving would not be in the public interest. The Brewers' Society does, therefore, recognize that in one area at least the connection between alcohol and sport may be harmful.

Local action

The participants in a local prevention strategy should not lose any opportunity to make their views about alcohol and sport sponsorship known to local sporting organizations. This includes the many bodies representing different sports in a locality, especially those which are affiliated to the CCPR and the regional, district, and local levels of the Sports Council. The aim should be to promote debate and discussion about 'alcohol and sport' at all levels within these important organizations.

Local prevention workers might wish to complain about advertisements for sports sponsored by alcohol companies. Such advertisements will, of course, be covered by the BCAP or the IBA Code. Complaints could be made about advertisements specifically directed at young people or which in any way suggest that alcohol can enhance physical prowess. When complaining, it should be emphasized that the notes of guidance on alcohol advertising which supplement the BCAP Code prohibit the use of 'heroes of the young'. It might be argued that it is difficult to see why brewery posters showing local football teams are acceptable in the high street and not on television screens. Many complaints will, undoubtedly, be rejected. But complaining may create an impetus for change.

BBC and ITV coverage of televised sponsored events could be monitored. A local consumers' group might be willing to help with this. Monitoring would be made much easier if the BBC could be persuaded to make its guidelines public and generally available as does the IBA. Complaints should be made to the BBC and the IBA about any deviations from their guidelines. The participants in a local prevention strategy might like to consider how these guidelines could be improved.

There is widespread agreement that sponsorship provides many sports with much-needed financial support and that, from the sponsoring company's point of view, it is a cost-effective way of promoting sales and good public relations. Any local prevention group could undertake to publicize the benefits of sports sponsorship among the business community in its locality in order to find alternatives to sponsorship by drink companies. Sporting organizations which have sponsorship arrangements with alcohol companies could be encouraged to ensure that any contractual arrangements which are made are limited to short periods and do not preclude other companies from sponsorship and advertising opportunities.

The presentation of alcohol in the media

Images of alcohol are presented in ways other than through direct and indirect advertising. Feature articles and documentary programmes about alcohol-related problems can help to remind people that there is another side to the pleasures of drinking which are constantly portrayed in advertising.

Chapter 2 provides some information and advice on how to establish links with local press and radio which can encourage these media to support and promote a local prevention strategy in terms of the way they feature alcohol. However, some of the most persistent and important images, which contribute to our stock of taken-for-granted ideas about drink and drinking, are those transmitted every night in television programmes. It is as important to monitor these as it is those projected by advertisements.

In 1977, the DHSS Advisory Committee on Alcoholism called for a more balanced representation of the effects of drinking, particularly in television programmes. This recommendation was 'noted' by the government in the 1977 White Paper *Prevention and Health* and 'brought to the attention' of the broadcasting authorities. The DHSS believes that the presentation of alcohol is an important component in a preventive strategy. As *Drinking Sensibly* puts it, this involves:

> 'Consideration by the broadcasting authorities, programme makers, producers and writers . . . to ensure that the presentation of alcohol . . . does not unwittingly encourage bad habits.'   (DHSS 1981: 66)

BBC TV and the presentation of alcohol

The BBC believes that, although alcohol consumption can regularly be seen in many BBC productions, care is taken to show it being used in moderation, as a harmless accompaniment to social intercourse and private relaxation. However, it is precisely this 'routinization' which many feel is unhelpful, since it reinforces the idea that pouring out a drink is one of the 'most natural things to do'.

Perhaps the most potent reason for much of the drinking portrayed in plays and serials is that the cast is involved in what is called 'business'. Dialogue must be accompanied by some sort of activity. The most obvious thing to do with the hands is pouring out a drink or lighting up a cigarette. Since television has ceased to portray cigarette smoking as 'natural' – and has thereby helped to contribute to the reduction of cigarette smoking – drinking has become even more important as 'business'.

The BBC does not have publicly available guidelines on the presentation of alcohol in its programmes. The BBC expects programme makers to show fidelity to their subject. If the context clearly requires drinking to be shown then it can be, but it expects 'commonsense' and 'maturity of judgement' to be shown. In cases of doubt a query can be referred 'upwards'.

The IBA and the presentation of alcohol

Unlike the BBC, the IBA has publicly available guidelines relating to the presentation of alcohol. The guidelines are contained in a paragraph of the *Television Programme Guidelines* which can be obtained from the IBA Information Department (see above). The paragraph reads:

> 'Tobacco and alcohol are social drugs whose consumption carries no particular stigma even though they can constitute a major health risk and may be as addictive as drugs which are less socially approved, or actually illegal. It is therefore desirable that programmes should not include smoking and drinking unless the context or dramatic veracity requires it.
>
> Particular care is needed with programmes likely to be seen by children and young people. Programmes made specially for children should not normally contain smoking, or drinking of alcohol, unless an educational point is being made, or unless their exceptional dramatic context makes it absolutely essential.

The existence of these written guidelines will not automatically guarantee that everyone will approve of the way alcohol is handled on independent television programmes. In the final analysis, ITV programme-makers, like those of the BBC, have to interpret the significance of 'context' and use their own 'commonsense' and 'good judgement'. They are subjected to the same pressures as their BBC colleagues to find 'business'. However, the public guidelines do make the independent television companies' concern over the presentation of alcohol visible. They provide a reference point and a 'handle' for complaints.

Local action

Chapter 2 underlined the need for local prevention workers to establish helpful working relationships with their local newspaper and radio and television stations. Links with independent television companies which, of course, cover specific regions could be used to ensure good 'presentation of alcohol' practices. Participants in a local prevention strategy might find it useful to sponsor a seminar on, for example, 'the presentation of alcohol in the media' and to invite programme makers from their local television station.

Media personnel are an 'at risk' group where alcohol problems are concerned. It may well be that their own attitudes towards drinking, and their own drinking habits, make it difficult for them to take those steps to reduce the depiction of drinking on television which many now feel is necessary. Chapter 6 contains material on alcohol and work policies which can help to change unhelpful attitudes. The value of these policies could be drawn to the attention of the television companies.

Complaints should be made about any unhelpful presentation of alcohol either on BBC or independent television. 'Unhelpful' can mean a number of things. It might mean that a particular context does not, strictly, require the portrayal of drinking. This is likely to be one of the most common situations. On the other hand, although relevant, drinking behaviour which is portrayed may be inappropriate or unwise. Characters in a public house who indulge in round buying, taking a drink before setting of to drive or, if it is 'a serial', who never appear to buy a soft drink, would fall into this category. So would the portrayal of drinking under stress or to build up nerve and courage.

As well as responding to individual portrayals or to the way alcohol is treated in particular programmes, a number of television programmes could be monitored over a period to assess the number of times in which alcohol is 'business'. Any complaint should clearly identify the programme, the incidents complained about and precisely why it is felt that the presentation of alcohol was unacceptable.

Complaints about BBC's television programmes should be addressed to the producer named in the credits. They are expected to respond directly to non-serious complaints. Complaints of a 'serious' nature are dealt with on a higher level. Complaints about the presentation of alcohol may be seen as 'serious' if sufficient complaints are received. The address is:

BBC Television
Television Centre
Wood Lane
London W12 8QT
(Tel: 01–743–8000)

Complaints about the content of independent television programmes should be sent to the programme director of the transmitting company. The producer of a programme on independent television may be an employee of another independent television company if the programme has been 'networked' or of an entirely independent production company. The complaint should refer to the relevant paragraph of the IBA *Television Programme Guidelines*, and could also be sent to the IBA.

This is intended to be a *living* 'guide to action'. Therefore, it needs to be revised and added to in the light of local needs and local experience.

The following two pages are for jotting down examples of good practice, and addresses relevant to the issues covered by this chapter.

We hope to update the guide, and would be delighted to receive any advice about corrections, new material or any other information which should go into the next edition. Please send all suggestions, before 31 December, 1987, to:

Philip Tether and David Robinson
Addiction Research Centre
University of Hull
Hull HU6 7RX

Examples of Good Practice

Useful Addresses and Telephone Numbers

Further reading

Advertising Association, *Alcohol Advertising in the Context of Consumption and Abuse*, Summary of principal points raised at Peterhouse Seminar, Cambridge, 1981, published by the Advertising Association, Abford House, 15 Wilton Road, London SW1V 1NJ

Advertising Standards Authority, *Annual Reports*, obtainable from Brook House, 2–16 Torrington Place, London WC1E 7HN

CCPR, 'Committee of Enquiry into Sports Sponsorship', (Howell Report), November 1983. Available from the Central Council of Physical Recreation, Francis House, Francis Street, London SW1P 1DE

Cook, J. and Lewington, M. (eds), *Images of Alcoholism*, British Film Institute, London, 1979

Dillin, J., 'TV Drinking', *Christian Science Monitor*, 11 July, 1975

Dorn, N. and South, N., *Message in a Bottle: Theoretical Overview and Annotated Bibliography on the Mass Media and Alcohol*, Gower, Aldershot, 1983

Duffy, M., 'Advertising, Taxation and the Demand for Beer, Spirits and Wine in the United Kingdom, 1963–1978', the University of Manchester Institute of Science and Technology, Occasional Paper no. 8009, 1980

EEC Draft Opinion of the Consumers Consultative Committee (CCC) on consumers, alcohol advertising, and codes of ethics, Commission of the European Communities, reference X1-225, 1982

Garlington, W., 'Drinking on Television', *Journal of Studies on Alcohol*, 38, 2199–205, 1977

Hagan, L. and Waterson, M., 'The Relationship between Alcohol Advertising and Consumption', report prepared for the *ITCA*, 1980

Harrison, L., *The Regulation of Advertising for Alcoholic Drinks*, Addiction Research Centre working paper, University of Hull, October 1984.

Independent Broadcasting Authority, *Annual Reports*, obtainable from 70 Brompton Road, London SW3 1EY

Institute of Alcohol Studies, *The Presentation of Alcohol in the Mass Media*, papers and summary of discussion at IBA House, Institute of Alcohol Studies, London, 1985.

Leathar, D. S., Hastings, G. B., and Davies, J. K., *Health Education and the Media*, Pergamon Press, Oxford, 1981

Loney, M., 'Why Drink Ads Are Never Curbed', *Community Care*, 22 January, 1981

Ogborne, A. and Smart, R., 'Will Restrictions on Alcohol Advertising Reduce Alcohol Consumption?', *British Journal of Addiction*, 75, 293–96, 1980

Plant, M. and Ritson, B., *Alcohol: the Prevention Debate*, Croom Helm, London, 1983

Small, J., 'Alcohol Portrayal in the Mass Media', *Alcohol, Health and Research World*, 5, 1, 1980

The Sports Council, 'Why Sponsorship of Sport?' handout produced by Sports Sponsorship Advisory Service, 16 Upper Woburn Place, London WC1H OQP

Williams, G. and Thompson Brake, G., *Drink in Great Britian, 1900–1979*, B. Edsall and Co., London, 1980, chapter 13: 'Liquor Advertising'

Appendix 3.A:

The British Code of Advertising Practice (BCAP) – Appendix J: Advertising for alcoholic drinks

Introduction

1.1 Moderate drinking is widely enjoyed and helps to make social occasions cheerful and pleasant.

1.2 The Alcoholic Drinks Industry, with others, is aware that a small, but significant minority cause harm to themselves and others through misuse of alcohol. They share the concern about this social problem, the causes of which are complex and varied. There is no evidence connecting such misuse with the advertising of alcoholic drinks.

1.3 The industry is concerned that its advertisements should not exploit the immature, the young, the socially insecure, or those with physical, mental or social incapacity. The industry accepts that its advertising should be socially responsible and should not encourage excessive consumption.

1.4 The industry believes that it is proper for advertisements for alcoholic drinks:

1. to indicate that they give pleasure to many, are of high quality and are widely enjoyed in all classes of society.

2. to seek to persuade people to change brands and/or types of drinks.

3. to provide information on products.

4. to employ such accepted techniques of advertising practice as are employed by other product groups and are not inconsistent with the detailed rules.

Implementation and Interpretation

2.1 The industry has therefore proposed the following rules for inclusion in the British Code of Advertising Practice. The CAP Committee has accepted this proposal and the Advertising Standards Authority has agreed to supervise the implementation of the rules.

2.2 The rules are to be interpreted in the light of the considerations set out in paragraphs 1.1 to 1.4 above. So far as the scope and general interpretation of the rules is concerned, the provisions of the British Code of Advertising Practice apply, as they do to those aspects of advertisements for drink not covered by the rules.

2.3 'Drink', for the purposes of this Appendix, is to be understood as referring to alcoholic beverages and their consumption.

Rules

3.1 *Young People*

Advertisements should not be directed at young people nor in any way encourage them to start drinking. Anyone shown drinking must appear to be over 21. Children should not be depicted in advertisements except where it would be usual for them to appear (e.g. in family scenes or in background crowds) but they should never be shown drinking alcoholic beverages, nor should it be implied that they are.

3.2 *Challenge*

Advertisements should not be based on a dare, nor impute any failing to those who do not accept the challenge of a particular drink.

3.3 *Health*

Advertisements should not emphasise the stimulant, sedative or tranquillising effects of any drink, nor imply that it can improve physical performance. However, references to the refreshing attributes of a drink are permissible.

3.4 *Strength*

Advertisements should not give the general impression of being inducements to prefer a drink because of its higher alcohol content or intoxicating effect. Factual information for the guidance of drinkers about such alcoholic strength may, however, be included.

3.5 *Social Success*

Advertisements may emphasise the pleasures of companionship and social communication associated with the consumption of alcoholic drinks, but it should never be implied that drinking is necessary to social or business success or distinction, nor that those who do not drink are less likely to be acceptable or successful than those who do. Advertisements should neither claim nor suggest that any drink can contribute towards sexual success, or make the drinker more attractive to the opposite sex.

3.6 *Drinking and Machinery*

Advertisements should not associate drink with driving or dangerous machinery. Specific warnings of the dangers of drinking in these circumstances may, however, be used.

3.7 *Excessive Drinking*

Advertisements should not encourage or appear to condone overindulgence. Repeated buying of large rounds should not be implied.

Appendix 3.B

Extract from 'The IBA Code of Advertising Standards and Practice'

Section 33 – Alcoholic Drink

(a) Liquor advertising may not be addressed particularly to the young and no one associated with drinking in an advertisement should seem to be younger than about 25. Children may not be seen or heard in an advertisement for an alcoholic drink.

(b) No liquor advertisement may feature any personality who commands the loyalty of the young.

(c) Advertisements may not imply that drinking is essential to social success or acceptance or that refusal is a sign of weakness.

(d) Advertisements must not feature or foster immoderate drinking. This applies to the quantity of drink being consumed in the advertisement and to the act of drinking portrayed. References to buying of rounds of drinks are not acceptable.

(e) Advertisements must not claim that alcohol has therapeutic qualities nor offer it expressly as a stimulant, sedative or tranquilliser. While advertisements may refer to refreshment after physical performance, they must not give any impression that performance can be improved by drink.

(f) Advertisements should not place undue emphasis on the alcoholic strength of drinks.

(g) Nothing in an advertisement may link drinking with driving or with the use of potentially dangerous machinery.

(h) No liquor advertisement may publicise a competition.

(i) Advertisements must neither claim nor suggest that any drink can contribute towards sexual success.

(j) Advertisements must not suggest that regular solitary drinking is acceptable.

(k) Treatments featuring special daring or toughness must not be used in a way which is likely to associate the act of drinking with masculinity.

CHAPTER 4

Alcohol and safety

CHAPTER 4

Alcohol and safety

'Alcohol-related impairment . . . means the dulling of senses and the loosening of normal inhibitions which immediately follow drinking. Even small degrees of impairment can be crucial and can result in accidental injuries or death.' (p. 10)

'It is estimated that one in five of all road deaths is related to excessive drinking. Road accidents cause roughly half of all male deaths between the ages of 15 and 24, and the largest factor in these casualties is alcohol.' (p. 14)   (*Drinking Sensibly*, HMSO 1981)

Alcohol in quite small amounts can impair co-ordination, affect judgement, and lead to accidents. The purpose of this chapter is to examine the part which alcohol plays in accidents of various kinds and to identify the local 'prevention resources' which could be mobilized in an effort to reduce alcohol-related accidental injury and death. The discussion is presented in three parts: home safety, water safety, and road safety. Two other alcohol and safety topics are discussed elsewhere in the guide: workplace accidents are dealt with in chapter 6 and road safety education for schoolchildren is covered in chapter 7.

Home safety

Each year, approximately 6,000 people die and over two million more are injured and require treatment because of accidents in the home. Of these, falls cause approximately 3,000 fatalities and 900,000 non-fatal injuries. Other common categories of accidents are poisonings, chokings, cuts and gashes, and electrocution. In general, elderly people are more susceptible to *fatal accidents* whilst young children are more prone to *non-fatal* ones. Up to the age of sixty-four males are more susceptible than females to fatal accidents but thereafter the position is reversed due to the greater susceptibility of elderly women to death as a result of falls.

Little publicity is given to home accidents despite the fact that there are as many fatalities as there are from road accidents. Even less publicity is given to the role which alcohol plays in accidents in the home.

The size of the problem

Information on the role of alcohol in home accidents is sparse. Most of it concerns *fatal accidents* and is gleaned from coroners' files. One analysis of the Birmingham coroner's files in 1980 revealed that out of 589 deaths, 165 were attributable to 'home accidents' of which nineteen were alcohol-related.

Another analysis of fatal home accidents, using coroners' files, entitled *Personal Factors in Domestic Accidents – Prevention Through Product and Environmental Design* was published in 1980 by the Consumer Safety Unit of the Department of Trade. This short but invaluable study revealed that out of a sample of 280 accidental deaths in the 15–64 age group no less than 102 (30 per cent) involved alcohol. The breakdown by type of accident was:

Alcohol and falls	29
Alcohol and fires	11
Alcohol, choking, and poisoning	7
Alcohol and overdose	21
Alcohol and carbon-monoxide fumes	2
Alcohol and drowning (in the home)	2
Alcohol and drugs	30
	102

The same report, again using coroners' files, examined in detail 173 cases of deaths from fire in England and Wales in 1973. It was found that alcohol was implicated in twenty-two (13 per cent) of these cases. The immediate cause of ignition in thirteen of these cases was 'dropped cigarettes'.

The contribution of alcohol to non-fatal home accidents is very difficult to establish, but appears to be substantial. The accident and emergency department at Edinburgh Royal Hospital breathalyzed 700 accident victims on seventeen evenings. It was found that 40 per cent of patients had consumed alcohol before attending, and 32 per cent had a blood/alcohol concentration exceeding the 'driving limit'.

Most discussion of accident prevention has tended to concentrate on particular sources of injury, or 'harm agents', and to draw attention to facts such as that faulty electric blankets can kill, that sharp edges of open food cans cut, or that slippery floors can cause falls. However, the Consumer Safety Unit's investigation of home accidents revealed the importance of personal and social factors in addition to the harm agents. In many cases, the victims lived in poor socio-economic conditions and the accidents involved not only alcohol but also illness: confusion, senility, stress, and drugs. Many accident victims, therefore, are people who are least likely to be reached by, or respond to, conventional education and publicity campaigns. Important though these are, such campaigns need to be supplemented with more imaginative local initiatives.

Local action

Local authorities, fire services, and district health authorities all have an important role to play in the home safety field and can contribute to this component of an integrated local prevention strategy. They can each develop their own good practices. Moreover, local authorities can establish Home Safety Committees which could provide a firm base, in any locality, for the development of 'alcohol and home safety' initiatives involving the fire service, the local health authority, and many other organizations and groups.

Home Safety Committees The Home Safety Act 1961 empowers all local authorities in England and Wales except the London boroughs to promote safety in the home. London has its own legislative arrangements. These powers can be exercised by district and metropolitan borough councils which are the authorities responsible for housing and environmental health. Some authorities have set up multi-disciplinary Home Safety Committees. Such a committee should, ideally, have a wide range of members including councillor and officer representations from the social services department of the County Council, voluntary organizations, the public utilities such as gas and electricity, and the local health authority. Where a committee exists, one or more local authority officers, usually from the environmental health department, will be given responsibility for home safety. However, since the promotion of home safety is not mandatory some authorities are not involved and even where a commitment exists there is not always a committee. Where committees do exist their membership is often restricted, their meetings sporadic, and their activities limited by their low status and low budgets. Some have no budget at all.

There are fourteen Area Home Safety Councils in the UK. These are loose federations of local authorities, including Home Safety Committees and other bodies concerned with home safety which meet on a regional basis to discuss matters of common concern. Each of these councils meets three or four times a year and sends two representatives – one officer and one elected member – to the National Home and Leisure Safety Committee (NHLSC) administered by the Home and Leisure Safety Division of RoSPA. The NHLSC also includes representatives of relevant government departments and of local government organizations such as the Association of County Councils and the Association of District Councils. Other bodies represented include British Gas, the Electricity Council, the British Standards Institution, the Association of Chief and Assistant Chief Fire Officers, and the Society of Health Education Officers. There is, therefore, a chain of committees concerned with home safety, linking the 'grass roots' with a wide variety of national organizations.

All areas should be served by a vigorous Home Safety Committee on which all important organizations, including those concerned with the prevention of alcohol problems, are represented. A vigorous committee could tackle the 'alcohol and home accident' problem in a number of ways which are discussed below.

Research   Home Safety Committees have an important role to play in encouraging the routine collection of more and better information on 'alcohol and home accidents'. Coroners' files are an important source of local information and may be available to anyone wishing to research this issue. The local university or college of higher education might have students who would be interested in understanding this kind of investigation for a project.

The Home Accident Surveillance System (HASS)   HASS was set up in 1976 to provide reliable and comprehensive information on home accidents with the aim of monitoring and costing trends and identifying areas in which preventive action could be usefully initiated. Data are drawn from twenty A and E departments in England and Wales. Each year ten of the departments are replaced by others, creating a 'rolling' sample. Accidents are analysed on HASS home accident report forms which are completed in the departments with the aid of extra clerical help paid for by the Department of Trade and Industry. These forms do not have questions dealing specifically with the alcohol component of an accident, although such information is sometimes volunteered by the patient. However, without systematic information on alcohol the HASS survey is seriously incomplete. Home Safety Committees might like to consider this issue and push for it to be considered further in the national, home safety committee structure. HASS Annual Reports can be obtained from:

Consumer Safety Unit
Department of Trade and Industry
Millbank Tower
Millbank
London SW1P 4QU
(Tel: 01-211-7521)

Alcohol poisoning among young people   One important dimension of alcohol and home safety concerns young people and alcohol poisoning. In the year to August 1982, eighteen alcohol poisoning episodes involving children under the age of ten years were recorded by the HASS survey. A study of all poisoning episodes in children under fifteen was carried out in Newcastle between 1974 and 1981. A total of 720 poisoning cases were recorded, seventeen of which involved alcohol poisoning in children under the age of five.

A Home Safety Committee might find it useful to conduct specific investigations in this area. Any results could be communicated to the national home safety network and the Child Accident Prevention Trust (CAPT). CAPT produces a *Register of Research into Child Accident Prevention* which a local Home Safety Committee might find useful. The address of the Trust is:

Child Accident Prevention Trust
Faculty of Clinical Sciences
University College London
University Street
London WC1E 6JJ
(Tel: 01-388-5652)

Public Education   Home Safety Committees can play an important role in public education programmes, which are an essential part of any comprehensive local prevention strategy. Since 'alcohol and home safety' is a largely unexplored topic it would, hopefully, raise interest and stimulate local debate. The need for parents to ensure that their young children do not gain access to alcohol in the home could form an important component of a committee's public education activities. Some basic information on educating the 'general public' via the press, radio, and TV is outlined in chapter 2.

GPs, alcohol, and home accidents   General medical practitioners deal with approximately 500,000 home accidents per year. Many GPs recognize that a proportion of these home accidents are alcohol-related. A Home Safety Committee could raise this whole issue with the Local Medical Committee (LMC) which represents local GPs. These LMCs usually produce a newsletter which could serve as a vehicle for an informative article on the subject. A member of the LMC could be invited to sit on the Home Safety Committee which could itself contribute to GPs' in-service training (see chapter 8).

Community health   If the deaths and injuries caused by accidents in the home were the result of infectious disease the NHS would probably mobilize all its preventive resources. However, home accidents attract very little publicity or attention. Since the whole topic of home safety is a community health issue, every Home Safety Committee should consider the inclusion of a specialist in community medicine in its membership. Such a link might help not only to encourage local research and changes in A and E procedures but also to increase the importance which the local health authority gives to the whole 'alcohol issue'.

The fire service   The fire service is well aware of the connection between alcohol misuse and fires. Experienced firemen can confirm that, in many cases, people who are present when fires start appear to have been drinking. Reseach sponsored by the Fire Research Station at Boreham Wood has confirmed this. The 1981 annual report of the Strathclyde Firemaster – the equivalent of a chief fire officer in England and Wales – estimated that 80 per cent of the fire fatalities within his authority involved alcohol. In Glasgow the fire service mounted a campaign to alert the public to the connection between alcohol misuse and fires.

A Home Safety Committee could encourage the local fire service to mention these specific 'alcohol and fire' connections in the extensive public information work which every service undertakes with groups ranging from schoolchildren to housewives and the elderly. In addition, a Home Safety Committee could seek the support and co-operation of its fire service in mounting local campaigns on the topic and in any training events for those workers who are in a position to safeguard groups who are particularly 'at risk'.

Protecting the vulnerable   The elderly, the ill, and the socially deprived are high-risk groups for accidents of all kinds but, at the same time, the least likely to respond to conventional education and publicity. Because of this, much accident prevention work is now focused on the physical and social contexts of 'at risk' individuals. The aim is to reduce risks in the physical environment and to improve care and supervision.

In every locality there are many workers, such as home helps, wardens of sheltered housing and homes for the elderly, health visitors, district nurses, and community psychiatric nurses in contact with people who are vulnerable. A Home Safety Committee could bring such workers within its orbit through the inclusion of a representative of the social services department and the district health authority's community nursing services in its membership. The aim would be to supplement preventive education and publicity with personal advice and, most importantly, identify hazards which may not be obvious to the potential victims. Workers who are aware of the potential 'alcohol and fire' risk – especially for clients who smoke – could reduce the risks by ensuring that there are, for example, well-guarded fires, sufficient ashtrays, and flame-resistant night attire. Links with social and nursing services could be used to influence pre-qualification and in-service training and to arrange multi-disciplinary events on home safety which would highlight the role alcohol can play in such accidents.

Alcohol and medicines   Alcohol and prescribed medicines can be a dangerous combination, causing the confusion and disorientation which precipitate many accidents. There is nothing in the Medicines Act 1968 or in any of the subsequent labelling regulations which requires a warning about alcohol use to be included on the label of a prescribed medicine. Any such warning is at the discretion of the prescribing practitioner or the dispensing pharmacist. The only legal requirement for 'alcohol warnings' on medicines applies to certain 'pharmacy medicines' which may only be sold in pharmacies but which are available 'over the counter' without a prescription. However, in 1984 the Pharmaceutical Society of Great Britain produced for the profession a guide to cautionary and advisory labels for dispensed medicines. The guide recommends twenty-eight cautionary and advisory labels and identifies the medicines which should carry them. Two of the labels make a specific reference to alcohol:

- 'Warning'. May cause drowsiness. If affected do not drive or operate machinery. Avoid alcoholic drink. (label 2)
- 'Warning'. Avoid alcoholic drink. (label 4)

The Pharmaceutical Society's guide recommends pharmacists to counsel patients on the use of the prescribed medicine and to ensure that the directions on the labels are understood. Details of the 'Guide to Cautionary and Advisory Labels for Dispensed Medicine' are in *The Pharmaceutical Journal*, 17 March, 1984. It is also hoped to include the guide in the *British National Formulary*, the compendium of available preparations produced by the Pharmaceutical Society in conjunction with the British Medical Association which is sent to all NHS doctors and pharmacists. Alternatively, information about the guide can be obtained from:

The Pharmaceutical Society of Great Britain
1 Lambert High Street
London SE1 7JN
(Tel: 01–735–9141)

It should be noted that the guide is only 'advisory'. While the Society fully expects its members to be in the forefront of 'good practice', it cannot enforce its new labelling system on them. A Home Safety Committee could monitor the situation in its area in order to see whether the guide is being followed by the local pharmacists. Enquiries could be initiated through the local branch of the Pharmaceutical Society or the local Family Practitioner Committee which is responsible for contracting with dispensing pharmacists for their services.

Education for young people   Chapter 7 outlines the need for more and better alcohol education for the young and how this might be promoted. Home Safety Committees could try to ensure that any educational programme includes at least some reference to 'alcohol and home safety' to illustrate the wide range of problems which can be caused by alcohol misuse. Such education might have an effect upon family behaviour if it alerted older children to the dangers of unsecured alcohol in the home and risks associated with, for example, parental drinking and smoking.

The Safety Education Department of the Royal Society for the Prevention of Accidents has some items on home safety and others are planned. Although none of these make any specific mention of the role of alcohol in home accidents, a Home Safety Committee might think it important to endorse the suggestion made in chapter 7 that individual schools or teachers should subscribe to the department's *Safety Education Journal* which will ensure that both home safety issues and materials become known locally. If a Home Safety Committee feels that the materials are inadequate they should inform the Safety Education Department at RoSPA. They might also consider devising their own leaflet for schools to supplement the alcohol education materials being promoted by an alcohol education committee, or held by local teachers' centres and by the health education unit. Full details of the various Safety Education Department's subscription schemes can be found in chapter 7. They can also be obtained direct from RoSPA at:

Royal Society for the Prevention of Accidents
Cannon House
The Priory
Queensway
Birmingham B4 6BS
(Tel: 021–233–2461)

Useful materials

An active Home Safety Committee will require regular information on home safety issues and on the materials available for use in publicity campaigns and exhibitions. These materials are available from two sources, the Royal Society for the Prevention of Accidents (RoSPA) and the Health Education Council.

RoSPA In addition to its Safety Education Department which specializes in educational material for young people, RoSPA has a Home and Leisure Safety Division. The division produces a range of audio-visual materials, posters, and leaflets and its catalogue is available to anyone on request. Organizations and individuals can take out either a 'One Star' or 'Three Star' subscription which currently costs £22 + VAT or £66 + VAT respectively. 'One Star' subscribers receive a

'Resource Pack' covering a home and leisure safety issue twice each year together with a quarterly magazine entitled *Care in the Home*. 'Three Star' subscribers receive the resource packs and the magazine plus a discount of one third on any materials purchased and the use of the division's information and library service. These subscribers can also call upon the services of the Division's home and leisure safety field staff. No Home Safety Committee can be fully informed and effective without using the services offered by RoSPA. Moreover, Home Safety Committees could encourage affiliated organizations to take out their own subscription with RoSPA.

The Health Education Council   This produces a resource list of home safety publications and teaching aids. This catalogues not only HEC materials but also items available from elsewhere. The HEC can only supply its own items and these can be viewed in the HEC's own resource centre. Some of the HEC materials will be held by local health education units where they can be viewed or borrowed. The address of the HEC is:

Health Education Council
78 New Oxford Street
London WC1A 1AH
(Tel: 01–631–0930)

Water safety

Each year approximately 700 people are drowned in the UK. About two-thirds of them are male. The drownings occur in all manner of settings from the bath to the beach. Contributory factors include mental stress, senility, heart attacks – and alcohol.

The Home and Leisure Safety Division of RoSPA is responsible for water safety in the home and its recreational use outside. Any issues involving safety and the recreational use of water outside the home are dealt with by the National Water Safety Committee serviced by RoSPA, on which government departments, local authorities and the major water sports bodies are all represented.

The size of the problem

Police forces use a 'drowning report form' to inform the Royal Life Saving Society (RLSS) of the drownings in their area. The RLSS produces an annual report entitled *Drownings in the British Isles*, which an be obtained from:

The Royal Life Saving Society
Mountbatten House
Studley
Warwickshire
(Tel: 052–785–3943)

The statistics of the Home and Leisure Safety Division of RoSPA suggest that in approximately 15 per cent of drownings drink was a contributory factor.

Since the Home Office abandoned the collection of statistics on aquatic fatalities there is no official reporting agency. Both RoSPA and the Royal Life Saving Society suspect that their separately collected figures of, on average, 700 deaths a year are less than the actual total.

RoSPA has also drawn attention to the increase in the number of people who drown in alcohol-associated circumstances in the home. This seems to be due, at least in part, to the growing popularity of 'leisure bathrooms' and jacuzzis and the increasing number of private pools. The combination of water, steam, and alcohol can be a dangerous cocktail, even for the young and fit.

Vigorous exercise, rather than reducing alcohol and water risks, can actually increase them. Sustained exercise such as board-sailing, canoeing, water-skiing, and swimming can use up carbohydrate reserves and as little as 30 ml of alcohol can, in these circumstances, produce a drastic fall in blood glucose causing weakness, confusion, and impairment of the normal homeostatic mechanisms. Victims may, therefore, be unable to survive even quite short periods in cold water. The BMJ has suggested that the routine advice about eating and swimming – which has not yet been shown to constitute a risk – should be substituted by clear advice on the risks of drinking and water sports.

In 1980 a Home Office analysis of 809 drownings reported specific contributory factors in 519 cases of which 148 were alcohol-related.

The Consumer Safety Unit's study of home accidents which was discussed above also examined 500 cases of accidental drownings in open stretches of water. It concluded that many drownings, including those due to illness and drunkenness, could have been prevented by appropriate environmental measures such as closing some paths at night, putting railings up at appropriate places, making the edges of water shallow, closing access to derelict land, and filling in disused reservoirs and canals.

Local action

In every locality, there are a number of organizations and groups of workers which have a role to play in promoting water safety. These organizations should be made aware of the issue and encouraged to take appropriate preventive action.

A local authority officer for water safety   The prevention of drownings outside the home is a local authority function, usually undertaken in conjunction with the local Water Board. All district authorities could appoint an officer with water safety responsibilities. Even if the authority is not on the coast and does not have any major areas of inland water which are used for recreational purposes it will still have drains, canals, waterways of various kinds, and public swimming baths. It would be appropriate to locate a responsibility for water safety within the local environmental health department which may already have an officer with specific home safety responsibilities. The task for such an officer for water safety would be to encourage public education, the systematic review of hazards, and the adoption of measures to prevent accidents occurring. The environmental health department of the London Borough of Hounslow has recently produced a comprehensive policy which reviews all the water hazards in the borough and the preventive strategies which should be adopted.

RoSPA and water safety   The Home and Leisure Safety Division of RoSPA includes a Water Safety Department. District authorities, other public authorities, commercial organizations, voluntary groups and individuals can all subscribe to the RoSPA Water Safety Department. These subscriptions are entirely separate from any to the division itself (see above). Subscriptions are currently:

District Councils – 25p per 1,000 head of population
Other public authorities – £50 per annum
Commercial organizations – £15 per annum
Voluntary groups – £15 per annum
Individuals – £10 per annum

Subscribers receive copies of the quarterly magazine, *Care in the Home*, which frequently deals with water safety issues. There is also a catalogue-pricelist of materials which can be used in publicity and education campaigns consisting mainly of posters, leaflets, and booklets. The main resource of the Water Safety Department is its advisory service which is available to all subscribers to help them to devise strategies and policies for the promotion of water safety.

Water safety and the advertising of alcohol   Advertisements in both the broadcast and the non-broadcast media frequently depict people drinking by the side of swimming pools, on exotic beaches, on yachts, and in the bath. Home Safety Committees, and officers with responsibility for home safety or for water safety, could complain about any advertisements which they feel are unhelpful. Details of the two advertising codes and information on how to register a complaint can be found in chapter 3.

Public swimming baths   Leisure and sports centres which provide a comprehensive range of recreational facilities, including swimming baths, are increasing. Many have bars. Is this appropriate? If so, then the local authority should display warning material both in the bars and by the poolside to ensure that everyone is aware of the risks from drinking and swimming – Don't Drink and Sink!

Alcohol and water safety: Education for the young   The Consumer Safety Unit's investigation revealed that a substantial number of drowning incidents involved young men who had gone swimming after drinking with friends at a pub or club. Information about the dangers of drinking and swimming should be part of a comprehensive local programme of alcohol education for young people, of the kind outlined in chapter 7.

Alcohol and work   Chapter 6 outlines the aims and contents of 'alcohol and work' policies which are designed to educate about alcohol, prevent accidents, and help individuals in difficulties. A water safety officer might try to ensure that those who work on or near water are covered by such a policy which should contain explicit recognition of the importance of environmental safety and a commitment to its promotion. Approximately one-fifth of the drownings reported in the Consumer Safety Unit survey involved drunken seamen falling into harbours. Interestingly, there were no such cases in floating harbours or docks where the water level is held constant and where ships are moored flush to the quayside in a fixed position. Measures to make the environment safer in tidal harbours and ports might include the introduction of railings, safety nets, floating jetties, and other means of making gangways safer, better lighting, patrols, and more safety and rescue equipment, including ladders and chains installed in the quay wall. These are all matters which could be taken up by a water safety officer.

Identifying drowning hazards   The Consumer Safety Unit's survey of drowning accidents was based on a study carried out for the Scientific Advisory Branch of the Home Office, in support of the working party for water safety. The original report by Poyner and Hughes entitled *Guidelines for the Identification of Drowning Hazards* identified, in detail, the various environmental precautions which could be taken to prevent different kinds of drowning accidents. The report was never published. However, some copies are still available from the authors and can be obtained by writing to:

The Tavistock Institute of Human Relations
120 Belsize Lane
London NW3
(Tel: 01–435–7111)

Road safety

Each year large numbers of people die or are injured on Britain's roads. The Department of Transport's annual reports *Road Accidents – Great Britain* provide a comprehensive analysis of every kind of road accident. The report for 1983 reveals that 5,445 died and 303,139 were injured in that year. It is well known that alcohol plays an important part in many of these accidents and, over the past two decades, strenuous legislative and educational efforts have been made to reduce alcohol-related accidents.

Alcohol and road safety

It is an offence to drive, attempt to drive, or to be in charge of a motor vehicle in a public place if impaired through drink. The Road Traffic

Act 1967 made it an *automatic* offence to drive, attempt to drive, or to be in charge of a motor vehicle in a public place if blood/alcohol content (BAC) exceeds 80 milligrammes of alcohol in 100 millilitres of blood (80 mg/100 ml).

The Road Traffic Act 1967 introduced the 'breathalyzer' as a roadside 'screening test' which, if a positive result was obtained, has to be followed by an 'evidential' blood or urine test at a police station. The Transport Act 1981 introduced evidential breath tests to be used in court proceedings in place of blood and urine analysis. The 'limit' remains the same but is now expressed as 35 microgrammes of alcohol in 100 millilitres of breath (35 ug/100 ml).

When blood/alcohol and blood/urine measurements were the evidential test the Forensic Science Laboratories routinely deducted 6 per cent from the mean result of the analyses when reporting their findings. The Blennerhassett Group recommended that a similar allowance be made for breath tests. In practice, then, readings between 36 ug and 40 ug do not lead to prosecution.

In the UK, the introduction in 1967 of the 'legal limit' is estimated to have saved 5,000 deaths and 200,000 other casualties. However, convictions in England and Wales for driving whilst under the influence of drink or drugs, which include those for failing to provide a specimen for analysis, have shown a regular year-on-year increase:

Driving whilst unfit through drink or drugs

Year	Offences
1973	61,000
1975	65,000
1977	53,000
1979	67,000
1981	71,000
1983	98,000

Home Office, *Statistical Bulletin*, 18/85

In part, these figures reflect changes in police practice and increasing determination on the part of many forces to respond to the drink-driving problem. However, these changes in approach have not created drunken drivers – they have merely uncovered them.

Alcohol-impaired pedestrians are a significant cause of accidents. A study carried out in the West Midlands Metropolitan area from 1969 to 1975 revealed that one-third of all fatally injured pedestrians had been drinking, that 22 per cent had BACs above the legal limit for drivers and

15 per cent had BACs above 150 mg/100 ml – the level regarded as indicative of the regular and heavy drinker. The study concluded that alcohol impairment had contributed directly to 27 per cent of the male and 7 per cent of the female fatalities in the sample.

Local action

Improving the driving environment   Accidents of all kinds can often be significantly reduced through improvements in the physical environment. This approach can complement conventional safety education. Well-documented research shows that low-cost engineering measures can be highly cost-effective in reducing road accidents. These measures include improved surface dressing, better signs and markings, and small changes to layouts, lighting, and the design of junctions. When accident 'black-spots' are examined it is often relatively straightforward for experienced highway engineers to devise improvement schemes, many of which cost less than £4,000 and few more than £15,000. A comprehensive guide to such schemes entitled *Accident Reduction and Prevention in Highway Engineering* was produced in 1980 by the Institute of Highways and Transportation. A revised edition is planned and can be obtained from:

> Institute of Highways and Transportation
> 3 Lygon Place
> Ebury Street
> London SW1W OJS
> (Tel: 01–730–5245)

It would be particularly useful if all members of the local Road Safety Advisory Committee and councillors on technical services committees at both district and county level have a copy of this report or, if not, a clear précis of its contents, in order to generate informed debate on the importance of environmental safety.

Improving car design   Just as the physical driving environment can be made safer, so can cars themselves. It has been argued that the motor industry has given little consideration to the design of a 'safe car' and that the application of existing technology could considerably reduce road deaths. Chassis construction, rear seat safety belts, better safety glass, cushions that inflate on impact, head restraints, and collapsible steering columns are all possible. This topic could be included in any local public education programme (see chapter 2). Councillors and Road Safety Advisory Committee members could also encourage their local Road Safety Officer to raise this issue with the County Road Safety Officers' Association which is part of the County Surveyors' Society.

More immediately, all those concerned with road safety issues at the local level might consider the content of car advertisements. These aim to sell glamour and the dream of a magic carpet. The speed of the advertised cars is often emphasized despite the fact that it would be illegal to drive them at full speed on any public road anywhere in the UK. Councillors, road safety officers, and members of Road Safety Advisory Committees could complain about these advertisements if they considered them to be unhelpful. Some of the more blatant have already been the subject of complaint. Chapter 3 describes the two codes governing advertising in the broadcast and non-broadcast media in the UK and how to frame and register a complaint. Members of Local Road Safety Advisory Committees might also consider whether or not there is a case for amending the codes in such a way as to reduce car advertisers' emphasis upon speed and power as a selling point.

Improving pedestrian safety   Research appears to indicate (see above) that a significant proportion of pedestrian deaths are directly related to alcohol impairment. Some minor environmental safety measures, such as the siting of railings, crossings, and lights in relation to the local configuration of public houses could be useful. However, much more could be done to prevent pedestrian drunkenness itself. Section 172(3) of the Licensing Act 1964 prohibits the sale of intoxicating liquor to a drunken person and yet such sales are common. Chapter 5 recommends the setting up of 'licensing forums' in every locality to promote debate about licensing issues, licensing law enforcement, and the development of comprehensive local liquor licensing policies. A number of liquor licensing issues have a 'road safety dimension' and every forum should include representatives with a concern for road safety.

Driving schools   Driving schools could be used as a platform for basic 'driving and driving-education' about such issues as the effect of alcohol upon co-ordination, skills, and stopping distances. Education might be particularly useful at this point in a driver's career, when driving habits are being formed. The current edition of *The Highway Code* makes no reference to the effect of drinking on driving performance or the penalties that may be incurred. The only mention of drinking and driving occurs towards the very end of the Code in a closely printed list of legislation affecting drivers. The Department of Transport's manual *Driving* is scarcely more helpful. Chapter 16 of the manual, 'Making Things a Little Easier', says merely 'apart from the penalties, these two things (drinking and driving) just do not mix'.

Because of schools' and instructors' preoccupation with getting people through the test rather than producing safe drivers, local road safety workers might find it difficult to gain their interest and co-operation. However, at the very least, a number might be persuaded to distribute a locally produced leaflet on the drink-driving law and the effects of alcohol on driving performance. Alternatively, the leaflet entitled *The Facts about Drinking and Driving*, produced by the Transport and Road Research Laboratory, could be used. The address is:

Transport and Road Research Laboratory
Old Wokingham Road
Crowthorne
Berkshire RG11 6AU
(Tel: 03446–3131)

Some of the larger driving schools run introductory 'classroom' sessions for pupils starting their course of instruction and some also run training courses for instructors. It might be possible to arrange an 'alcohol education' contribution to these courses from the local Road Safety Department, or other local group. The alcohol education materials identified in chapter 7 could be used.

Alcohol and work   Many people drive for a living, employ drivers, or have a special responsibility to discourage drinking and driving. RoSPA's Road Safety Division has produced a series of booklets about drinking and driving for: the licensed trade; coach, minibus, and taxi operators; organizers of young people's groups; voluntary organizations; and employers and employees. Each booklet contains factual information and, most importantly, a section entitled 'What You Can Do To Help'. RoSPA's address is given above.

Alcohol and work policies underline the importance of the workplace in the identification and management of alcohol-related problems, and a properly constructed policy should contain a specific drinking and driving component. Chapter 6 describes the origins, purpose, and workings of these policies, and lists other drinking and driving educational materials which can be used in the workplace. Employers may also find that some of the materials identified in chapter 7 are useful, particularly where young people are concerned.

Development of devices to prevent drunk driving appears to be well advanced, and may soon be a practical option for employers. In 1985, General Motors NZ launched what is claimed to be the world's first commercially manufactured unit specifically designed to prevent drunken driving. Before the vehicle can be started, the driver must blow into a small hand-held sensor. If the breath sample is below the legal limit, the car can be started, but if over the legal limit, the ignition system remains locked. The device can be run on a twenty-four hour control, or on a timing mechanism which automatically switches on between 6 pm and 6 am (the high risk time). It can be fitted to any petrol-powered vehicle, including motor cycles. The company involved in international distribution is:

Stevens and Hall Ltd
PO Box 705
Auckland
New Zealand

Community initiatives   Public attitudes towards the drunken driver have been hardening. However, for many the drunken driver is guilty of no more than a misdemeanour. Changing local attitudes will be an important part of any local road safety initiative. A variety of 'local' community initiatives in the USA over the past decade have been designed to raise public awareness of the drink-driving issue, to pinpoint legislative weaknesses and to foster a social climate in which drinking and driving is discouraged. Various strategies adopted in the USA suggest an approach and a 'style' which could be considered at the local level in the UK.

USA community initiatives seek to saturate a community with drink-driving mesages and to identify the many different ways in which drinking and driving can be discouraged. Public education campaigns are central but these involve much more than the local media. Such campaigns might include 'fact sheets' for opinion leaders, local groups, organizers of entertainment, and senior high school pupils. Posters, lapel badges, and bumper stickers with messages such as 'I ♥ sober drivers' are widely distributed to back up the campaign. Some of the specific initiatives which have been developed by the Office of Alcohol and Other Drug Abuse Programming in St Paul, Minnesota, include:

• Plotting the home addresses of drink-driving offenders with a view to encouraging community groups in localities where the largest number of offenders live.

- Persuading local licensed victuallers' associations to award prizes to licensees who reduce alcohol-related incidents in their bars and taverns.
- Persuading insurance companies to offer lower premiums to licensees who keep well controlled bars and taverns.
- Encouraging local licensed premises to understand the importance of the 'environment' of drinking. This includes emphasizing the fact that appropriate lighting, seating arrangements, decor, table service, mixed clientele, management, clear posting of rules, drink-driving posters, non-alcoholic drink, food and other entertainment, helps to reduce heavy drinking.
- Subsidized taxi rides home for people who become intoxicated in public places such as bars and restaurants. Taxi companies sell coupons to participating bars and restaurants which entitle customers to a discount on the fare home.
- 'Roadside jingles' based on the Burma Shave roadside advertisements of the 1920s and 1930s which had the lines of an advertising jingle on separate roadside posters spaced along the highway. Some of the original Burma Shave highway advertising featured drinking and driving jingles such as:

It's Best For
One Who Hits
The Bottle
To Let Another
Use The Throttle (1940)

Competitions to write new jingles have been run using the local media and schools, sometimes with a small prize of Savings Bonds. Signs are erected by sponsors, who may be a local company, public agency, or citizens' 'action group'. Their name appears on the last sign of all. The signs can be sited at city limits, outside trading estates, or in areas with a large number of bars. Some towns in the UK do have drinking and driving warning signs but local companies, the Chamber of Trade or other public-spirited organizations might be interested in adopting or adapting the 'Burma Shave' idea.

Many community initiatives and programmes in the USA are entwined with the work of local groups of 'Mothers Against Drunken Drivers', founded in 1980 by Ms Candy Lightner shortly after her thirteen-year-old daughter had been killed by a hit-and-run drunk driver. She began a one-woman crusade against the court system which, she alleged, 'looked the other way'. For four years, Ms Lightner and MADD worked diligently to secure a minimum drinking age of twenty-one for each state. When President Reagan signed the National Minimum Drinking Age Act of 1984, Candy Lightner was at his side.

The United Kingdom equivalent of MADD was formed in 1985, 'dedicated to the reduction of deaths and injuries caused by drinking and driving'. CADD, the Campaign Against Drinking and Driving, expect to form local groups throughout the country to press for measures 'which will remove drunken drivers from our roads', such as:

- Only allowing bail on condition that they do not drive before their case is heard in court.
- Working toward a reduction in the allowed blood-alcohol level until it is zero alcohol.
- Monitoring court cases and protesting when sentences are only token or trivial.
- Allowing victims the same rights of appeal as are allowed to the criminal drunken driver.

CADD can be contacted at:

Action on Alcohol Abuse
Livingstone House
11 Carteret Street
London SW1H 9DL
(Tel: 01–222–3454/5)

This is intended to be a *living* 'guide to action'. Therefore, it needs to be revised and added to in the light of local needs and local experience.

The following two pages are for jotting down examples of good practice, and addresses relevant to the issues covered by this chapter.

We hope to update the guide, and would be delighted to receive any advice about corrections, new material or any other information which should go into the next edition. Please send all suggestions, before 31 December, 1987, to:

Philip Tether and David Robinson
Addiction Research Centre
University of Hull
Hull HU6 7RX

Examples of Good Practice

Useful Addresses and Telephone Numbers

Further reading

Chandler, S.E., Chapman, A., and Hollington, S.J., 'Fire Incidence, Housing and Social Conditions – the Urban Situation in Britain', *Fire Prevention*, 172, 1984

Department of Trade, *Personal Factors in Domestic Accidents: Prevention through Product and Environmental Design*, 1980. Available from Consumer Safety Unit, Millbank Tower, London SW1P 4QU

Editorial, 'Drinking and Drowning', *British Medical Journal*, vol. 1, 70, 1979

Home Office, *Fire Statistics, United Kingdom 1982*. Published by the Home Office, London, 1983; copies can be obtained from S3 Division, Home Office, 50 Queen Anne's Gate, London SW1H 9AT

Lawson, G.R., Craft, A.W., and Jackson, R.H., 'Changing Pattern of Poisoning in Children in Newcastle, 1974–81', *British Medical Journal*, vol. 287, July 1983

Perry, B., 'FPA Large Fire Analysis for 1982', *Fire Prevention*, 166, 1984

Pharmaceutical Society Working Party, 'Guide to Cautionary and Advisory Labels for Dispensed Medicines', *The Pharmaceutical Journal*, 17 March, 1984

Poyner, B. and Hughes, N., *Guidelines for the Identification of Drowning Hazards*, commissioned by the Scientific Advisory Branch of the Home Office for the Working Party on Water Safety, Tavistock Institute of Human Relations, 1977

RoSPA, *Water Safety Outdoors: Advisory Notes for Local Authorities and Others*, reference number WS39 (no date), and *Home Safety: What's It All About?: A Guide for Professional Officers, Policy Makers, Speakers and Students*, reference number ISBN 9 900635 576, 1982. Available from RoSPA, Cannon House, The Priory, Queensgate, Birmingham B4 6BS

Whittington, R.M., 'Alcohol-related Deaths: Birmingham Coroner's Records 1980', *British Medical Journal*, Vol. 284, 17 April, 1982

Woolley, D.W., 'Synthetic Materials and Alcohol are Culprits in Fire Death Study', *Fire*, September 1979

CHAPTER 5

Alcohol and liquor licensing

CHAPTER 5

Alcohol and liquor licensing

'Available evidence . . . suggests that licensing restrictions may have a broad influence on both the level of average consumption per head of alcohol and the incidence of alcohol-related harm.'
                    (*Drinking Sensibly*, HMSO 1981: 43)

An important aspect of any local community's alcohol prevention strategy concerns liquor licensing. This chapter considers the prevention potential of liquor licensing. Good practice is identified at two levels: at the overall *strategic* level of liquor licensing policies and the involvement of the broader community in liquor licensing issues, and at the level of detailed aspects of the licensing *process* itself.

Liquor licensing and prevention

Alcohol is held to be a special substance and its retail sale is regulated by the licensing laws. In order to retail alcohol, licences and certificates of various kinds must be obtained and regularly renewed. Current practice and procedure has meant that the prevention potential of liquor licensing is to a large extent unfulfilled.

Liquor licensing

The law which applies to England and Wales is for the most part contained in the Licensing Act of 1964. This Act was a consolidating

117

measure which has since been amended in 1980, 1981, and 1983.

Licensing justices are charged with administering the liquor licensing law. Every year the magistrates for each petty sessional division appoint from among their number the licensing justices who make up a licensing committee.

Licensing sessions   The work of licensing justices is carried out at licensing sessions which are held at regular intervals throughout the year. The minimum requirement is four sessions in any one year and eight is the maximum. The first session of the year is held in the first fortnight of February. This is the general annual licensing meeting – commonly known as the 'Brewster Sessions'. All the powers of the justices may be exercised at this meeting but the most important are the powers to renew liquor licences of all kinds and to make orders modifying the general licensing hours in the district. Licensing matters throughout the rest of the year are dealt with at ordinary licensing sessions – commonly known as 'transfer' sessions because of the preponderance of applications for licences to be transferred to the new occupant of licensed premises. Other licensing business of the transfer sessions include the 'removal' of a licence to different premises, decisions about alterations to licensed premises and the granting of new on- or off-licences.

Each year the police provide for the licensing justices a report on licensing matters. These reports vary greatly from locality to locality but most would, at least, include details of the numbers of each type of licence granted or in operation, together with information on all licensing law offences which have taken place in the previous year.

Liquor licences   The two major kinds of licence are 'on-licences', permitting the sale of alcohol for consumption either on *or* off the premises – unless a condition is attached to the licence prohibiting off sales – and 'off-licences', where alcohol is sold only for consumption *off* the premises.

A variety of on-licences authorize the sale of particular kinds of liquor. The number of licences in operation in June 1984, was:

- Intoxicants of all descriptions   96,178
- Cider and wine only⎱
- Beer and cider only⎰   257
- Cider only ⎱
- Wine only ⎰   458

In 1983 the number of off-licences was 40,853.

There are three further kinds of licence, which are, strictly speaking, on-licences. They relate to the use to which the licensed premises is put. These are known as 'Part IV Licences' after the section of the Licensing Act 1964 which controls their issue:

- Restaurant   14,666
- Residential   5,345
- Combined restaurant and residential   3,668

A restaurant licence is granted on the condition that the sale or supply of intoxicating liquor is confined to those taking table meals and for consumption as an ancillary to such meals. A residential licence is granted to enable residents to drink on the premises of a guest house or hotel.

In addition, there were just over 30,000 licensed or registered clubs in 1983. The licensing law also enables justices to grant occasional licences and a variety of orders and certificates dealing with special hours, supper hours, and extended hours, and certain other exceptions from usual licensing requirements.

Unfulfilled prevention potential

There are many current debates in the alcohol field in which liquor licensing issues are prominent. One concerns the relationship between the number of outlets in a locality and the overall amount of alcohol consumed. Others concern variations in licensing law and their impact. Does the extension of hours undermine the symbolic value of liquor licensing laws as a control on excessive drinking? Would an extension of hours late at night avoid the problem of drinking quickly just before closing time? Have the 'more relaxed' licensing hours introduced in Scotland in 1976 had any impact on the overall level of alcohol-related problems, in particular those concerned with public order? Are levels of alcohol-related harm in locality linked to the number, types, or geographical distribution of outlets?

These and many other issues continue to be debated. Every licensing committee will come to its own conclusions about these matters in the light of its own local experience. These conclusions will have a bearing on the justices' decisions about the 'need' for any new licence. The right of licensing justices to assess the need for outlets in their locality was stated by Lord Halsbury in *Sharp-v-Wakefield (1891) 55 JP 197*: 'it is within the power and even the duty of magistrates to consider the wants of a neighbourhood with reference both to its population, means of inspection by proper authorities and so forth'.

The licensing justices' absolute discretion over the granting of on- and off-licences and their right and 'duty' to consider the needs of their locality appear to offer considerable opportunities for the exploration and exploitation of the prevention potential of the liquor licensing law. However, there are a number of reasons why liquor licensing law does not have the impact which might be expected.

The *first* is that justices, by and large, do not have any special knowledge and understanding of alcohol-related problems. Some justices recognize this deficiency and attempt to gain some understanding of alcohol problems and related issues and bring this knowledge to bear in their licensing work. 'Alcoholism and Crime' and 'Liquor Licensing' are two of the approved training topics for magistrates laid down by the Lord Chancellor's office (see chapter 10).

Since these are approved topics rather than 'required' topics, many licensing justices are in need of basic education about alcohol problems and about liquor licensing law itself. Among some there is misunderstanding and, in some cases, plain ignorance of the law. Although justices make every effort to carry out their tasks properly and efficiently they are often overwhelmed by the complexity of the law. The absence of clear guides is one difficulty, although any licensing justice who cares to will find a variety of texts which explain in detail the complexities, possibilities, and practices associated with liquor licensing law. Some of these texts are listed in 'Further reading'.

The *second* difficulty which justices face if they seek to develop the prevention potential of their work concerns the concept of 'need'. The need in any locality for a liquor outlet can be expressed in relation to the total number of outlets, the density of outlets, the quality of outlets, the range of types of outlets, and any combination of these features. It is very difficult, therefore, to quantify and specify 'need' with any precision. This means that applicants for licences who are turned down by the licensing justices can appeal to the Crown Court against the decision and challenge the justices' assessment of 'need'.

The *third* reason why licensing law does not have the prevention impact it otherwise might have is due to the fact that all licensing decisions must be excercised *judicially*: 'that is to say according to the rules of reason and justice and not a private opinion. It must not be arbitrary, vague or fanciful but legal and regular,' *The Justices' Clerks'*

Society, 1983. This case-by-case approach by licensing committees to each application for the grant or renewal of a licence means that appeals are often upheld if there is any suggestion that the justices are making their decisions in terms of some broad policy about the 'needs' of a locality rather than in relation to the merits of the particular case under consideration.

The *fourth* reason why the prevention potential of liquor licensing is unfulfilled stems from aspects of the liquor licensing process itself. These are discussed later.

An overall local licensing strategy

If the prevention potential of liquor licensing is to be exploited a locality needs an overall strategy. The strategy must be well thought out and known to all interested parties. It must be based on adequate information and the full involvement of all relevant local organizations. It must also receive their support.

Licensing policies

Whatever the licensing committee concludes about the issue of need and other core licensing matters these conclusions would carry more weight if they were informed by local experience and local debate and then codified in a local liquor licensing policy.

Spread, purpose, and content   At present only a minority of licensing committees have a written liquor licensing policy even though the Justices' Clerks' Society has produced a model policy (see Appendix 5.A). Extracts from some existing local policies are contained in Appendix 5.B.

A policy is important since it draws attention to those dimensions of liquor licensing that justices take to be important. These may be relatively minor matters concerned with the formulation of the application or the amount of time required prior to the session for the justices to inspect property. But they may also be concerned with major issues such as the nature and range of licences desired in the locality or the question of the need for new on- or off-licences.

Only a minority of existing policies attempt to define 'need' and those that do have different approaches (see Appendix 5.B). Putting the task of demonstrating need in the hands of the applicant is probably the least satisfactory way of approaching the problem. It opens the way to strategies such as petitions in support of specific licences which are difficult to evaluate. It is also not unknown for applicants to produce very large-scale maps showing how their proposed outlet is needed because it is, apparently, a considerable distance away from existing ones!

There is obviously no magic formula which will define need for any and every locality in England and Wales. Licensing justices must come to their own decisions. They must decide what weight to give to such factors as overall numbers, geographical distribution, and types of outlet. Just as there are no overall formulas which will define need for every locality so justices may not want to operate with the same criteria for every part of the area under their jurisdiction.

Zoning   Some licensing committees are now operating with zoning policies which help to determine whether a particular kind of licence or aspect of a licence is appropriate. For example, in certain inner city zones it may be less appropriate for a licence to include a 'children's room or family room facility', whereas this might be felt to be more appropriate and acceptable in outlying or country areas where alternative provision for children may not be possible.

Given that the Crown Court is interested in the 'judicial' merits of the justices' decisions it is important for licensing committees to emphasize that their policy provisions in relation to need, zoning, or other matters are guidelines not rules. They do not constitute a means of routinely assessing applications. The onus is then on the applicant to make out a case for why, on merit, the broad guidelines of the licensing policy should not apply in relation to the particular licence being applied for. If this principle is emphasized in the text of the policy as well as in the presentation of case judgements, there might be less likelihood of decisions being taken to appeal and of those appeals succeeding.

Public disorder   Policies could identify those factors which justices consider are related to heavy drinking and public disorder. These might include the recognition that young licensees may be less able to avoid violent incidents than older and more experienced ones, that the diversification of facilities within a public house can help to undermine the pre-occupation with heavy drinking, that the disposition of public transport systems and taxi services have a bearing on the amount of public disorder at closing time, and that overcrowding and the ambience of licensed premises can contribute to public disorder.

It would be helpful if policies emphasized that licencing justices have significant responsibilities in relation to the prevention of alcohol misuse. The promotion of sensible, moderate drinking results in less public disorder. The long-term effect of liquor licensing policy and practice is to make a contribution to 'the social welfare and health of the community' as the report of the Northern Ireland Interdepartmental Review Body on Liquor Licensing puts it. Justices should not be afraid of indicating the broad aims which lie behind their local licensing activities. The annual Brewster Session would provide an opportunity for the chairman to draw attention to these responsibilities and to the policy which flows from them.

Appeals However, even if there is a carefully constructed, public, written liquor licensing policy containing guidelines rather than 'rules' and even if the licensing justices take seriously their responsibility and authority to help to prevent alcohol misuse, there will still be 'appeals' against the justices' decisions.

The gap between local justices and applicants will be exploited at the appeal court. An important question, therefore, is: 'How can those justices who take the prevention of alcohol misuse seriously make it less likely that their decisions will be overturned on appeal?' One answer is to ensure that their decisions are not based solely on the work, ideas and intentions of justices alone without the support of other related, interested, and concerned organizations.

Licensing forums

A key requirement of any local licensing strategy is for it to be community-based and not merely justice-based. In any local community there are a number of agencies which have an interest in licensing decisions and are affected by the consequences of them. Social services departments, the probation and after-care services, agencies concerned with the care, rehabilitation, and counselling of those with alcohol problems, various sections of the alcohol trade itself, the police, local road safety departments, Home Safety Committees, the local authority, and district health authority all have views, information, and expertise on various drinking issues which could usefully be shared.

Membership and purpose   Given all the organizations which have a legitimate interest in and concern with licensing decisions and their impact, a 'licensing forum' would be an ideal place for these organizations to meet to discuss specific issues such as licensed premises and public disorder and to discuss the introduction, implementation, and support for an overall local licensing strategy.

To be effective, a local liquor licensing policy and an associated local licensing forum must be informed by relevant data and information upon which to have discussions and make decisions. The kind of information that is required goes beyond the simple aggregate figures for licensing and drunkenness offences which are normally found in the chief constable's year-end report to the local liquor licensing committee. For instance, it is essential that public order incidents are 'mapped' so that the justices and their licensing forum colleagues from other organizations can see which types of offences are clustering at what time in relation to which licensed premises in which locations. This information is vital if justices are to make sensible decisions about the granting or renewal of licences and if the locality is to develop an effective, co-ordinated response to disorder problems.

Funds for research   Any well-organized local licensing forum which contains representatives from relevant local organizations and agencies should be in a position to gather information and raise funds to conduct research. One source of such funds would be the Alcohol Education and Research Council which was established in 1982 with the money from the licensing compensation fund. The address is:

Alcohol Education and Research Council
Abell House (Room G6)
John Islip Street
London SW1P 4LH
(Tel: 01–211–8513)

'Judicial' decisions   The existence of a licensing forum would not mean the erosion of the justices' obligation to act 'judicially' and examine every application carefully on its merits. The value of a licensing forum would be to ensure that the justices' overall licensing strategy is informed by discussion with other interested parties.

Justices may feel more confident in refusing licences which they feel to be inappropriate or unnecessary, and appeals might be less likely to succeed, if powerful local coalitions of interested agencies were willing to offer their support for licensing decisions.

Objecting to an application Members of the licensing forum can monitor applications for new licences and the effect of existing outlets. It may be that forum members themselves may want to object to an application for a new licence or to the renewal of a particular licence in the light of problems in the previous year. The process of objecting to a licence is straightforward. A clearly written guide entitled *The Private Citizen's Powers in the Field of Liquor Control* is referred to in the list of 'Further reading'.

Focused activities A number of forums are being set up. Their task is to develop a consistent way of working and responding to licensing issues, to undertake background monitoring and play a part in ensuring that licensing issues are fully debated in the locality. It is important to ensure that the business of a licensing forum is strictly concerned with licensing and licensing-related issues. There has been a tendency for some embryo forums to become 'talking shops' for local agencies with interests in alcohol problems. This is understandable, given the fact that in most localities it will be those who are already involved with alcohol issues who form part of the core of the forum membership – but it should be avoided.

One way of focusing attention is for the forum members to undertake specific licensing tasks such as the construction of an outline licensing policy – if there is not one already – based perhaps on an analysis of policies from half a dozen other localities. Another task would be to construct a map of all liquor licence and public order offences over the previous five years. Such exercises would concentrate attention on specific licensing issues and, if done properly, would raise background matters which any licensing forum needs to come to terms with, such as its attitude to need, the range and nature of outlets, the ratio of outlets to population, and questions such as whether or not it would be helpful to have licensing 'zones', whether or not breathalyzers in pubs are a good idea, and how local practice can be altered to respond to the fact that licensing law is being broken every time someone who is drunk is served on licensed premises and yet in 1983 there were only fourteen convictions for this offence in England and Wales.

Harmonizing policies

Licensing appeals are heard in the Crown Court by a judge or recorder sitting with four licensing justices, two of whom must be from the defending committee and unconnected with the original decision. It is not unknown for applicants to put in a 'trial' application to the justices in the expectation of proceeding to appeal when the full range of arguments can be brought to bear by experienced counsel.

Problems with appeals   Sometimes the applicant's success in convincing the Crown Court can be achieved by the production of a petition which purports to show that consumers want the outlet. Arguments may be advanced that the area is insufficiently served by outlets of a particular type or quality. Often a skilled barrister will simply ask for an explanation of why the line has to be drawn at this application. 'If there are already twenty – or thirty – or forty – outlets within the area what difference will one more make?' If a local licensing committee has a formal liquor licensing policy then the applicant's appeal may be upheld on the grounds that the application was not considered 'judicially', i.e. on its merits.

It has been held that the mere existence of a body of customers patronizing a shop or department which has applied for an off-licence demonstrates a need for that outlet. Similarly, the existence of an application for a new licence has been held to demonstrate a need since, runs this argument, an applicant will have assessed the state of the market and identified a gap in provision because otherwise, on market grounds, the application would not be made.

Faced with all these difficulties, many liquor licensing committees give up the struggle with the concept of need and consider that they have discharged their duties if they ensure that the applicant for a new on- or off-licence is fit to hold a licence and that the premises are suitable.

Developing local consistency   The aim of licensing policies and their adjunct, licensing forums, is to restore 'weight' to justices' decisions. Any initiatives in these areas would be reinforced by more communication across petty sessional divisions so that local policies are built upon fairly common criteria, assumptions, and perspectives.

Any move to harmonize policies across petty sessional boundaries should, on educational grounds, involve Crown Court judges, many of whom have little experience in licensing matters and issues. The development of a broader regional approach would reinforce the operation of particular policies in petty sessional divisions. Licensing justices who sit with Crown Court judges to hear licensing appeals would be less likely to come from divisions where very different local licensing criteria and approaches are applied.

There are now some localities where inter-divisional discussions on policies and licensing issues are taking place. All those involved have found these discussions to be useful for promoting agreement on basic issues and for gaining understanding of the reasons for variations between local policies.

The licensing process

The establishment of an overall licensing strategy provides the framework within which licensing decisions are made and the context within which local discussions about licensing can take place. In addition to these broad examples of good practice there are more detailed aspects of the licensing process which, if altered, could make a contribution to the establishment of coherent licensing practices, encourage sensible drinking and make less likely the development of alcohol problems.

Fit and proper people

The Licensing Act 1964 requires licensing justices to ensure that applicants for a licence are 'fit and proper persons'. In addition the Justices' Clerks' Society points out that justice's licences should only be granted to persons who can be made the subject of control by the licensing committee. Although there is no statutory requirement that it should be done, licensing justices in many parts of the country insist that the person in day-to-day charge of licensed premises should be the holder of the licence and so directly accountable to the licensing committee for the conduct of those premises.

Accountability This principle of accountability should apply equally to on- and off-licensed premises. Several licensing committees insist that the licence-holder, or at least one of the co-licensees, should be *on* the premises during permitted hours. Many committees insist that all shop and supermarket off-licensees are seen to be running those premises. With large supermarket chains this can cause difficulties but these can be overcome if the licence is granted in the joint names of a local 'on-the-spot' manager and the appropriate regional or other executive.

Insistence that the holder of an off-licence should be the manager of the premises can cause extra transfers, since managers tend to be mobile within large networks of organizations. But, in the words of the clerk to one north-eastern committee, 'if it is worthwhile having a control it is worthwhile doing the job properly'.

Education of licensees   Some training for aspiring managers and tenants is provided by the Brewers' Society at a number of centres in the United Kingdom. However, the vast majority of training for public house managers and tenants is now provided by the brewery companies themselves.

In-company training covers, among other things, the managers' and tenants' responsibilities under the law. However, the broader topic of alcohol abuse, how to recognize it in oneself and in others and how to respond to people with problems is seldom dealt with. Only a few breweries offer specific problem drinking modules in their in-company training programmes. Even where it is on offer such information is seldom handed on to other staff.

Training is an area which could benefit from the attention of the licensing forum or other participants in the local prevention strategy. It would be possible, for example, for a number of interested parties in a locality to come together to provide training on alcohol-related problems and how licensees can help to reduce alcohol misuse. Managers of specialist off-licences could be included in such events. One area in which licensees can do much to help is drinking and driving, and RoSPA has a booklet on this topic produced especially for the licensed trade. RoSPA's address is:

Royal Society for the Prevention of Accidents
Cannon House
The Priory
Queenway
Birmingham B4 6BS
(Tel: 021–233–2461)

Licensing justices, when considering applications for licences, could enquire whether the applicant's training has covered alcohol misuse; whether, if a licence is granted, any realistic training will be given to bar staff; and whether any training which may be provided makes use of the valuable RoSPA booklet.

Alcohol and work policies   It is widely recognized that workers in the drinks trade are especially susceptible to alcohol problems. The Registrar General's statistics place publicans and innkeepers at the top of the occupational list for mortality from cirrhosis of the liver.

Many of the larger breweries have well-developed alcohol and work policies which state that drinking problems will be regarded as a health issue and that sick leave and job protection will be extended if the individual in difficulty agrees to seek help. In a fully operationalized alcohol and work policy (see chapter 6) supervisors and others are instructed in how to recognize the signs of problem drinkers and where to seek help for anyone discovered to be in difficulties.

Licensing justices, in hearing applications for new licences and transfers involving managers and tenants, could enquire whether the proposed licensee is covered by a written alcohol and work policy and whether, if such a policy exists, other staff are also covered.

It may be argued that there is a significant difference between managers and tenants where alcohol and work policies are concerned. Tenanted staff are not, of course, employees in the strict sense of the word and so any control which the companies are able to exercise over them is limited and governed entirely by the tenancy agreement. However, there is no reason why managers and tenants should not receive the same training where alcohol abuse is concerned nor why policies should not cover tenants and their staff. This could easily be written into a tenancy agreement and is the kind of local good practice which should be pushed for by members of a licensing forum or other local prevention group.

Local action

Liquor licensing law is complex. There are many licences and certificates, and licensing practice in relation to their application, operation, and supervision varies widely from area to area. In this section a number of specific items of good practice are suggested.

'Happy hours' and 'pub crawls' An increasing number of licensed premises advertise cheap drinks in a 'happy hour' or its equivalent, usually early in the evening or at similar slack times. There will be those who argue that encouraging people by the offer of cheap alcohol to drink more than they otherwise would, or over a longer period of time than they would otherwise spend in licensed premises, is not helpful.

A similar question can be raised about sponsored 'pub crawls' which often contain the implicit or even active endorsement of breweries. Again it could be argued that anything which encourages people to drink more than they otherwise would or to move, sometimes by car, between licensed premises is not compatible with an overall licensing strategy geared to the encouragement of sensible behaviour in relation to alcohol.

Entertainments licences   Entertainments licences were previously called singing, music, and dancing licences and in many areas were issued by the licensing justices. Entertainments licences are now issued by local authorities. The granting of such licences obliges licensing justices to extend drinking time on those premises. Some committees fear the consequences of this change of responsibility and have established liaison arrangements with their local authorities to ensure that applications for entertainments licences are first referred to the justices for their comment and advice. This sensible procedure goes a long way toward avoiding the situation in which a licensing committee is under obligation to grant a liquor licence although it has reservations about the desirability of licensing those particular premises. Any committee which does not liaise formally with its local authority in relation to entertainments licences should urgently review its practice.

Transfers   The transfers of justices' licences can be granted by the licensing committee at the annual Brewster Session or at transfer sessions throughout the year. The applicant must give formal notice to the court but need not advertise in the press or on the premises. Some people have suggested that it is a waste of licensing court time to listen to unopposed applications for transfers which, it is argued, could be handled purely administratively.

There is strength in this argument. Anything which streamlines the licensing process and cuts down on court time is to be welcomed. However, transfer sessions do offer justices an opportunity to meet licensees, to impress their policies upon them, to question them about their training, and to enquire about such things as alcohol and work policies. Committees could consider taking advantage of transfer sessions in this way. To handle transfers administratively may save some time but the price of this convenience may be high.

Clubs   The term 'club' lacks a legal definition. But in terms of the way in which they can be authorized to sell or supply intoxicating liquor clubs are divided into two distinct categories which should not be confused. First there are licensed or proprietary clubs; second are registered or members' clubs.

A justices' licence to sell intoxicating liquor is required for a licensed or proprietary club. In a proprietary club, as the name suggests, the stock and premises belong to a proprietor or group of proprietors. When a customer orders and pays for a drink a sale takes place. This is not the case in a registered or members' club. Here the property, including the stock of liquor, belongs to the members jointly. When members obtain a drink they are not, therefore, in the strict sense, 'buying' a drink even if they pay. The drink is being supplied rather than sold. And since no sale takes place a justices' licence is not required. In law a members' club must hold a registration certificate to authorize the supply of intoxicating liquor on the premises. These registration certificates are granted by magistrates, not by the licensing justices.

Given this separation between licensed and registered clubs, and the separation between the granting of licences by licensing justices and the granting of registration by magistrates, there are several problems which arise:

- The fact that registered club certificates are granted by magistrates means that those who are granting the permission to supply drinks may have inadequate knowledge of – or little sympathy with – local licensing policy.
- Many registered clubs are coming more and more to resemble public houses. The provisions of section 49 of the Licensing Act 1964 – allowing sales to non-members – are being increasingly adopted under club rules as clubs seek outside custom to enable them to keep going in hard economic times.
- There is much confusion in the minds of many club committees between an on-licence and a club registration certificate. The operation of many registered clubs in relation to drink suggests that they are not operating wholly within the law
- It is becoming increasingly common for registered clubs to forget to renew their certificates – particularly in those local authority areas which grant ten-year certificates during which time there may be several changes in club officers.

There are several good practices which can overcome most of these difficulties. For example, some courts make provision for licensing justices to sit in the magistrates' court when applications for registration certificates are being dealt with. This simple practice could be adopted by all licensing committees.

Section 49 of the Licensing Act 1964 allows the sale of intoxicating liquor to non-members if the rules of a registered club so allow. If this provision exists in the rules then when the registration certificate is granted or renewed the court may attach to the certificate such conditions restricting sales of intoxicating liquor to non-members as it thinks reasonable. However, if the club rules are altered to incorporate section 49 provisions during the period of a registration certificate then the court has no opportunity to impose conditions.

Some magistrates' courts have attempted to overcome this problem by imposing conditions under section 49 upon the grant or renewal of the registration certificate *whether or not* a club indicates a wish to avail itself of the section 49 provisions. Certain other courts have an arrangement whereby a section 49 provision will be accepted only on condition that the occasions on which drink can be sold to non-members do not exceed a specified number. This is another practice which goes some way toward stopping the gradual transformation of registered clubs into public houses.

All applicants for registration certificates should be closely questioned about the liquor licensing law and their duties and responsibilities under it. It is helpful if a club has codified these and if that document is publicly displayed and given to all incoming club officers and committee members.

A new club registration certificate remains in force for one year after the date it is granted. However, courts may renew an existing certificate for any period up to ten years. This, it could be argued, is not a helpful practice. The annual renewal of club registrations, as in the case of on- and off-licences, would give the magistrates and the officers and committees of registered clubs the opportunity to consider regularly the operation of the clubs. Fire authorities have urged that certificates should be granted for no more than three years so that safety of premises can be checked regularly.

Licences for special occasions   An occasional licence is granted by a magistrates' court and can be obtained by an on-licensee in order to sell alcoholic drink at a place other than that authorized by virtue of the on-licence. Occasional licences are sought for dances, sporting events, and other occasions held at a public hall or unlicensed premises. Occasional licences cannot be granted for Christmas Day, Good Friday, or any day of public thanksgiving or mourning.

An occasional licence is different from the parent on-licence and not subject to its conditions. Nevertheless, the occasional licence is granted to a licensee who is responsible under the Licensing Act for proper conduct under the licence. The Licensing (Occasional Permissions) Act 1983 allows those representing voluntary organizations to apply directly to the justices for up to four occasional licences a year allowing them to organize events at which alcohol is sold. Licensees can also apply for exemption orders which allow an extension to normal closing time for a special function.

Many committees are concerned at the frivolity and regularity of applications for occasional licences and exemption orders for parties, darts matches, and other questionably 'special' occasions. Some committees have incorporated guidelines into their policies and make a point of closely questioning applicants about the 'specialness' of the event and, where occasional licences are concerned, the bar structure, staff arrangements, staff instruction, liquor security, and the management of the licensee's own premises whilst absent at the 'event'. Some refuse to grant a licence or an order for an event already advertised with such phrases as 'licence applied for' or 'extension applied for'.

Licensed Premises (Exclusion of Certain Persons) Act 1980 This act empowers magistrates to ban potential trouble-makers from specified premises for up to a year. Many juctices, and the licensed trade, are concerned that magistrates are not using this power enough. Reference to this power in the licensing policy might give it greater 'visibility'.

A 'shop-within-a-shop' A major concern for many licensing committees is that off-licence premises should be properly supervised and that stock is secure and sales handled by mature staff who will ensure that, for example, minors and drunks are not served. Many committees express a preference, often incorporated in their publicly stated licensing policies, for a 'shop-within-a-shop' system.

A shop-within-a-shop system means that alcohol is either sold from behind a specialist counter or that, where it is only available by self-service, it is within physically demarcated sales areas with separate checkouts. This kind of arrangement is one way of discouraging theft. It also provides for a check on illegal sales to under-age purchasers. An additional consideration for many licensing committees is the fact that a separate alcohol sales area may discourage 'impulse' or ill-considered purchases.

Having a separate display area, or paying at a separate till, is a clear recognition that alcohol is a different kind of commodity from vegetables or soap powder. The fact that licences are needed to sell alcohol is reflected in the structure of the sales area and no one is left in any doubt that alcohol is not just an ordinary commodity, conveniently available, for all purchasers. The model licensing policy, drawn up by the Justices' Clerks' Society, specifically recommends the shop-within-a-shop arrangement.'

It is not possible for licensing justices to attach conditions to off-licences as they can with on-licences. Nevertheless, most off-sale retailers 'undertake' to comply with a shop-within-a-shop arrangement. Although applicants are under no legal obligation to abide by any undertaking made in connection with shop-within-a-shop or other arrangements, the case of *Regina-v-Edmonton Licensing Justices* in 1983 (2 A11 ER 545) does indicate that if a licensee departs from an undertaking the matter *might* be relevant if there is an *objection* to renewal of that licence. This is a matter which the licensing forum could monitor and on which it could develop a policy.

Nevertheless, most major retailers are certainly not in favour of a shop-within-a-shop approach. They have successfully argued against its provision and claimed that they have no record of trouble from operating with alcohol on open shelves alongside other non-licensed commodities. The argument that there has been no trouble with serving minors nor have there been any incidents of public disorder associated with the open sale of liquor is a strong one. However, there is little police surveillance of off-licensed premises so the detection of under-age purchasing is extremely unlikely. Justices may care to consider how they assess the adequacy of off-licence premises in relation to compliance with the law. In addition, it would be interesting for justices to monitor shoplifting cases passing through the courts in which they sit. Cases involving theft of liquor from off-sale retail outlets that do not operate a shop-within-a-shop arrangement might be noted.

It is also important that the staff of off-licences should be adequately trained to understand the nature of their activity and that they should have sufficient maturity to deal with under-age purchasers. This is something about which licensing committees may care to question potential licensees. They could seek reassurances at least.

Wholesale without justices' licence   An area of potential difficulty concerns the fact that a justices' licence is not required for the sale of liquor in wholesale quantities. For wine, the wholesale amount is not less than nine litres or one twelve-bottle case; the wholesale amount for spirits is the same, while the amount for beer and cider is not less than twenty-one litres or two cases totalling twenty-four bottles. Given that wholesale amounts are relatively small, almost any shopkeeper, grocer, supermarket, or newsagent could open a wholesale department without any licence being needed.

Until 1982 wholesale outlets had to pay an excise licence which cost £5.00. The purpose of excise licensing was to aid the customs and excise department to verify duty payment on alcohol. But it also provided a register of all wholesale outlets in a locality. Now that the excise licence is no longer needed, wholesale outlets are unrecorded. Any licensing forum which wants to map *all* alcohol sales would need to find other sources of information on the location of wholesale outlets.

Alcohol and garages It is illegal to sell alcohol from motorway service stations. However, an increasing number of justices' licences are being granted to ordinary roadside garages – in September 1985 there were fifty-two such garages selling alcohol to motorists and, indeed, non-motorists. Where licences to sell retail have been refused some garages now sell in wholesale quantities. For this they do not require a licence of any kind (see above). The Motor Agents' Association defends these developments by claiming that it promotes safer driving because it encourages more drinking at home. Opponents see the association of drink and driving in this way as being unhelpful, unnecessary, and dangerous. Licensing justices, forum members and, indeed, all the participants in a local prevention strategy, might think it important to formulate a view on this issue. Any consideration they give to this question could note that the two codes of advertising practice which govern advertising in the broadcast and non-broadcast media respectively forbid any association of drinking and driving, and that the Brewers' Society has recommended that its members do not sponsor motor sports (see chapter 3).

Visiting by licensing justices Licensing committee members make visits to licensed premises in connection with new licences, to maintain a 'presence' where existing premises are concerned and in connection with alterations to licensed premises.

Before the initial grant of a new licence it is common practice for one or more of the committee to inspect the premises. This has been found to be valuable, since the submitted plans of the premises do not always reflect what is actually there on the ground.

Licensing justices have differing views on the value of regular or systematic visiting but an increasing majority see some supervisory exercise as one component of good committee practice. The opinion is

that regular visiting leads to increased bar supervision, good relationships between the justices and the licensees, and a better understanding by licensees of local issues, local problems, and the licensing
committee's overall licensing strategy.

The pattern and frequency of visiting will vary from district to district
depending on whether the area is predominantly urban or rural, the
numbers of licensed premises within the locality, and the workload and
particular problems of the licensing committee. It is usual for visits to be
unannounced. The procedure adopted by many committees is that if
premises do not meet with the committee's satisfaction the clerk will
inform the licensee by letter. The premises are then revisited, again
unannounced, to see if the particular problem has been resolved. Clerks
can prepare a list of those premises which have been recorded as
unsatisfactory during any licensing year. A further visit to clarify the
position may be needed prior to the licence renewal at the annual
Brewster Sessions in February.

It is the justices' responsibility to approve plans for alterations to
licensed premises and, if the plans are accepted, to ensure that the work
has been carried out in accordance with them. But in neither case are
committee members obliged to inspect premises. However, many
committees visit the premises to get 'the feel' of the proposed changes
before the application is heard, and to check that alterations have been
implemented as agreed.

The police and licensing   All police forces exercise some supervision
over licensed premises, although the quality and quantity of supervision
varies enormously. The value of a well-thought-out police supervisory
strategy was demonstrated in an experiment conducted in 1978 by the
police in Torquay. Prior to the introduction of the experiment the police
in the resort had been organized to respond to outbreaks of public
disorder during the high summer season as these outbreaks occurred.
This involved the creation of a seasonal task force which was kept busy
at closing time dealing with drunkenness, violence, and other acts of
rowdyism.

During the summer of 1978, frequent but irregular visits by two or
more uniformed officers were made to those premises where there was
the possibility of trouble. The police talked to the bar staff and
conspicuously checked for under-aged drinking and drunkenness. The
frequency of visits to any particular premises was determined by the
perceived potential of those premises for alcohol-based, illegal activities.

To gauge the effect of this supervision the rates of recorded crime and public order offences in the summer of 1978 were compared with the summer preceding the experiment and in the summer following when policing reverted to its normal pattern. In the experimental year, all arrests in the resort decreased by 21 per cent and increased in the following year, when usual practice was resumed, by 20 per cent. It might be thought that the reliance on arrest figures as the marker for change would merely reflect the changes in policing practice. However, reported crime figures – those reports of crime made by the general public to the police – also showed a confirming substantial drop during the 1978 experiment.

The Torquay experience suggests that comparatively minor alterations in policy supervisory practice can have a significant influence on alcohol offences. A planned and systematic programme of visiting by uniformed officers to key premises appears to have a deterrent effect. It also provides the opportunity for licensees and the patrons to be reminded of the law within which they sell and consume alcohol.

The deployment of scarce police resources and consideration of the best way of preventing rather than just responding to alcohol-related offences and disturbance is something which could usefully figure on the agenda of a licensing forum.

Applications for new licences are processed by the police who investigate the status of the applicant and the quality of the premises. Their recommendations carry considerable weight with the justices. The police are also responsible for enforcing all the provisions of liquor licensing law relating to such things as permitted hours and sales to minors and to drunks.

Police forces vary widely in the way in which they view their responsibilities and organize their practice. A small number of forces give a very high priority to liquor licensing issues. Specially designated, full-time officers work in licensing divisions with a senior officer co-ordinating activities and policy across divisions. These forces emphasize the value of focusing responsibility and developing specialist expertise in relation to liquor licensing matters. This enables the trade and licensing committees together with solicitors who act in licensing cases to recognize and respect the police expertise. These forces tend to see their administrative responsibilities of screening and processing applications and their regulatory responsibilities in connection with enforcing the law as two sides of the same licensing coin.

Forces which give licensing issues a high priority usually call regular meetings of licensees, representatives of the trade and their own specialist officers to consider how best to tackle public disorder difficulties. These meetings are embryonic licensing forums and may benefit from having a wider group of people involved. Emphasis is also placed on the importance of developing closer relationships with licence-holders which can be important for enabling licensees to turn to the police when they feel they need advice, help and support. Court initiatives in relation to alcohol and offenders are outlined in chapter 10.

Those forces which have seen the importance of developing licensing expertise and which have integrated the administrative and regulatory functions are, by and large, those forces which have mounted other interesting initiatives in the liquor licensing area. One force has an officer specifically appointed to supervise and liaise with registered and proprietary clubs. Another has developed check-lists of points to watch for on its regular cycle of visits to these clubs. These questions include how many people are eating, how many are dancing, how many are drinking, the ratio of males to females, the broad age profile of participants, and other points of interest in relation to the operation of proprietary clubs and other licensed premises.

One force gives lectures on the law to licensees. Another provides a handout for all licensees – prepared in conjunction with a local brewery – which deals with the design of premises, equipment, staffing, supervision, and the issue of public disorder. A 'designated' officer has been appointed in another force. This officer, who has a high level of expertise in relation to alcohol problems generally, is a key resource for his force where such problems are concerned.

A well-developed licensing presence in a police force would be measured by the existence of liquor licensing departments, the recognition of the need for licensing expertise, the integration of administrative and regulatory functions, awareness of alcohol problems within the police itself, the encouragement of forums, training and educational materials, and the development of close working relationships with the licensed trade.

Some police forces, by contrast, are essentially reactive. They have no department or specially designated officer concerned with licensing issues. The vetting and processing of applicants, transfers, alterations to premises, and other licensing issues will be dealt with, as one officer put it, 'by any shift inspector who happens to be around'. One force believes that a licensing department would be 'a luxury'. Some 'reactive' forces do have licensing departments but their work is seen to be purely administrative. There is no attempt to develop the various initiatives and relationships established by the more pro-active departments. The regulatory licensing function is not integrated into the licensing department's work. A number of reactive forces actually reject the idea of integrated pro-active approaches on the grounds that the police's task is the detection of offences. Other forces carry out very little supervision of licensed premises on the grounds that there are many more pressing calls upon their time.

The question of allocation of police time, the balance between a pro-active and a reactive stance in relation to liquor licensing issues, and the degree to which the police could or should become involved in broader licensing issues are all policy matters for the police themselves. But they are matters which ought to concern other organizations in any locality as well. The local licensing forum would be the ideal place to discuss the role of the police in relation to both administrative and regulatory licensing practice.

But whatever position is taken by the police in a locality it would be helpful for the annual report from the chief constable to the licensing justices to contain an outline of the force's liquor licensing organization and supervisory strategies. This could include details on the supervising of off-licence as well as on-licence premises and could also contain as much up-to-date information as possible on licensing offences and alcohol-related offences in relation to licensed premises.

This is intended to be a *living* 'guide to action'. Therefore, it needs to be revised and added to in the light of local needs and local experience.

The following two pages are for jotting down examples of good practice, and addresses relevant to the issues covered by this chapter.

We hope to update the guide, and would be delighted to receive any advice about corrections, new material or any other information which should go into the next edition. Please send all suggestions, before 31 December, 1987, to:

Philip Tether and David Robinson
Addiction Research Centre
University of Hull
Hull HU6 7RX

Examples of Good Practice

Useful Addresses and Telephone Numbers

Further reading

Anthony, E., Acred, C.J., *Guide to Licensing Law for Betting Shops, Bookmakers, Clubs and Licensed Premises*, Barry Rose, Publishers, Chichester, 1976

Baker, E.R. and Dodge, J.B., *Police Promotion Handbook No. 3*, 7th edn, Butterworth, London, 1979

Brewers' Society, 'Licensing Law and the Young', a Brewing Review Reprint from an article which first appeared in the *Brewing Review*, 1, 4, 1978. Published by and available from the Brewers' Society, 42 Portman Square, London W1H OBB

Daly, J.M., *Club Law*, Butterworth, London, 1979

Davies, A.C., *The Private Citizen's Powers in the Field of Liquor Control*, United Kingdom Temperance Alliance, London, 1979

Field, D. and Pink, M., *Liquor Licensing Law*, Sweet and Maxwell, London, 1983

Jeffs, B.W. and Saunders, W.M., 'Minimising Alcohol Related Offences by Enforcement of the Existing Licensing Legislation', *British Journal of Addiction*, 78, 1, 67–77, 1983

Justices' Clerks' Society, *Licensing Law in the Eighties*, Ref. 70.0026, April 1983. Copies can be obtained from: Gerard Sullivan, P.O. Box 107, Nelson Street, Bristol BS99 7BT

Martin, J.N. (ed.), *Paterson's Licensing Acts 1985*, 93rd edn, Butterworth, London, 1984

National Union of Licensed Victuallers, *The Case for Change*, submission on licensing legislation reform, Reedprint Ltd, Windsor, 1980. Available from: NULV, Boardman House, Farnham, Surrey, GU9 7NX

Pain, K.W., *Licensing Practice and Procedure*, Fourmat, London, 1984

Report of the Departmental Committee on Liquor Licensing (the Erroll Report), HMSO, London, 1972

Report of the Interdepartmental Review Body on Liquor Licensing (the Blackburn Report), HMSO, London, 1980

Underhill, M., *Licensing Guide*, 9th edn, Longman Professional, London, 1985

Whiteside, G.L., *Handbook for Licensing Justices*, 3rd edn, Barry Rose, Publishers, Chichester, 1982

Appendix 5.A:

Model licensing committee statement of policy – Justices' Clerks' Society, *Licensing Law in the Eighties,* Annex 'C'*

Overriding considerations

1. In considering applications for the grant or renewal of a licence the following factors will be regarded as overriding:

    (a) *Public Safety.* No licence will be granted for premises which are or are likely to represent a substantial risk to the public from the point of view of structure, fire hazard or hygiene.

    (b) *Public Order.* No licence will be granted for premises which are or are likely to represent a substantial risk to public order, whether on the basis of their clients, management or layout.

    (c) *The Avoidance of Public Nuisance.* No licence will be granted for premises which are or are likely to represent a substantial risk of nuisance to the public from drunkenness, noise or misbehaviour, particularly late at night and in residential areas.

    (d) *Compliance with the Law.* No licence will be granted for premises where there is or is likely to be a substantial risk of law breaking, whether of the licensing laws or dishonesty.

    (e) *Where alcohol abuse is a problem in the area.*

Liquor security

2. The committee will always wish to be satisfied that adequate arrangements have been made for the security of the liquor on display and in stock.

Generally

3. Factors which will be borne in mind by the committee are:

    (a) the suitability of the public part of the premises, its means of access to the street and any arrangements for car parking;

    (b) the amenity effects of the premises on the surrounding neighbourhood.

*Reproduced with the kind permission of the Justices' Clerks' Society.

Suitability of applicant

4. No licence will be granted to an applicant of bad character or to anyone who is otherwise unfit to hold a licence.

Multiple licensees

5. The licensing justices will not grant a licence to two or more persons unless at least one of them is in day to day management and control of the premises.

Note: If it should transpire that the licensee in day to day control of the premises has ceased to exercise that control and that sales of intoxicating liquor have continued under the authority of a licensee who is not in day to day control and that prompt action has not been taken to obtain a licence for someone in day to day control this will be regarded by the committee as a ground for failing to renew the licence at the next general annual licensing meeting.

Off licences

6. The justices will wish to be assured that all sales will be conducted by competent and responsible staff of eighteen years of age or more.

7. For premises engaged in the sale of general foodstuffs the licensing justices prefer the 'shop within a shop' type of operation. Where that method is not to be adopted then the following practices are preferred:

(a) counter service methods of sale, to the exclusion of self-service methods of sale;

(b) intoxicating liquor to be out of the physical reach of customers;

(c) intoxicating liquor not to be presented for sale amongst other commodities of a general nature; and

(d) all purchases of intoxicating liquor to be paid for over the counter at the point of selection.

8. In exceptional circumstances the provisions of paragraph 7 may be departed from in the case of a self-service store if it is shown by evidence to the committee's satisfaction that the methods of sale, display, security, supervision and staff training are such as to prevent so far as possible:

(a) pilferage;
(b) illegal sales.

9. Where there is any change of the part of the premises in which intoxicating liquor is sold or in respect of a matter mentioned in paragraphs 7 and 8 above, the applicant must attend the next licensing sessions to report it to the licensing committee.

Appendix 5.B:

Extracts from three local liquor licensing policies*

Nant Conwy Petty Sessional Division: Extracts from Licensing Policy

'In the first place it is important that it should be realised the Justices have very much in mind the fact that they act for a busy tourist centre, and that in such connection they realise the great importance of the provision of facilities to cater for the needs of the holiday maker, recognising the ever changing nature of such needs. At the same time they are aware of their duty to preserve within the area – surely one of the most pleasant in the country – the air of dignity which remains one of its hall marks, and to prevent rowdyism and hooliganism which unfortunately dominates many holiday centres today.

Secondly, it is emphasised that every application will be considered on its individual merits, and that the policy contained in this document is for the guidance of those concerned.' (Introduction)

'It is believed that generally speaking, the needs of the public in the area for on and off-liquor licences are fully met, and applications for new licences will be carefully considered for special merits justifying their grant.' (Item 1)

'Where special hours certificates are granted, there will normally be a provision imposed limiting permitted hours to midnight.' (Item 3)

'The Justices will not look favourably on applications for engagement parties, retirement parties or 18th birthday parties.' (Item 4 (h))

---

*Extracts reproduced with the kind permission of the Clerks to the Nant Conwy, Slough, and Poole Licensing Justices.

'The Justices recognise the growing popularity of certain sporting activities, darts and snooker in particular, but they view with certain alarm the number of applications for extensions of hours in connection with matches particularly when such extensions mean that those who are not actually participating as contestants take advantage of the facility. The position will be kept under constant review, but licensees and club owners are reminded that the frequency of such applications may well bring these to a category of functions which cease to be possible to be regarded as special.' (Item 6)

Slough Petty Sessional Division: Extracts from Licensing Policy

'In accordance with the dicta in *Regina-v-Torquay Licensing Justices ex parte Brockman (1951) 2KB 784*, Slough Licensing Justices have a general policy relating to licensed premises and require certain criteria which are set out below to be satisfied. These apply where appropriate to applications for "On", "Off", "Restaurant" or "Club" licences.' (Introduction)

'Slough Licensing justices have laid down a "shop within a shop" policy for "off" licences. This means that there must be a check-out for licensed goods separate to any check-outs for other items.' (Item 4)

'There should be no self selection except in off-licence shops which sell only licensed goods, unless the area licensed is separate from the remainder of the shop.' (Item 5)

'Where a proposed off-licence is to be incorporated in a store selling other goods, the licensed goods should be sold from an area which is capable of being completely secured and separated from the rest of the shop, by means of a lockable grill.' (Item 6)

'If granted, off-licences should clearly display the opening hours outside the premises.' (Item 8)

'The Justices require the person or persons (if different from the applicant) responsible for the sales to be included on any licence application.' (Item 12)

'In all cases the applicant will have to demonstrate to the committee a need for the type and location of the particular licence applied for.' (Item 14)

Dorset Magistrates Courts: Extracts from Licensing Policy

'The following is a statement of the committee's policy concerning applications for the grant and renewal of licences. In examining any particular application however, the committee will always look to the merits of the particular case. To this extent the policy statement amounts to guidelines only which are published for the information and assistance of all concerned.' (Introduction)

'In considering applications for the grant or renewal of a licence the following factors will be considered:

- Public safety . . .
- Public order . . .
- The avoidance of public nuisance . . .
- Compliance with the law . . .
- Liquor security
- The needs of the area – particularly where there is a high concentration of licensed premises and where alcohol abuse is a problem.' (Item 1 (a) – (f))

'Other factors which will be borne in mind by the committee are:

- the suitability of the public part of the premises, its means of access to the street and any arrangements for car parking:

- the amenity effects of the premises on the surrounding neighbourhood.' (Item 2 (a) – (b))

CHAPTER 6

Alcohol and work

149

CHAPTER 6

Alcohol and work

'Many problem drinkers are in regular employment, and can be helped by companies which adopt policies for problem drinkers and encourage initiatives to help them while at work.' (*Drinking Sensibly*, HMSO 1981: 60)

Contrary to popular belief most problem drinkers are *in* work. Many bring their problems *to* work. Some develop their problems *at* work. It has been estimated that problem drinkers take over five times the average sickness absences a year and are three times more liable to have accidents at work. The adverse economic consequences of alcohol problems for both public and private employers are obvious.

The typical workplace responses to problem drinking are collusion and dismissal. Ignorance about the nature and extent of problem drinking, the inability to recognize the warning signs, ambivalent attitudes towards drink, and an understandable – but unhelpful – personal loyalty often lead to problem indicators such as frequent lateness, increased absenteeism, and deteriorating work performance being covered up or ignored. If the problem is left to develop then the first official workplace response is often dismissal. For the employer, losing staff in this way can mean personnel problems, a lost investment in training, and the need for more resources to train replacements.

This chapter sets out the main components of an alcohol and work policy, stresses the importance of monitoring, and identifies some of the many groups and organizations which have a role to play in encouraging policies and good practice at the local level.

151

Alcohol and work policies

In 1981 the Health and Safety Executive, the Health Departments, and the Department of Employment jointly published *The Problem Drinker at Work* which outlined the extent of the 'alcohol and work' problem and urged management and unions to co-operate to 'develop policies to make it possible for employees who are problem drinkers to come forward and be given help' (p. 4).

Policies: aims, types, and spread

Aims In its outline an 'alcohol and work' policy is simple. It is a statement, agreed by *both* employer and employees, which emphasizes that problem drinking is a 'health problem'. A policy promises employees that those coming forward for help and those identified by disciplinary procedures as being in need of help will be given the opportunity to obtain appropriate aid and support, and that if they do so, their job and job rights will be preserved.

Depending on the severity of the problem and the facilities available, help may be provided by the organization's own medical or welfare department or from any one of a number of community sources – general practitioners, specialist treatment units, or local counselling services.

No legislation governing the relationship between employers and employees inhibits an employer from adopting an 'alcohol and work' policy. Employers have a common law duty to 'take reasonable care' to ensure the health and safety of their employees. In addition, the Health and Safety at Work Act 1974 imposes a joint duty on employers and employees to promote a safe working environment and the Act requires a written statement of general policy with regard to health and safety at work.

The case for 'alcohol and work' policies is reinforced by the drift of legal decisions in cases of dismissal for problems arising from drinking. These dismissals come under the headings of 'capability' – physical incapacity or deteriorating competence – and 'conduct' – intolerable behaviour on or off duty, unauthorized absences, and persistent lateness. If 'incapability' or inappropriate 'conduct' is due to alcohol, then a sickness rather than a disciplinary approach is more appropriate.

A number of cases of unfair dismissal have held that employers should give chronically sick employees – including problem drinkers – their patience and time, and that they should investigate the medical position and consult and discuss rather than issue warnings and arrange disciplinary hearings.

Policies are especially appropriate where certain 'at risk' groups are concerned. It is now recognized that there are many occupations whose members are particularly susceptible to alcohol problems. The 'risk' factors include stress, uncertain hours, separation from family and home, and unsupervised opportunities for the consumption of alcohol. 'At risk' groups include publicans, bar staff, those manufacturing and selling alcoholic beverages, sales people, those who have to entertain others as part of their job, seafarers, doctors, and those who drive for a living. However, epidemiological evidence indicates that approximately 5 per cent of the population has a serious drink problem and so *every* workplace can *expect* to have employees in difficulties due to alcohol.

A well-rounded and comprehensive alcohol and work policy will be concerned with *inappropriate* drinking as well as with helping problem drinkers. 'Inappropriate drinking' includes drinking at work or coming to work under the influence of drink. Inappropriate drinking should be the concern of employers for two reasons. In the first place, inappropriate drinking behaviour can be the precursor of serious alcohol problems – which emphasizes that policies should be as much about *prevention* as about helping those who have developed problems. Unfortunately, most discussion and literature about 'alcohol and work' has tended to concentrate solely on the problem drinker. As a consequence, alcohol and work policies often contain references to 'alcoholics' and 'alcoholism' which unhelpfully diminish the extent of the alcohol and work problem by focusing exclusively on a small group of grossly damaged drinkers from whom the majority of the workforce can disassociate itself.

The second reason for taking inappropriate drinking seriously is that quite small amounts of alcohol can lead to impaired judgement and inefficiency. As well as decreasing skills, alcohol can promote false confidence which in many work situations can be, quite literally, a fatal combination. Amounts of alcohol which, in another context, would be considered moderate can be excessive and dangerous if the workplace task calls for competence, fine judgement, and concentration. Unfortunately, data on the relationship between workplace accidents and alcohol is sketchy. This is a matter for health and safety representatives, the Health and Safety Executive, management, insurance companies, trades unions, and health and safety at work officers.

Policies should apply to every employee without discrimination or favour. Confidence in a policy will be undermined if, for instance, executives and manual workers are treated differently and receive different amounts of care, attention, and help. A policy should command the confidence and respect of *all* employees.

Types   Workplace policies for problem drinkers can be developed in isolation or as part of a wider Employee Assistance Programme (EAP). EAPs are designed to identify and help employees with any health, personal, or social problems. A well-developed EAP will have an 'alcohol and work' component which details the workplace response to those employees whose problems are primarily alcohol-related and the help and support which can be provided.

EAPs with an 'alcohol and work' component have several advantages over policies which focus exclusively upon problems relating to alcohol. First, any of the indicators of a developing alcohol problem such as lateness, absenteeism, sickness, and poor work performance, can be the result of difficulties quite unrelated to alcohol. A policy geared solely to alcohol problems may lead to other employee problems being down-graded, ignored, or dealt with in an inappropriate way. Second, those whose responsibility it is to spot the problem indicators may feel that their task is less 'sensitive' and difficult if they are looking for signs of general personal or health problems rather than just drink-related ones. Third, those employees with an alcohol problem may well have other difficulties and a broad EAP might be better able to help with these than a specific 'alcohol and work' policy. Finally, a workplace response to problem drinking embedded in an EAP may prove more acceptable to employees. Certainly, many trade unions prefer a workplace response to problem drinkers to be incorporated within an overall EAP.

This does not mean, however, that specific 'alcohol and work' policies are worthless. Far from it. Well-thought-out workplace responses to alcohol problems are urgently needed. Moreover, the value of any policy, whether specific or as part of an EAP, depends on the way it is implemented. A well-implemented 'alcohol and work' policy will be more useful than a wide-ranging, but poorly implemented, EAP.

The aims and content of good 'alcohol and work' practice are the same whether they are part of an alcohol and work policy or part of a general EAP. The material in this chapter applies equally to both.

Spread   Policies are common in the USA. The aerospace firm Pratt and

Whitney claimed to have saved $1.5 million in the first year of its policy. The USA Post Office calculates that its policy has saved $17.5 million. Progress in the UK has been slow, with the drink and transport sectors leading the way. A small number of district health authorities and an even smaller number of local government authorities have adopted policies. The civil service is now covered by a national agreement reached between the trades unions and management which is designed to encourage the development of local policies. The Department of Trade and Industry and the DHSS have built on this general agreement and issued departmental policies. British Telecom, the Post Office, Marks and Spencer Ltd and several other major concerns in both the public and private sectors have adopted policies (see, for example, Appendix 6.A). It is less easy to establish how many small organizations have adopted alcohol and work policies, although policies appear to be quite widely spread in Scotland.

CBI and TUC   The CBI has no official attitude towards policies and offers no guidance to its members on the subject of 'alcohol and work'. It believes that individual companies should make up their own minds about the need for such policies. The Trades Union Congress (TUC) displays greater interest. The TUC began a survey of jointly negotiated alcohol and work policies in 1981 as a response to the publication of *The Problem Drinker at Work*. As a result, the TUC has produced a set of recommendations on policies which should be of interest to all trade unionists. They are entitled *Problem Drinking: TUC Guidelines for a Workplace Policy* and can be obtained from:

> Social Insurance and Welfare Department
> Trades Union Congress
> Congress House
> Great Russell Street
> London WC1B 3LS
> (Tel: 01-636-4030)

Implementing policies

Where they do exist, alcohol and work policies are often poorly implemented. The tendency to concentrate upon 'alcoholics' means that many policies serve merely as a 'safety net' for the exceptional 'problem cases'. The issue of inappropriate drinking is usually ignored.

Even the concern for 'alcoholics' will often not be effectively realized because policies usually fail to spell out the contribution which specific workplace groups and professionals can make towards the identification of problem drinkers. However, problems of implementation do not always result from the inadequate content of the policy. Some trade unions, whose interest and co-operation are essential, can be reluctant to participate in case their involvement is interpreted as 'taking the management's side'. As a result, many 'policies' are merely statements of good intent. They fail to have any impact upon workplace activity or on the prevention, identification, or handling of alcohol problems.

Good practices   For any alcohol and work policy to be more than just a statement of good intent requires the active participation of many different categories of workers in a number of good practices. The categories of workers include managers, foremen and supervisors, personnel officers, shop stewards and trade union representatives, health and safety at work officers, members of health and safety committees, and occupational health staff. The good practices cover the three basic components of a comprehensive alcohol and work policy: alcohol in the workplace, educating about alcohol, and responding to alcohol problems.

Good practices are outlined below and should be identified, at least in outline, in any alcohol and work policy so that the employer, trade unions, and key workers are committed to promoting them, and so that employees understand the main purposes of the policy and how these can be achieved.

Sets of good practices can be developed in any workplace without the introduction of a fullyfledged, written, public, alcohol and work policy. Indeed, it may well be more sensible in many workplaces to encourge a policy to evolve out of an accumulation of good practices rather than to construct a policy and expect the necessary good practices to emerge all at once. Building policy 'from the periphery' might well result in one which is more durable and better understood by everyone.

Good alcohol and work practices

The three sets of good practices relate to:

- Alcohol in the workplace;

- Educating about alcohol;
- Identifying and responding to problem drinkers.

Since a sensible stance on alcohol in the workplace and education about alcohol can help to prevent serious problem drinking, and since problem drinking is inappropriate drinking writ large, all these 'good practices' are about *preventing* inappropriate drinking *and* helping the problem drinker.

Alcohol in the workplace

Every workplace provides a number of opportunities for developing consistent attitudes toward alcohol which will help to reinforce the alcohol and work policy. If these reinforcing good practices in relation to alcohol are not developed then important opportunities for making the policy visible in the daily life of the workplace will be lost, and unhelpful or contradictory messages will be encouraged. Some of these good practices are outlined below. Every workplace is different. It is the task of all personnel to identify the good practice possibilities.

Workplace bars   Many workplaces have bars and clubs in which alcohol is sold at lower prices than in public licensed premises. Is a policy of subsidizing drink compatible with an alcohol and work policy? Moreover, many works bars are open during the day. These include bars open during the day in police and civil service canteens and, even, one serving a large northern city's public transport staff. Management could review the wisdom of what amounts to an encouragement to inappropriate drinking – mixing alcohol and work.

Soft drink alternatives   If there are workplace bars and clubs then there should always be plenty of non-alcoholic drinks; and similarly, these should be available in directors' dining rooms and at 'social' occasions such as long-service, leaving, retirement, and Christmas parties. Whatever the occasion and wherever drinking takes place, the ready availability of soft drinks as an alternative to alcoholic beverages is important not only for drivers but to underline the fact that alcohol is not, necessarily, an indispensible adjunct to every social occasion. It also reinforces the fact that the alcohol and work issue is being taken seriously.

Lunchtime drinking   Many employees go to a public house at lunchtime. It might be that the lack of company facilities encourages employees to go off the premises for a drink. If canteen food is unattractive or too expensive and there are no thirst-quenching drinks then employees will, understandably, seek the nearest pub for their lunchtime relaxation. One northern private firm which has experienced considerable problems as a result of lunchtime drinking has made it a condition of employment that employees will not drink at lunchtime. It has also reorganized its own canteen arrangements to provide cheap, attractive, and varied food in pleasant surroundings.

Concessionary prices   Many firms, particularly shops, offer their employees the chance to purchase goods at reduced prices. This may include alcohol. Management may want to review such a policy. When can the drink be purchased? Should it be available for purchase during the day? How big are the discounts and are these positive inducements? Should discounts be offered at all on this particular commodity? Is a financial encouragement to employees to drink more alcohol than they otherwise would consistent with the spirit of an alcohol and work policy?

Drinking and disciplinary procedures   The aim of an alcohol and work policy is to discourage inappropriate drinking and to help problem drinkers. A policy benefits from having a clear attitude to alcohol and work expressed through workplace rules, regulations, and disciplinary procedures. Handbooks outlining these rules, regulations, and procedures provide an opportunity, by way of explanation and amplification, to reinforce the policy.

Workplace regulations should make clear statements about whether alcohol can be brought on to the premises and whether it can be consumed on the premises. They should also indicate exactly what will happen if any employee is found to be intoxicated during working hours.

The disciplinary rules, regulations, and procedures, in addition to being clear about alcohol, drinking, and intoxication, should refer to any existing 'alcohol and work' policy. Disciplinary procedures which make appropriate reference to alcohol and an alcohol and work policy are two complementary aspects of a sensible workplace approach to alcohol issues.

Driving for the company   Terms of employment and the disciplinary code should spell out the consequences of a drunken-driving conviction for an employee who drives for the firm. Many organizations deal with individual cases as they arise. This is unsatisfactory if the aim of disciplinary procedures and alcohol and work policies and practices is to develop sensible, clear, and codified responses to alcohol problems.

Responses to drunken-driving vary. But the alternatives are clear. If there is no alcohol and work policy then the issue is disciplinary and management must decide how it will respond after a conviction. Should they dismiss? Should alternative work be found? Should the driver be allowed to drive again when the licence is returned? And if so, what would be the consequences of a subsequent conviction?

Where a policy exists, the question arises of whether the drunken-driving is symptomatic of an alcohol problem. If it is not then it is a disciplinary matter. If an alcohol problem does exist then the employer is committed, through the alcohol and work policy, to providing alternative work until such time as the employee is fit and legally eligible to resume driving. Then a decision can be made about returning the employee to the previous job.

Development of devices to prevent drunken-driving appears to be well-advanced and may soon be a practical option for employers. In 1985 General Motors NZ Ltd launched what is claimed to be the world's first commercially manufactured unit specifically designed to prevent drunken-driving. Before the vehicle can be started, the driver must blow into a small hand-held sensor. If the breath sample is below the legal limit the car can be started, but if it is over the legal limit the ignition system remains locked and the vehicle cannot be started. The device can be run on a twenty-four hour control or on a timing mechanism which automatically switches on between 6 pm and 6 am (the high-risk time). It can be fitted to any petrol-powered vehicle, including motor cycles. General Motors do not, at the moment, plan to instal this device during manufacture although their New Zealand dealer network is selling and installing it. The company involved in international distribution is:

Stevens and Hall Ltd
PO Box 705
Auckland
New Zealand

Health and safety at work   Employers and employees have a joint duty to promote health and safety in the workplace. Health and safety at work officers, Health and Safety Committees, and occupational health staff have specific duties and responsibilities and 'alcohol issues' cannot be ignored. All three groups should have a direct interest in 'alcohol in the workplace' issues involving, for example, the supply of non-alcoholic drinks at parties, bar facilities on the site, and workplace regulations concerning alcohol.

Health and safety officers could include alcohol as a routine health-and-safety-at-work topic and it would be useful if they regularly analysed the time, type, and place of workplace accidents. Are accidents tending to cluster in the mornings – the hangover effect – and in the early part of the afternoon – after lunchtime drinking? Such simple, basic information might be useful in stimulating debate about alcohol issues in the workplace.

The Health and Safety at Work Act 1974 states that safety representatives may be appointed in any workplace by a recognized trade union. A joint Health and Safety at Work Committee will be made up of these representatives together with management. The functions of safety representatives are numerous but the most important are: to represent the membership on health and safety issues; to investigate potential hazards, the causes of accidents, and complaints by employees; to make representations to the employer; and to inspect the workplace. Clearly, a joint Health and Safety Committee is an ideal forum for the discussion of alcohol issues.

One of the most useful discussion topics for a joint Health and Safety Committee would be the routine identification and cataloguing of specific problem indicators among employees (see below). To date, this is an aspect of alcohol and work policies which many trade unions baulk at.

Health and safety at work officers, members of Health and Safety Committees, and occupational health staff could between them establish the case for an alcohol and work policy and outline the kind of policy they would like to see adopted. Or they could agree between themselves to promote a variety of good practices which would establish a *de facto* policy as an alternative to, or a precursor of, a formal policy.

Educating about alcohol in the workplace

Workplace education about alcohol should, at least initially, be of two kinds. First, key groups and professionals such as health and safety at work officers, personnel officers, occupational health staff, managers, shop stewards, and supervisors need education about alcohol and work policies – why they are necessary, their content, and how they should be introduced. Second, general alcohol education for the entire workforce should be introduced as an integral part of the policy to underpin and reinforce it. These two educational 'strands' cannot be completely separated. Some educational material on policies which is suitable for managers and others is also suitable for general workplace education.

Any workplace education programme should take into account the possibility that some workers might be specifically 'at risk' because of lack of supervision, proximity to alcohol, or the nature of their employment. These 'at risk' groups might include salesmen, drivers, or those working with dangerous and delicate machinery. If there are women employees then the topic of alcohol and pregnancy could be included in any general alcohol education programme.

There are a number of useful *guides for management and unions* to introducing and running an alcohol and work policy. These guides are outlined below.

Alcohol Problems in Employment This was produced by the Alcohol Education Centre and the Scottish Health Education Group and is a multi-media resource pack. It is for use by all those in industry concerned with the prevention and treatment of alcohol problems. The pack contains a number of papers on the formulation of a company policy, an analysis of the significance of recent legislation with regard to drunkenness and problem drinking, and basic information about the range of treatment services for problem drinkers which are available in most localities. It also contains three training audio-tapes. The Alcohol Education Centre is no longer in existence. Its responsibilities have been taken over by:

Alcohol Concern
305 Gray's Inn Road
London WC1X 8QF
(Tel: 01-833-3471)

Enquiries about the pack should be addressed to Alcohol Concern or, alternatively, to:

Scottish Health Education Group
Wcodburn House
Canaan Lane
Edinburgh EH10 4SG
(Tel: 031-447-8044)

The Industrial Pack This is produced by the Institute of Alcohol Studies and is a set of guidelines for supervisors, occupational health and welfare services, management, and trades unions. It identifies the ingredients of a successful workplace response and pinpoints the information and appropriate skills which specific groups in the workplace must acquire to make a policy successful. The address is:

> Institute of Alcohol Studies
> 12 Caxton Street
> London SW1H 0QS
> (Tel: 01-222-4001/5880)

The Problem Drinker in the Workplace This is produced by the Brewers' Society and is a video-tape with a supporting booklet dealing with alcohol problems in the workplace and how to respond to them. This video-tape has been widely used outside the brewing industry and has helped to persuade a number of major employers to adopt alcohol and work policies. The price to non-members is currently £60 with supporting booklets at £1.50 each or £1 each for orders of 100 or more. The address is:

> Brewers' Society
> 42 Portman Square
> London W1H 0BB
> (Tel: 01-486-4831)

The posters, pamphlets, and other materials identified in chapter 2 can be used for *general education in the workplace*. Some more specialized material is described below.

Sensible Drinking This is a Brewers' Society video-tape with a supporting booklet. The video-tape is an extract from *The Problem Drinker in the Workplace*. It is designed to alert employees to the problems which excessive drinking can cause and indicates that the company is willing to help employees who are in difficulties. The current price to non-members is £40 with supporting booklets at 30p each or £25 for 100.

Alcohol Education Syllabus An alcohol education syllabus has been jointly produced by TACADE, the Teachers' Advisory Council on Alcohol and Drug Education and the Health Education Council. The syllabus consists of two separate packages, one for 11–16-year-olds and the other for 16–19-year-olds. Employers might find the second package appropriate for their young workers. Each package has an introductory booklet and five separate teaching units, each of which comes in its own folder and can be used independently. The packages are supported by six 'trigger' films designed to stimulate discussion. The address is:

TACADE
2 Mount Street
Manchester M2 5NG
(Tel: 061-834-7210)

The Facts about Drinking and Driving This is a four-page pamphlet produced by the Transport and Road Research Laboratory. It covers a number of important topics including the effects of alcohol on driving performance and the legal consequences of drinking and driving. This is an ideal publication for an employer seeking specific education literature to give to drivers of company cars and other vehicles. In addition, the Transport and Road Research Laboratory has a library which contains a range of audio-visual material on drinking and driving. The address is:

Transport and Road Research Laboratory
Old Wokingham Road
Crowthorne
Berkshire RG11 6AU
(Tel: 0344-773131)

Posters Posters on drinking and driving have been sponsored by and are available from the Brewers' Society. One poster is entitled 'Don't Gamble with Your Licence'. This is part of a wide range of materials dealing with the dangers of drinking and driving which the Brewers' Society has been producing now for many years. Another appropriate poster is one of a range recently sponsored by the Society especially for motor cyclists and the caption reads 'Don't Drink and Ride'.

Other materials Video-tapes on drinking and driving have also been sponsored by the Brewers' Society. Three have been produced by the Road Safety Education Unit of the University of Reading, in collaboration with RoSPA and the Road Research Laboratory and with help from the Metropolitan Police and ambulance service. They are entitled *Driven to Drink?*, *Who's Sorry Now?*, and *What's the Limit?* Further details of these video-tapes can be found in chapter 7. The Department of Transport and the Brewers' Society have provided funds so that any educational institution can borrow the video-tapes free of charge from:

Central Film Library
Chalfont Grove
Gerrards Cross
Bucks SL9 8TN
(Tel: 0753-885991)

RoSPA's Road Safety Division has produced a series of booklets on drinking and driving. Each one is aimed at a specific group and there is one for *Employers and Employees*. All the booklets contain common material on the effects of alcohol on driving and the law. Each booklet contains an individually designed section entitled 'What You Can Do to Help'. Details of these important and helpful publications can be obtained from:

Road Safety Division
RoSPA
Cannon House
The Priory
Queensway
Birmingham B4 6BS
(Tel: 021-233-2461)

Problem drinkers: identification and responses

Policies, as well as helping to prevent inappropriate drinking and to educate about alcohol, should be designed to help problem drinkers. All policies should include procedures for identifying problem drinkers and for helping them to overcome their problems.

Indicators of problems The mere existence of a policy will not automatically lead to problem drinkers in a workforce coming forward for help. Management and unions have to devise objective measures of workplace activity and work performance which will help to identify problem drinkers. No supervisor, foreman, or line manager can be expected to diagnose a drinking problem; but with the aid of straightforward indicators they can establish *prima facie* evidence of a problem which can be investigated by trained personnel.

Problem indicators include patterns of absences – such as on Monday mornings; work accidents; lateness – especially at lunchtime; mood changes; irritability; depression; decreased ability to co-operate with fellow workers; and reduced or ineffective work performance. Sickness absences for such problems as stomach upsets, abdominal pains, ulcer, indigestion, depression, or anxiety *may* be due to alcohol problems. Workplace experience suggests that the deterioration in work performance combined with personality changes are significant indicators although they may be linked to health or personal problems which are quite unrelated to alcohol.

Screening Some workplaces have comprehensive health screening programmes. The British United Provident Association (BUPA) have several screening centres and over 1,000 companies now send their staff for routine examination. Companies and individuals do not have to belong to BUPA to use the screening centres but BUPA members do enjoy reduced fees. The centres screen for, among other things, problem drinking. Employees complete a questionnaire, either on paper or direct to a computer in London, which contains standard questions for the detection of alcohol abuse. The centres carry out bio-chemical and haematological tests for alcohol problems and the examining physician looks for the signs and symptoms of problem drinking (for further discussion of screening see chapter 8).

Clearly, regular health screening as part of an alcohol and work policy is one way of identifying problem drinkers, but employers should make sure that any company-paid participation in the screening programme is fully compatible with the workplace response to problem drinking. Policies must apply to all employees not just senior staff who are sent for 'check-ups'.

Responding to problem drinkers Once problems are identified help can be offered. Some help, such as sick leave or movement to another, less demanding job, can be organized in the workplace. Where there are occupational health and welfare staff, specialist advice and counselling may be available which could be all that some problem drinkers require. However, most company medical staff will have had no special training for diagnosing or treating problem drinkers. Similarly, most nurses who hold an Occupational Health Nursing Certificate will not have had any specialist training in 'alcohol and work' issues. Companies which do not have their own occupational health staff often employ a part-time retained GP to carry out any necessary medical examinations and to advise management generally, and the health and safety officers in particular, on occupational health issues. Few GPs have been trained to identify or respond to alcohol problems (see chapter 8).

Because of this it would be useful if occupational health staff participated in the 'Drinking Choices' training course (see chapters 2 and 8) which imparts not only the knowledge and skills to educate other educators but also provides the education component of the treatment of problem drinkers. Although the tendency is to refer most problem drinkers to community services outside the workplace, occupational health staff could usefully develop educational skills to assist in the rehabilitation process. In many cases simple advice may be all that is required. Alcohol education within the workplace will carry authority if it comes from workplace medical personnel.

In the great majority of workplaces, no specialist occupational health staff will be available and problem drinkers will have to seek help outside. When an alcohol and work policy is established, contact should be made with the local Council on Alcoholism, Alcoholics Anonymous, and any other source of counselling help and support. Some of the local bodies which may have appropriate counselling skills are identified in chapter 9. In any particular case, the employee's GP should always be contacted.

Some alcohol problems might be dealt with through health insurance. In the UK over four million people are covered by private health insurance. Many organizations organize cover for their own employees through either a group scheme under which individuals qualify for reduced premiums or through a company-paid scheme. Neither of these schemes requires an automatic pre-insurance medical. Applicants are merely asked some simple and straightforward questions about hospital and GP contact over a number of previous years. More elaborate 'screening' operations involving automatic medicals and detailed questionnaires which might, among other things, probe drinking habits are difficult and costly to administer. If treatment through health insurance is one response to problem drinkers then, again, insurance must cover all employees to maintain the even-handedness of an alcohol and work policy.

Monitoring alcohol and work policies

Every alcohol and work policy should be carefully monitored to ensure that the various provisions of the policy are being consistently and properly *implemented* and to gauge their *impact*.

Monitoring the implementation of the policy

A comprehensive alcohol and work policy includes several different activities involving a wide range of workplace groups and professionals. When a policy is established, responsibility for implementing different parts of the policy or sets of good practice must be clearly established. Who has overall responsibility for organizing and mounting educational activities? Who is responsible for dealing with the alcohol and work issue in any induction programme? Who is responsible for ensuring that all those driving for the company are fully aware of the 'alcohol and driving' provisions in the disciplinary code? Who is responsible for ensuring that any 'good practices' in relation to the provision of soft drinks in the works bar, or at any works function, are carried out?

Once these responsibilities have been established, regular monitoring should be conducted to ensure that they are being carried out, to identify any problems and to see where adjustments need to be made. Failure to do this will result in the policy remaining merely a statement of good intent.

Monitoring inappropriate drinking

Monitoring inappropriate drinking in the workplace will be difficult. At an impressionistic level, it may be possible to get some idea of whether the number of employees going to public houses at lunchtime is decreasing, whether more people are having soft drinks at works functions, and whether fewer employees appear to be exhibiting signs of drunkenness or reduced efficiency. But most of these and other improvements in 'alcohol and work' behaviour will be diffused and difficult to pinpoint. One area, however, in which benefits could be quantified and costed is work accidents. Have those accidents which appear to be alcohol-related – either as a result of taking place at a 'high-risk' time or as a result of individual investigation – decreased since the implementation of the alcohol and work policy?

The overall benefit to an organization of reducing inappropriate drinking is, at base, a matter of commonsense. Surely, few would argue that personnel are safer or more efficient after drinking or that boardroom or management decisions are improved if those involved are partly intoxicated.

Monitoring the workplace response to problem drinkers

It may be easier to monitor the helping component of a policy than to monitor inappropriate drinking or the implementation of the policy itself. Where there is no alcohol and work policy most alcohol-related problems which come to attention will surface through the disciplinary procedure. If an alcohol and work policy is in operation people with problems will be encouraged to refer themselves. In some cases, people with problems will be identified through good case-finding practices and encouraged to seek help before disciplinary proceedings come into play. After a policy has become established and has gained the confidence of the workforce, it might be expected that the number of self-referred, as opposed to identified, cases would increase. Later still, it would be hoped that the number of both self-referred and identified cases would decline as the good educational and preventive practices of the policy take effect.

It would be unrealistic to expect the number of problem drinkers at work to reach zero. Although the workplace, with its procedures and good practices, can make a major contribution to the prevention and identification of problem drinking, it can never be expected to control the outside pressures and problems which may cause or contribute to employees' alcohol problems.

In order to monitor the impact of a work policy, records need to be kept of case-finding activities, the total number of cases that emerge, how they are responded to, and the outcome of the help. The numbers of individuals identified and helped can form one component of a simple cost-benefit analysis of the alcohol and work policy. What would be the cost of recruiting and training new workers to replace those who have been identified and how does this compare with the cost of implementing the policy?

Encouraging policies and good practice at the local level

One way of encouraging the spread of policies is to concentrate upon individual workplaces, particularly those covering large sections of the population such as local government, the NHS, or important 'at risk' groups such as the police, the licenced trade, and seafarers. There are many other local workplaces which would benefit from the introduction of policies and good practices but it would be impossible for local prevention workers to reach them all individually. Nevertheless, they can be influenced through key local organizations and groups.

The Health and Safety Executive The Health and Safety at Work Act 1974 created a Health and Safety Commission (HSC) and a Health and Safety Executive (HSE). The HSC is a six-to-nine-member body made up mainly of employers and employees' representatives. Its duty is to encourage training and research, and to advise government departments, employers, and employees' organizations on the promotion of safety. The HSE is the working arm of the Commission.

There are twenty-one area offices of the HSE Factory Inspectorate, each responsible through a senior principal inspector – under the overall direction of an area director – for dealing, on a national basis, with one specific industry or sector of employment. These National Industry Groups (NIGs) enable the Factory Inspectorate to parallel the structure of particular industries. There is no specific alcohol NIG. Alcohol is an issue relevant to every workplace and the problems that it can create are not restricted to one particular kind of industry. There is, however, a Drinks Industry NIG which is part of Scotland East area based in Edinburgh.

In addition to a NIG, each area office has several other groups under principal inspectors which deal with specific sections of industry such as steel, general engineering, and construction. The particular pattern of groups in any office reflects the industrial activities of the surrounding area. Some areas have shipbuilding groups, some steel, while in others textile groups may predominate. A few of the area offices have 'out station' officers. For instance a Carlisle office is out-stationed from Preston whilst Hull is out-stationed from Sheffield.

Area officers are supported by six Field Consultant Groups serving large regions. For instance, the North East Field Consultant Group serves the three area offices in Sheffield, Newcastle, and Leeds. The Field Consultant Groups are linked to a series of Health and Safety Executive HQ departments dealing with a range of special topics such as electrical safety, occupational hygiene, and lifting plant mechanical handling. The Field Consultant Groups act, therefore, as links between area offices and HQ.

The HSE structure of specialized inspectorates and Factory Inspectorate area officers with their NIGs and other industry groups could play an important role in raising alcohol awareness in a wide variety of workplaces. The specialized inspectorates have access to their own particular type of workplace. The Factory Inspectorate is primarily responsible for health and safety issues in workplaces in which mechanical processes predominate. The responsibility for health and safety in offices, shops, and other 'non-mechanized' workplaces lies with the local environmental health departments (see below).

Although the HSE was jointly responsible with the health departments for the 1981 report on *The Problem Drinker at Work*, the local HSE organization is not vigorous in pressing for policies and good alcohol and work practices. Local prevention workers might find it difficult to draw in a member from the local HSE. It might be easier to involve a physician from the Employment Medical Advisory Service (EMAS) which is part of the HSE. EMAS provides information and advice on employment and extends this service to all employees. It could well include alcohol information.

Environmental health departments   Environmental health departments (EHDs) are part of local government and share health and safety at work responsibilities with the HSE. EHDs are basically responsible for health and safety in 'non-mechanized premises' such as offices and shops. The only blurring of this distinction is where local authority premises are concerned. Since EHDs are part of local government the HSE has oversight of health and safety issues in this sector.

EHDs vary in size from those employing over fifty environmental health officers (EHOs) to the smallest department in the country which contains only three. Their internal structure is varied. Some are functionally organized with specialists in different branches of environmental health. In others officers have all-round responsibility for a geographical area. A great deal of an EHO's work is concerned in some form or other with education and most departments are developing an explicit health education component to their work. This is most advanced in those departments which are functionally organized, where it has been a relatively easy matter to add health education to the existing list of specialisms.

Like the HSE and EMAS – both of which are a source of advice – EHDs have access to a wide range of local workplaces and the potential to generate increased knowledge about, and interest in, alcohol issues. In addition, their developing health education function provides these departments with a ready-made opening for promoting alcohol work policies.

Coroners   All sudden or unexplained deaths are investigated by coroners who are usually experienced doctors or lawyers. The cost of the service is met from the rates, but coroners are judicial officers who are quite independent from local and central government and who are required to act in accordance with specific laws and procedures. They are assisted by a small staff whose number depends upon the size of the population and district in which they serve.

When someone dies as a result of an accident at work a coroner's inquest is held before a jury. If death occurs within twelve hours of the incident a blood/alcohol analysis may be made by the pathologist who, at this point, may not be aware that a coroner's post-mortem is being conducted. A blood/alcohol test carried out more than twelve hours after the accident would serve no purpose since any alcohol would, by this time, have been dissipated. However, even if death occurs within twelve hours after the accident it is not always possible to ascertain a reliable blood/alcohol level. In many severe accidents – especially those involving internal injuries such as might be sustained in a bad workplace incident – massive transfusions of blood and plasma are often given. Moreover, any blood/alcohol test is challengeable on the basis that, after death, the body generates a certain amount of its own alcohol.

Obviously, coroners and those interested in establishing the causes of workplace accidents should attempt to ensure that blood/alcohol testing is done wherever possible. Nevertheless, any alcohol connection with the accident must be established by the coroner's own enquiries. Coroners could devise certain standard 'alcohol' questions to ask in all cases of industrial accidents such as 'What time did the accident take place?' and 'Where did the deceased have lunch?' and so on. If the coroner's enquiry discovers a state of affairs which might lead to further deaths from the same cause the public's attention can be drawn to it. In this way a coroner is well placed to give useful publicity to workplace accidents involving alcohol. Like all the other key local organizations and groups identified in this section, coroners should be acquainted with the alcohol and work issue and the need for sensible policies and practices.

Participants in a local prevention strategy could raise the whole issue of alcohol and work accidents with their local coroner.

Personnel managers   Most personnel managers are members of:

Institute of Personnel Management (IPM)
IPM House
Camp Road, Wimbledon
London SW19 4UW

The IPM is locally orientated and its forty branches are regarded as important. All members of the IPM, from student members upwards, are entitled to belong to local branches and to vote in elections.

There are three stages in the IPM examination and any prospective student must be a registered IPM student member. Stages 1 and 2 are gained by examination while stage 3 consists of a project. The content, conduct, and organization of all courses leading to stages 1, 2, and 3 is the responsibility of the Education Committee of the IPM which is a committee of the institute's central council. The Education Committee is pursuing a policy of educational devolution by encouraging suitable institutions of higher education to set their own examination papers.

In addition to contacting the local branch of the IPM a local prevention group could seek to highlight the alcohol issue by approaching local institutions of higher education which run IPM courses. Most tutors would welcome a contribution on alcohol and work. Similarly, students undertaking stage 3 projects could be urged to consider alcohol and work as a suitable topic.

Currently, there is no specific mention of alcohol and work issues in the approved outline curriculum but the IPM is aware of the topic and is developing teaching on it. The outline curriculum is flexible and the subject could be introduced at a number of points. Perhaps the most appropriate would be under 'Employee Resourcing' in stage 2 of the examinations which covers health and safety and employee services.

Health and safety at work officers   The national organization for health and safety at work officers is:

> The Institute of Occupational Safety and Health (IOSH)
> 222 Uppingham Road
> Leicester LE5 0QG

There is a two-tier examination structure leading to associated membership and full membership of the IOSH. Five topics are covered at each examination level: law; techniques of safety management; behavioural science; occupational health and hygiene; and general science. The full curriculum is specified by the National Examinations Board in Occupational Safety and Health (NEBOSH) in its 'Outline Syllabus in Objective Form'. There is no specific mention within this syllabus of alcohol and work issues.

Currently, some twenty-five institutions of higher education offer courses leading to associate and/or full membership of the Institute. NEBOSH sets the papers and organizes the examination at a number of centres throughout the UK. There is, therefore, much less scope for local influence on curriculum content than for the IPM. Nevertheless, alcohol and work issues could be raised locally with health and safety at work officers. Such interest might lead to appropriate changes in the outline syllabus.

Occupational nurses   Nurses working in occupational health are urged by the Royal College of Nursing (RCN) to organize themselves locally into groups in order to exchange information, organize study days, and keep abreast of developments in the discipline. Most localities will have such a group.

There are currently fifteen centres offering courses leading to examinations for the RCN's Occupational Health Nursing Certificate (OHNC). The outline syllabus for these courses is devised by the RCN in conjunction with the Education Board of the United Kingdom Central Council (UKCC) (see chapter 8). Nurses working in industry and commerce receive little specific occupational health training. In order to assist these nurses an Occupational Practice Nursing Course has been devised and is currently offered in five centres. The course involves practical training but does *not* prepare a nurse to take the RCN's OHNC examination. The addresses of all the centres offering courses leading to the OHNC and the Occupational Practice Nursing Course can be obtained from any local director of nurse education or direct from:

Royal College of Nursing
Henrietta Place
London W1N 0AB
(Tel: 01-409-3333)

Centres offering occupational nurse training will be pleased to discuss a teaching contribution on alcohol and work. Although the alcohol issue is being steadily introduced there is a particular need for more specific information on the aims, content, and implementation of alcohol and work policies.

Occupational health and safety groups and RoSPA.   There are eighty-two occupational health and safety groups spread throughout the UK. Membership includes not only health and safety at work officers but personnel officers, supervisors, and managers of all descriptions. The groups meet regularly, often with a visiting speaker, and are brought up-to-date on the latest health and safety issues and regulations. The exact titles of the groups vary. Some call themselves a safety group, others an occupational health and safety group or an environmental health and safety association. But whatever their title they offer an excellent opportunity for discussing alcohol and work issues with key local officials.

Approximately two-thirds of the groups are affiliated to the Royal Society for the Prevention of Accidents (RoSPA). They have an Occupational Health Safety Groups Advisory Committee (OHSGAC) within RoSPA's Occupational Safety Division. Local occupational health and safety groups send delegates to OHSGAC which, in turn, selects three of its members to sit on the RoSPA National Occupational Health and Safety Committee. This committee, on which sit senior safety professionals from the HSE, the medical profession, the unions, employers' organizations, and insurance companies, provides important links with a wide variety of governmental and other national organizations. Any interest in alcohol issues generated at the local level among occupational health and safety groups, or any concern about the alcohol education of any particular occupation or profession, could reach a wide and important audience, not only through the committee network but also via RoSPA's many health and safety at work courses and its links with over 8,000 companies.

Anyone can buy books, leaflets, posters, and other materials from the Occupational Safety Division of RoSPA and go on their training courses. Any public or private sector organization can subscribe to the division and receive a variety of magazines, guides, bulletins, the RoSPA year book, catalogues, materials, course details, planning guides for various campaigns, and the use of RoSPA's enquiry service and library. The subscription cost to any educational establishment is currently £41.30 plus VAT per annum. For trade unions, employers' organizations, and all firms with less than 2,000 employees the cost is £53.30 plus VAT. All appropriate local groups and organizations should be encouraged to subscribe.

Trades Councils In each locality individual TUC-affiliated trade unions are members of Trades Councils. The aim of a Trades Council is to make TUC policy more widely known and to promote local trade union co-ordination and co-operation. They also nominate trade union representatives to a number of local committees, tribunals, and other organizations such as Community Health Councils.

It is a condition of recognition by the TUC that a Trades Council must affiliate to a local County Association of Trades Councils and play an active part in its work. These County Associations are responsible for expressing trade union views to County Councils on issues that affect the community, such as public transport, consumer protection, education, and youth employment. Clearly, through these connections members of a trades council are well placed to raise alcohol and work issues with key local organizations.

Trade unions Participants in a local prevention strategy may wish to approach a trade union to enlist its support in devising and promoting a policy for a particular workplace or 'at risk' group. The outline structure of most trade unions is similar. Local branches, based on workplaces or particular trades and occupations, are represented on area or district committees which have full-time officers. The district committees have a supporting and advisory role *vis-à-vis* their branches. In the larger trade unions there will probably be an additional, regional tier. This too will provide support and advice but will usually, in addition, have responsibilities for education.

Most trade unions appoint health and safety experts, who can be contacted at union head offices or who are located within the regional structure. However, an approach to an individual trade union over any alcohol and work issue is best made to its district committee through which any contacts with the regional tier, an HQ specialist, or any special structure parallel to a given industry, can be made.

There are opportunities for participating in trade union organized education for health and safety at work representatives and shop stewards. The TUC has a regional council in each of the eight economic planning regions composed of representatives of affiliated unions and representatives of the County Association of Trades Councils.

The TUC's regional councils have close links with the TUC Education Service which has grown rapidly in recent years. TUC regional education officers are assisted in the preparation of their educational and training programmes by Regional Education Advisory Committees consisting of regional council delegates, local full-time officers of affiliated unions, and representatives of local Trades Councils, tutors in further and higher education establishments, and the Workers' Education Association. The Regional Education Advisory Committee play an important role in identifying the educational needs of a local trade union community and the local educational resources that are available to meet them.

Training is provided largely through TUC sponsored day-release courses run in local colleges of further and higher education or by the

Workers' Education Association. Members of all affiliated unions may take part in the TUC postal courses run from the Tillicoultry Centre in Scotland, while full-time officers are trained through a series of one-week courses held in the TUC Training College at Congress House.

TUC regional councils, regional education officers, and Regional Education Advisory Committees are all points of contact in any local programme seeking to raise the alcohol and work issue with trade unions and to make a contribution to the local training of trade unionists.

Chambers of Trade   Every locality has a Chamber of Trade consisting of members engaged in retailing and in other service industries ranging from small, street-corner enterprises to banks and department stores. In addition to trade membership every Chamber will have a number of affiliated associations such as the local Credit Cheque Traders' Association and the Retail Fruit Trade Federation. There are some 500 local Chambers of Trade representing approximately 200,000 members. All Chambers of Trade are members of the National Chamber of Trade which is a major pressure group. Chambers produce magazines, newsletters, and 'annual' reports. These can be used in any local initiative aimed at raising alcohol and work awareness and an initiative in this area might well supplement any approach to the local environmental health department which has the responsibility for health and safety in the premises of Chambers of Trade members.

Chambers of Commerce   Like Chambers of Trade, Chambers of Commerce are also found in every locality. Their membership is mainly drawn from business as opposed to retailing, although there is usually some overlap in membership. The local Post Office, for instance, is usually a member of both the Chamber of Commerce and the Chamber of Trade.

A Chamber of Commerce can be a member of the CBI (see below). Even where a Chamber of Commerce is not a direct member of the CBI there will be close links and liaison over issues of common concern. Individual businesses and undertakings can join a local Chamber of Commerce but most of the membership will be provided by the subscriptions of a wide variety of trade organizations. Again, like Chambers of Trade they will usually produce newsletters, digests, or reports for the membership.

The Confederation of British Industry (CBI)   The CBI represents a wide range of organizations which between them employ over twelve million people. The CBI draws its members from almost every sector of business – manufacturing, retailing, agriculture, construction, mining, finance, and transport. The CBI has officers based in thirteen regional locations and these serve as two-way communication points. Each region has its own elected council for which members are elected to the CBI's central council. The CBI regional offices will usually maintain standing groups concerned with major issues of continuing importance and interest to all members. These will include, for example, a standing group on training. Regional councils will form *ad hoc* groups to look at some particular issue as it arises.

There is also an important informal sub-regional organization of senior staff from member companies – often personnel directors – who meet to keep an eye on the local industrial scene and to discuss any issues of importance which may arise. The regional CBI office will frequently use these informal groups as a sounding board when a policy stance is being developed.

The CBI does not place as much emphasis as the TUC does on formal motions. Any issues of importance which emerge from the 'grass roots' and which receive the endorsement of a regional council would probably be discussed at the monthly meeting of all the chairmen of the regional councils and then be fed into one of the CBI Policy Directorates which are standing committees of the central council. It is always open to any individual member company to raise any matter from the floor during the annual CBI conference.

Local prevention workers could contact either the informal sub-regional group or the regional office to raise the alcohol and work issue. A lead from the CBI could increase the appreciation among employers of the nature, range, and extent of the alcohol problem at work and the need for sensible policies and good practices.

This is intended to be a *living* 'guide to action'. Therefore, it needs to be revised and added to in the light of local needs and local experience.

The following two pages are for jotting down examples of good practice, and addresses relevant to the issues covered by this chapter.

We hope to update the guide, and would be delighted to receive any advice about corrections, new material or any other information which should go into the next edition. Please send all suggestions, before 31 December, 1987, to:

Philip Tether and David Robinson
Addiction Research Centre
University of Hull
Hull HU6 7RX

Examples of Good Practice

Useful Addresses and Telephone Numbers

Further reading

Allsop, S. and Beaumont, P.B., 'Dismissal for Alcohol Offences', *Employee Relations*, 5.2 and 5.5, 1983

Argyropoulos-Grisanos, M.A. and Hawkins, P., *Alcohol and Industrial Accidents*, Christian Economic and Social Research Foundation, 1980, 12 Caxton Street, London SW1H 0QS, from where copies can be obtained

Beaumont, P.B. and Allsop, S., *The Safety Representative and Alcohol Policies*, 1983, mimeo, can be obtained from the Department of Social and Economic Research, University of Glasgow

Cohen, J., Deanarley, E.J., and Hansel, C.E.M., 'The Risk Taken in Driving under the Influence of Alcohol', *British Medical Journal*, 1, 1, 1438–442, 1958

Engel, H.O., 'Do We Need Policies for Alcoholism?', *Journal of The Royal Society of Medicine*, 70, 79–81, 1983

Health and Safety Commission, *Health and Safety at Work: Safety Representatives and Safety Committees*, HMSO, London, 1977

Health and Safety Executive, *The Problem Drinker at Work*, the Health Departments and the Department of Employment, HMSO, London, 1981

Hore, B.D. and Plant, M.A., *Alcohol Problems in Employment*, Croom Helm, London, 1981

Labour Research Department, *Alcohol Policies at Work, A Bargaining Report*, Trades Union Congress, London, 1983

Price, D.L. and Hicks, T.G., 'The Effects of Alcohol on Performance of a Production Assembly Task', *Ergonomics*, 22, 1, 37–41, 1979

Scottish Council on Alcoholism, *A Joint Union-Management Approach to Alcoholism Recovery Programmes*, produced by the Scottish Council on Alcoholism, 147 Blythswood Street, Glasgow G2 4EN, 1977

Scottish Council on Alcoholism, *Alcohol and Employment*, report of a working party, the Scottish Council on Alcoholism, Glasgow, 1981

Smith, D.J. and Gray, J., *Police and People in London*, Policy Studies Institute, London, 1983

Trades Union Congress, *Safety and Health at Work: a Handbook*, 2nd edn, TUC, London, 1978

Ward Gardner, A., 'Identifying and Helping Problem Drinkers at Work', *J. Soc. Occup. Med.*, 32, 171–79, 1982

Appendix 6.A:

Metropolitan Borough of Rochdale Policy on Alcohol and Drug Abuse Among Staff*

Introduction

1.1. The Metropolitan Borough of Rochdale, in common with any other major employer, is faced with the problem of alcohol and drug abuse at all levels within the organisation

1.2. It is felt that, when any member of staff becomes dependent on alcohol or other drugs, there should be a procedure, known to all, whereby that person can be offered help

1.3. The purpose of this document is to indicate the alcohol and drug abuse policy which has been jointly agreed between the Council and the locally recognised Trade Unions. It spells out the objectives and procedural arrangements and commits both Management and Staff Sides to use the policy for the mutual benefit of the workforce and the Authority

Objectives of the Policy

2.1. There is a joint recognition of the need to consider alcohol and drug abuse as primarily health problems. It is appreciated that prevention is better than cure and educational measures will be instituted to make staff at all levels aware of the dangers of alcoholism and drug addiction and of the help available to prevent the development of these conditions

2.2. The aim of the Authority is to ensure that advice and specialist help is made available to staff at an early stage so that their medical conditions can be investigated and treated with the utmost confidentiality

*Reproduced by the kind permission of the Metropolitan Borough of Rochdale.

2.3. Staff who suspect or know they have an alcohol or drug abuse problem are to be encouraged to make that problem known voluntarily. The Authority agreed to train a number of its employees as counsellors to advise their colleagues and to arrange for those with particular problems to be referred to the Medical Officers of the District Health Authority or to outside agencies such as Alcoholics Anonymous. Staff will be given every possible encouragement to pursue an agreed recovery programme

2.4. Because staff may feel that, if their problem is known, there may be a threat to their future employment, even though their previous standard of performance at work had not been recognisably affected, the Authority gives an assurance that those who seek help voluntarily will be dealt with in confidence and will not be liable for dismissal on grounds of incapability

2.5. It is imperative that there is an early recognition of an alcohol or drug abuse problem to increase the possibility of recovery and to minimise the effect on the service which is being provided to the ratepayers

Alcohol and drug abuse may be suspected in the following circumstances:-

(I) *Evidence of inadequate work performance*

(a) Frequent lateness, repeated brief periods of absence for trivial or inadequate reasons, poor productivity, impaired concentration and memory;

(b) Absenteeism – uncertified or certified – particularly related to weekends, holiday, etc;

(c) Accident proneness – minor accidents on the job and accidents away from the job – mistakes, errors of judgement

(II) *Observations of Behaviour and Appearance*

(a) Smelling of drink or under the influence of drink during working hours;

(b) Mood changes, irritability, lethargy;

(c) Deterioration in relationships with fellow workers, borrowing money;

(d) Hand tremor, slurred speech, facial flushing, bleary eyes, poor personal hygiene.

Whilst these are only POSSIBLE signs of abuse and may be

caused by other medical conditions, staff at all levels, who exhibit these signs, should be offered assistance in accordance with the policy.

2.6.   If abuse is suspected, the Chief Officer of the Department in which the member of staff concerned is employed, will arrange for that person to meet one of the counsellors. Because the Authority wishes to encourage staff to seek help, the same assurance with regard to job security will be given to any person who, after the meeting, agrees to pursue any recovery programme, which the counsellor might propose. In addition, should a referral for specialist help be declined, the individual will be advised at the meeting to discuss the matter with an appropriate trade union representative, before making a final decision.

2.7.   The policy is designed to provide a workable basis for the care and treatment of any member of staff who requires help with conditions which can have a devastating effect on the personal and family life of the individual, and which may, if allowed to progress untreated, result in serious disciplinary action or even dismissal.

Procedural Arrangements

3.1.   The following arrangements will apply in respect of the policy:-
(a)   Staff, who suspect or know they have an alcohol or drug abuse problem, should seek advice from one of the Authority's trained counsellors, whose names can be obtained from the Social Services and Personnel and Management Services Departments;
(b)   Immediately a member of Departmental management suspects, because of inadequate work performance or observed behaviour, that a particular employee might have an alcohol or drug abuse problem, the matter should be drawn to the attention of the appropriate Chief Officer. The Chief Officer (or his representative) will have an informal discussion with the member of staff concerned, avoiding any judgement as to whether or not the person has an alcohol or drug abuse problem and offering an early opportunity for the individual to meet one of the Authority's trained counsellors. If the meeting is declined, the Chief Officer (or his representative) will advise the particular employee to

discuss the matter with an appropriate trade union representative;
(c)   Counsellors will outline to staff, who have sought help voluntarily, the range of specialist advice, which is available from the Medical Officers of the District Health Authority and from other outside agencies. They will attempt to reach agreement with regard to a referral on which a recovery programme can be based. If agreement is not possible, counsellors will advise the member of staff concerned to discuss the proposed referral with an appropriate trade union representative;
(d)   At any meeting arranged by a Chief Officer, counsellors will seek the views of the member of staff concerned with regard to the inadequate work performance or observed behaviour, which has led to the suspicion of alcohol or drug abuse. They will attempt to diagnose the contributory factors so that there is agreement with the particular employee on a future course of action. If counsellors consider that an alcohol or drug abuse problem is confirmed, they will proceed in the same way as with staff who sought help voluntarily. Should a referral for specialist help be proposed and declined, counsellors will advise the member of staff to discuss the matter with an appropriate trade union representative;
(e)   Staff will be granted time off with pay, if referred by a counsellor to a Medical Officer of the District Health Authority. Attendance at a specialist treatment centre in the course of an agreed recovery programme will be considered to be sick leave and will be dealt with in accordance with the appropriate Sick Pay Scheme;
(f)   Staff, who either have been suspected of having an alcohol or drug abuse problem and, after a meeting with a counsellor, have declined to accept referral, or who have discontinued a recovery programme before its satisfactory completion, will be subject to the normal and recognised disciplinary procedures, if, thereafter, inadequate work performance or observed behaviour occur.

3.2.   The attached Appendix summarises the arrangements diagrammatically.

3.3.   If, in the course of the application of this policy, a dispute arises between an individual employee and a Chief Officer as to whether or not there is a health problem the matter will be resolved in the usual way by a referral to a Medical Officer of the District Health Authority.

3.4.   The Authority will make every endeavour to ensure that staff, who have suffered from an alcohol or drug abuse problem when considered fit for work, will return to their current post. A suitable alternative will only be offered in a particular case, if a return to that post might carry with it a risk of the recurrence of the condition or a risk of jeopardising the welfare and safety of others.

3.5.   Staff with an alcohol or drug abuse problem should have no fears about seeking advice, help and treatment to effect a recovery. The Authority undertakes to give them every assistance, willingly, and in complete confidence. The confidential nature of any records or correspondence relating to staff, who have undergone recovery programmes for alcohol or drug abuse problems, will be strictly preserved.

CHAPTER 7

Alcohol, education, and young people

CHAPTER 7

Alcohol, education, and young people

'To be successful, health education must have a lasting effect on people's behaviour. A long-term objective of this kind is more likely to be achieved if health education "catches people young".' (*Drinking Sensibly*, HMSO 1981: 33)

Everyone concerned with the prevention of alcohol-related problems recognizes the importance of alcohol education for young people. However, although a wide range of excellent material is available, alcohol education in schools is patchy and often dependent upon the enthusiasm of individual teachers, while opportunities for alcohol education in colleges, polytechnics, and universities are under-exploited.

The success of alcohol education, which has to change both attitudes and behaviour and contend with many other influences, cannot be guaranteed. Doing something about preventing alcohol-related problems should never be seen solely in terms of such education but it is, nevertheless, an important component of any local prevention programme, especially where young people are concerned. They are particularly susceptible to unhelpful ideas about alcohol which could create problems for them at a crucial period of their lives. Second, the young are the citizens and parents of tomorrow. Attitudes and beliefs formed whilst young could influence their subsequent behaviour and the 'messages' they pass to others.

This chapter identifies the various local organizations and groups which have a major part to play in the promotion of alcohol education

189

for the young and some of the materials which they could use. It also suggests ways in which local workers can be encouraged to develop their alcohol education activities.

Opportunities for alcohol education

In every locality there are many opportunities for providing alcohol education for the young. Schools, youth clubs, colleges of further and higher education, polytechnics, and universities can all contribute. They cover every age group and many specific sets of young people, including those on youth training schemes. All these organizations provide opportunities for at least some form of alcohol education for young people as they progress towards adulthood.

It is important not only to promote alcohol education in a variety of settings but to promote the right kind. Alcohol education is a part of health education, the focus of which is personal and social development. The Assessment of Performance Unit, set up by the Department of Education and Science (DES) in 1977 to monitor progress and standards in education, describes personal and social development as:

'The pupil's understanding of himself, his development as a responsible person and his moral response to his social and physical environment.'

Developing this kind of informed awareness and decision-making ability requires more than what all too often passes for 'alcohol education': the provision of a few 'facts' and the distribution of leaflets.

Schools

Education is compulsory up to the age of sixteen and is provided by Local Education Authorities (LEAs). There are 104 LEAs in England and Wales. Each has an education committee consisting of local government councillors and co-opted members drawn from groups such as the churches, employers' organizations, trades councils, and teachers' groups.

Many schools now have a place in their curriculum for health education although its development is uneven. The prominence given to alcohol education within any health education programme also varies considerably. Health education has been called the 'soft under-belly of the curriculum'. Parental interest is not great, teachers rarely specialize in it, it is rarely examined, and it has to compete with other 'new' subjects for a place in an already crowded curriculum.

The development of health education in the curriculum has been largely due to the Health Education Council (HEC) and health education officers employed by local health authorities. Together with others, the HEC has sponsored a number of major school health education projects with the result that there is now health education material for all ages and most of it includes material on alcohol.

The HEC has sought not only to encourage the introduction of health education into schools but also to move away from traditional, didactic teaching methods towards more experientially based learning in which the young are encouraged to analyse their own attitudes, discuss situations, role-play, and make decisions. Best practice now seeks to integrate health education – along with social, moral, political, career, and parenthood education – into the school curriculum as part of a coherent and planned programme of personal and social education. A number of schools now have health education 'co-ordinators' who, among other things, identify the opportunities for promoting health education (see below).

Experientially based learning and personal and social development come together in 'tutorial work' when time is set aside for teachers to involve their pupils in group discussion on issues relevant to their personal development and self-confidence. This pastoral work has two aims – the care of pupils as developing adults and the creation of an efficient environment for learning. Topics include the transition to secondary education, tensions with parents, and how to handle a visit to a GP. Active tutorial work provides teachers with an important opportunity for promoting health education and alcohol education.

Colleges of further education

LEAs are responsible for school education and post-compulsory education. Post-compulsory education includes 'further' education which is described as 'non-advanced' to distinguish it from 'higher' education. Most areas have a separate college of further education although in a few areas the two are amalgamated into colleges of further and higher education.

Every college is divided into a number of departments such as engineering, construction and building sciences, business studies, catering, and general liberal studies. These departments offer a wide range of qualifications to both full-time students and part-time students on 'day release'. Most courses in most departments will have a 'general education' input and these provide an opportunity for providing health education. A number of courses in most colleges of further education will, almost certainly, have a health education ingredient. These are the 'caring' courses which may well include the following – although titles will vary slightly from college to college:

- A Nursery Nurse Course for young people intending to work with children;
- A Preliminary Certificate in Social Care Course for workers looking after children in care, old people, and the disabled;
- Home Economics for Family and Community Care for social workers caring for families in difficulty;
- A pre-Nursing Course for young people who intend to make nursing their career.

Colleges of further education are heavily involved in the education of young people on youth training schemes. Every locality now has a wide range of youth training schemes covering, among other things, retailing, hairdressing, joinery, clerical and office work, and engineering. Employers participating in such schemes receive a grant for each youth training place and pay a set weekly allowance. Employers are expected to provide relevant work experience and training. Training schemes are categorized according to where the responsibility lies for organizing and managing the work activity and the 'off the job' training and education which every young person on a scheme must receive.

- 'Mode A' schemes are employer-based and whilst many larger employers provide the mandatory 'off the job' training and education themselves, others elect to use the local college's facilities.
- 'Mode B' schemes are located in colleges of further education which provide training and education and organize work experience with suitable local employers.
- 'Mode B1' schemes are based upon local workshops which provide training in lathe-work, pottery, photography, joinery, bricklaying, and so on. The young people in these workshops attend a local college for their 'off the job' training and education.

A major ingredient of the educational component of youth training schemes is the development of personal and social life-skills. The schemes insist that young people must not only learn how to use a typewriter or lay bricks, they must also be prepared to cope with the complexities of modern life and the responsibilities of adulthood. Personal and social education provided in colleges for young people on youth training schemes can cover everything from how to manage money and open a bank account to handling interviews and understanding the basics of the social security system. Health education in some form is provided by many colleges since learning to take responsibility for health matters is an important part of personal and social education. However, the amount and quality of the education that is provided varies from college to college. Alcohol is often handled, along with tobacco, from the point of view of 'dependency' which is not the most helpful approach. Much could be done in local colleges to provide more imaginative alcohol education for this particular group of young people.

'Mode A' and 'Mode B1' youth training schemes

'Mode A' schemes are employer-based and 'Mode B1' schemes are workshop-based. Major employers may elect to provide, in whole or in part, the 'off the job' work training and the compulsory life and social skills education which the schemes demand.

Many such employers attach great importance to the life and social skills component of 'off the job' training. Whilst the jobs themselves may be relatively straightforward, 'foundation work' needs to be done to turn many of the young people into competent employees. Employers have found, for example, that some of their trainees have never used a telephone. The best employers on 'Mode A' schemes go to a great deal of trouble to mount extensive and well-thought-out programmes for their trainees. One bakery and food retailing chain in Humberside, during a six-month period, included in its life and social skills programme the following events:

- A day trip to a sports centre some sixty miles away arranged by the trainees themselves, which required them to make the telephone booking, write the letter of confirmation, obtain quotes for transport, calculate VAT and other sundries to establish a total cost, and attend to all the organizational details.
- A police visit to learn about general police work and to stimulate

discussion about the role of police and their relationships with young people.

- Sessions with outside speakers and audio-visual materials on drugs and glue sniffing, crowd violence at football matches, avoiding trouble in pubs, first aid, and basic personal hygiene.

'Mode B1' workshop schemes provide multi-skill training. Many, but not all, are set up and run by local authorities. Others are privately sponsored but, of course, meet criteria laid down by the Manpower Services Commission. Like the other schemes, 'Mode B1' schemes will use the local college of further education for relevant 'off the job' training for young people seeking, for example, a City and Guilds or other form of qualification. However, like many of the employers in 'Mode A' schemes, many workshops provide their own life and social skills education for their trainees. A privately sponsored workshop in Humberside has recently included the following:

- A talk and discussion on the role of trade unions in the workplace.
- A video-tape on personal hygiene followed by a discussion and group work to identify how hygiene in the workshop could be improved.
- A session on how to open a bank account, use a cheque book, and pay bills

Employers and workshops providing life and social skills training for young people clearly offer an important opportunity for promoting and developing alcohol education. A number of employers and workshops were asked whether they would welcome information on the available materials and on any local teaching inputs from individuals, groups, or organizations interested in promoting alcohol education. All responded enthusiastically to the idea.

The youth service

Every LEA is required to provide a youth service as part of its post-compulsory education responsibilities. There are three categories of wholly maintained youth centres and clubs:

- Senior youth clubs (over-fourteen-year-olds);
- Junior youth centres and clubs (9–14-year-olds);
- Play centres (5–14-year-olds).

Maintained youth centres and clubs have paid staff assisted by voluntary workers.

However, the youth service is more than just the statutory provision of centres and clubs. It is a partnership between the statutory and voluntary sectors, providing a wide range of facilities and activities geared to the informal social education of young people. A local authority can provide grant aid for voluntary youth service premises, staff, and grants for training youth club leaders. Along with the voluntary sector, it will seek to monitor provision and attempt to maintain a balance between statutory and voluntary youth services.

The youth service undertakes informal social education, the aims of which are to give young people the opportunity to practice being adults and to develop both physically and morally. This personal and social development can be promoted in any number of ways – sports, group projects, informal discussions, and community work.

All youth leaders and organizers prior to their appointment are required to attend a Youth Service Training Course which is usually run by a college of further education. This course introduces workers to topics such as group work, adolescent development, running a club or centre, and ways of handling problems in clubs.

The wide range of statutory and voluntary organizations and facilities, activities and groups of young people which are brought together in each locality by the youth service provides another important setting for the development of health education generally and alcohol education in particular.

Materials and help for alcohol educators

There is no shortage of alcohol education materials for the young. There is a wealth of packs, games, leaflets, posters, audio-visual aids, and discussion materials. Anyone seeking to develop alcohol education in the school curriculum, in colleges of further education, in the workplace, or in youth centres and clubs, will find something suitable.

Two major sources of materials and help

Details about this range of valuable materials – and, if needed, further help and information – can be obtained from two organizations, the

Health Education Council and the Teachers' Advisory Council on Alcohol and Drugs Education.

The Health Education Council The HEC regularly publishes a catalogue of alcohol education materials and teaching aids, many of which are suitable for use with young people. The HEC can supply only those items for which it is itself the source, although many can be viewed at or borrowed from the offices of the local health education officer. The catalogue can be obtained from the HEC at:

Health Education Council
78 New Oxford Street
London WC1A 1AH
(Tel: 01-631-0930)

The Teachers' Advisory Council on Alcohol and Drug Education (TACADE) is devoted almost entirely to encouraging the development of alcohol and drug education in schools, although it is now expanding its concern to cover non-school health education. TACADE's staff work closely with health education officers, teachers, LEAs, and anyone interested in developing health education skills. Advice on developing health education and appropriate training – often based on TACADE's own materials – is provided through TACADE's director of training and development. A quarterly magazine, *Monitor*, is available and the publications department produces a comprehensive list of materials which are fully annotated. Like the HEC, TACADE has a resource centre where these materials can be viewed. Again, many of TACADE's materials can be examined at or borrowed from the local health education unit. TACADE is located at two addresses:

TACADE
Head Office
2 Mount Street
Manchester M2 5NG
(Tel: 061-834-7210)
(Training – North Midlands, consultancy,
resource centre, publications department)

Southern Office
202 Holdenhurst Road
Bournemouth BH8 8AS
(Tel: 0202-295874)
(Training – south)

Teaching materials: some major items

Since there is such a wide range of materials available the problem arises of choosing the most appropriate. There are several tried and tested educational items suitable for specific groups and teaching situations. Not all are devoted to alcohol. Indeed, some – especially those for younger children – make little or no mention of alcohol at all. However, they are useful insofar as they seek to enhance, from an early age, self-esteem and confidence – both of which are needed to take sensible health decisions.

Some of these items are listed in the HEC and TACADE catalogues. Others are not. Of course, health educators may not agree about the usefulness of particular materials. Nevertheless, the items outlined below will, we hope, provide alcohol educators with a starting point from which to develop their teaching and a stock of information with which to judge other materials.

Active Tutorial Workbooks 1–5 and 16–19 This is a series of six workbooks for teachers to use in pastoral work covering secondary and sixth form education. The first five (1–5) were developed out of pioneering work in Lancaster LEA carried out with the support of the HEC, and were published in 1979/80. The 16–19 workbook has just recently been produced. Together with a resource pack containing photocopy matters, work cards, and ready-drawn illustrations, the workbooks are obtainable from TACADE and from:

Basil Blackwell Limited
108 Cowley Road
Oxford OX4 1JF
(Tel: 0865-724041)

Since the publication of the first Active Tutorial Workbooks in 1979/80 the HEC has funded a project to train teachers in personal and social education, its aims and techniques, and to disseminate the scheme. This project has been based at:

The HEC Active Tutorial Work Development Unit
St. Martins College
Barnham Road
Lancaster LA1 3JD
(Tel: 0524-63446)

The Unit now has five project trainers in addition to two co-directors.

Over 12,000 teachers have been introduced to the Active Tutorial Work methodology, and training teams have been established in thirty-eight LEAs in England and Wales. Teachers who have been trained in Active Tutorial Work philosophy and techniques are able to act in schools as 'co-ordinators', promoting the development of personal and social education across the curriculum.

An HEC-commissioned study of this training and dissemination process was carried out by R. Boalan and P. Medlock at Bristol University. Their report entitled *Active Tutorial Work – Training and Dissemination – An Evaluation*, will be of interest and value to all those concerned with personal and social education in schools. It is available through Basil Blackwell.

The Schools Health Education Project 5–13 This material was originally sponsored by the HEC and the now defunct Schools Council. It is divided into two parts:

- *All About Me*, for ages 5–8;
- *Think Well*, for ages 9–13.

Each part contains a teacher's guide and pupils' materials.

Both *All About Me* and *Think Well* are designed to develop individual awareness and decision-making and focus on topics such as food, smoking, and exercise. *All About Me* does not make any specific reference to alcohol although it could be introduced. However, section 4 of *Think Well*, entitled 'Deadly Decisions', does cover alcohol use. These publications are particularly important since it is often assumed that health education in general and alcohol education in particular are only suitable for older children. However, children are learning about both health and alcohol from the earliest age and it is important to encourage their awareness of the issues involved. It should be possible to borrow these materials from any local health education unit. They are published by:

T. Nelson and Son Ltd
Nelson House
Mayfield Road
Walton-on-Thames
Surrey KT12 5PL
(Tel: 0932-246133)

The Schools Health Education Project 13–18 This material complements the Schools Health Education Project 5–13 packs. Again, support for the project came from the HEC and the Schools Council. It is based on work carried out by teachers in more than seventy schools and colleges. The multi-disciplinary nature of the material encourages its integration into the curriculum. The pack is divided into three age-levels: 13–14, 14–16, and sixteen plus. Nineteen health topics are covered including smoking habits, dental health, sexually transmitted diseases, nutrition, teenage lifestyles, and alcohol. Training for teachers is funded jointly by the HEC and LEAs. This important and well-known project should be available from any local health education unit. Alternatively, it can be obtained from the publishers:

Forbes Publications Ltd
120 Bayswater Road
London W2 3JH
(Tel: 01-229-9322)

Free to Choose – An Approach to Drug Education This material has been produced by TACADE and its aim is to encourage personal autonomy in relation to health behaviour. The package caters for the range of ages and abilities in secondary schools. It is divided up into ten units each dealing with a different topic. Units 3 – 'The Party', 4 – 'On Holiday', and 10 – 'Want a Lift Home?' each deal with a different aspect of alcohol use.

Alcohol Education Syllabus 11–19 This has been produced jointly by TACADE and the HEC. Unlike the other materials described in this section it is a *syllabus* – a comprehensive programme based on the progressive needs and development of young people during their formative years. The syllabus consists of two packs, one for 11–16-year-olds and the other for 16–19-year-olds. Each contains five individual units, consisting of a teaching plan and pupils' materials.

The 11–16 pack has been written with secondary schools in mind, so the units are labelled 'Year 1', 'Year 2', and so on. The syllabus can be supplemented with a series of six HEC 'trigger films' designed to stimulate discussion. The films which can be integrated with the syllabus for 11–16-year-olds are:

- *In the Middle*;
- *Losing Out*;
- *Happy Birthday*.

The films which can be integrated into the syllabus for 16–19-year-olds are:

- *Rounds*;
- *Rules of the Game*;
- *It's Up to You.*

Finding Out . . . What Happens When I Drink/Finding Out . . . About Drinking and Driving These are two CSE Biology and General Studies Resource Books produced by the Brewers' Society. The Brewers' Society has a strategy for the prevention of problem drinking which recognizes three principle target groups – young people, drinking drivers, and problem drinkers in the workplace. *Finding Out . . . What Happens When I Drink* covers twelve topics including 'Why Do People Drink?' and 'Advertising'. Each section has a number of questions to stimulate debate and learning.

Finding Out . . . About Drinking and Driving has eight sections ranging from 'Why Do People Drink and Drive?' to 'Accidents'. Each topic has a 'What You Can Do' section designed to stimulate pupils' thinking about drinking situations and road safety. *What Happens When I Drink* sold over 100,000 copies in the eighteen months up to December 1984. *About Drinking and Driving* was first produced in May 1984 and by the end of the year some 30,000 copies had been sold. Copies of both books cost 37p each or 30p each in an order of ten or more. They are obtainable from:

Hobsons Press (Cambridge) Ltd
Bateman Street
Cambridge CB2 1LZ
(Tel: 0223-354551)

One for the Road film series and One for the Road teaching unit 'One for the Road' is a series of three films sponsored by the Brewers' Society and supported by the Royal Society for the Prevention of Accidents (RoSPA). The films deal with different aspects of drinking and driving and are designed to be used in conjunction with a 'One for the Road' teaching pack which is part of a comprehensive traffic education course entitled 'Teenagers and Traffic' (see below).

The three films are entitled:

- *Driven to Drink?*
- *What's the Limit?*
- *Who's Sorry Now?*

The first film looks at influences on young people's decisions about drinking and driving. The second examines the effects of alcohol on motoring performance. The third is concerned with the new breath test and the arrest and charge procedure introduced in 1983 and looks at the possible consequences of a drinking and driving offence on all those involved. Each film is accompanied by teachers' notes to enable adequate preparation, discussion, and follow-up work. The whole 'One for the Road' film series is available in VHS, BetaMax, U-Matic, and 16 mm from:

The Royal Society for the Prevention of Accidents
Cannon House
The Priory
Queensway
Birmingham B4 6BS
(Tel: 021-233-2461)

- Separate 16 mm films £75 each + postage + VAT.

The Department of Transport and the Brewers' Society have provided funds to enable any educational institution to borrow the series free of charge from:

Central Film Library
Chalfont Grove
Gerrards Cross
Bucks SL9 8TN
(Tel: 0753-885991)

Teenagers and Traffic This is a comprehensive traffic course designed by the Road Safety Education Unit at the University of Reading. Its development was funded by the Transport and Road Research Laboratory and RoSPA is organizing and funding publication of the complete course. The course consists of four teaching packs each of which costs approximately £20. They contain students' discussion sheets and a set of teachers' notes. The four packs are:

- *One for the Road* which deals with all aspects of drinking and driving. It contains six discussion sheets and has been designed to be used with the series of 'One for the Road' films (see above).
- *Ready for the Road* deals with preparing to use a powered vehicle: documentation, insurance, finance, and training.

- *Accidents on the Road* deals with the causes, consequences, and prevention of road accidents and what to do if involved either as a victim or a witness.
- *Reading the Road* is based on a video-tape, with accompanying discussion sheets and teachers' notes. It deals with how riders and drivers get information from the road and what this information tells them.

Further information about the 'Teenagers and Traffic' course can be obtained from the local road safety officer at the town hall or civic offices. Information can also be obtained from RoSPA.

Drinking and Driving: A Guide to All Organizers of Young Peoples' Groups RoSPA's Road Safety Division has produced a series of booklets on drinking and driving, one of which has been written specifically for organizers of young people's groups. It describes the extent of the problem and the drink-driving laws and, most importantly, spells out clearly and simply how organizers can help to reduce this major cause of death and injury among the young.

Understanding Alcohol   This is a traffic education pack sponsored by Ansvar Insurance Company and produced by the School Traffic Education Programme (STEP). STEP was founded in the early 1970s by the motor cycle industry to promote the development of traffic education in schools. In 1984 the industry decided to put all its support into promoting a national motor cycle training programme – the 'Star Rider' scheme. STEP's publication and consultancy work was taken over by the British Institute of Traffic Education Research, a wholly independent organization with a subscribing membership of road safety officers, teachers, and others concerned with road safety education. Sponsors such as insurance companies given support in several ways, such as by funding specific publications.

'Understanding Alcohol' is available in a video-tape version costing £22.50 + VAT and a tape/slide version costing £15 + VAT. Each pack contains teachers' notes, work sheets, and suggested activities. The pack and a wide range of other traffic education material is available from:

BITER Publications Department
Kent House
Kent Street
Birmingham B5 QF
(Tel: 021-622-2402)

Just to be Sociable   A new health education film/video-tape, showing Jimmy Savile OBE, actor Martin Shaw, and pop star Lynsey de Paul, was launched in September 1984. It was sponsored by Ansvar Insurance Company Ltd which is the UK's only insurer dealing exclusively in policies for non-drinkers. The twenty-minute dramatized documentary looks at the problems caused by alcohol and interviews the show-business personalities about their reasons for choosing to be non-drinkers. It won a prize at the 1984 New York Film Festival as the best health education film of the year. *Just to be Sociable* has been acquired by the Guild Organization for world-wide distribution. It is available for hire and sale on 16 mm film and video-tape in VHS, BetaMax, and U-Matic formats. The video-tape and film versions can both be hired for £12.50 + VAT, the film for £260 + VAT. The address of the Guild Organization is:

Guild Organization
Guild House
Peterborough PE2 9PZ
(Tel: 0733-63122)

Alcohol and higher education

'Higher education' includes colleges of higher education, polytechnics, and universities. A young person's higher education involves, often, their first break with home and the beginnings of an independent life. This new independence brings with it many unfamiliar pressures and makes both emotional and intellectual demands. Alcohol, for some students, is a cheap and readily available way of coping with these pressures. Subsidized drink is the norm in student union bars and alcohol is an integral part of 'student culture'. Although only a small minority of students get into serious difficulties, using alcohol as a relief from stress is clearly unwise and, for some, may create difficulties later in life.

Pastoral services in higher education

Unlike schools, colleges of further education, youth training schemes, and the youth service, institutions of higher education do not offer many opportunities for developing alcohol education as part of the curriculum. However, virtually all institutions of higher education have a number of services devoted to the pastoral welfare of students, and workers in these services regularly have to deal with alcohol-related problems.

Student counselling services   Most institutions of higher education will have a student counselling service. Its exact place in the organizational structure will vary between institutions. In some it will be part of an 'umbrella department' dealing with various aspects of student welfare such as accommodation, careers, and health. In others it will be quite separate although, of course, it will liaise closely with other services.

Many of the problems seen by student counselling services in institutions of higher education appear to involve alcohol. Counsellors recognize that the student culture encourages regular and occasionally excessive drinking. Problems involving female students are becoming more common. Whilst counsellors will usually include specific questions on alcohol use when talking to a client, most have had no specific training on the nature, range, and extent of alcohol-related problems nor about the advice and assistance which they can provide or which they can help the client to find. Some student counselling services are fortunate enough to have professional on-campus help available from a clinical psychologist. Difficult problems will usually be referred to the student medical services where psychiatric help may be available (see below).

'Night line' services   Student unions offer their members a variety of welfare and advice services and will refer people with personal problems to the student counselling service. However, most campuses operate some kind of 'listening service' for students, staffed by student volunteers. Although some students may use the night line in preference to the counselling service, the two services should complement each other. Night lines provide cover when the trained counsellors of the counselling service are not available to cope with sudden crises. Where appropriate, callers will be referred to the counselling service or to other local services and agencies which may be able to help them with their problems.

A night line, or equivalent, service in an average-sized provincial university will have up to one hundred student volunteers on call. Training is usually provided via a short programme of talks given by members of the student counselling service and other appropriate local agencies such as the Samaritans. However, the student volunteers are not expected to act as counsellors. They are there to provide a sympathetic ear and information. Such services are usually well-publicized with, for example, leaflets supplied to all freshers and posters sited in every department.

Chaplaincies Universities, colleges of higher education, and poly-technics will have chaplains representing different denominations. Some will be full-time, others, with their own churches and congregations, will be part-time. There is a growing emphasis in theological training on developing pastoral skill. Chaplains with these special skills will usually be members of the Association of Pastoral Care and Counselling division of the BAC. However, like the night line services, most chaplains will provide a sympathetic ear and general support but will refer students whom they think need specialist help to the student counselling service or other appropriate local agencies.

Student medical services Students have access to medical services on the campus. At a university this often consists of a health centre with beds and staffed by nurses and full-time NHS doctors whose practice is, in effect, the student population. Some campuses 'buy in' a psychiatrist to do a weekly session in the health centre although economies are making such an arrangement difficult. The extent to which a student medical service takes an interest in students' drinking and alcohol-related problems and co-operates with the campus student counselling service depends very much upon the attitudes of the doctors in the centre.

'Good practices' in higher education

Although higher education does not offer as many opportunities as schools and colleges of further education to develop alcohol education as part of a curriculum, the various groups responsible for the pastoral care of students can help to 'educate' young people through a variety of 'good practices'.

Readiness to talk about drinking, the ability to recognize the early signs of problems, and the confidence to offer sensible advice are important. Workers concerned with the pastoral care of students may find the materials identified in chapter 2, especially *Drinking Choices*, useful in developing both knowledge and confidence and the 'self-help' materials listed there offer students the chance to examine and reflect upon their own drinking behaviour. Pastoral workers of all kinds might find it useful to have stocks of these. *That's the Limit* could be included in the pack of induction material received by 'freshers'.

One issue which all pastoral workers on a campus might consider is the availability of cheap drink in student union bars. Student unions usually have a policy of making drink as cheap as possible as a 'service' to their customers and quite considerable reductions are often possible through a combination of discounts available from the brewery for bulk purchases and low overheads. Pastoral workers might find it useful to make this policy a public issue on campus with a joint approach to the student union to discuss the pricing of alcohol in its bars. At the very least, the fixing of prices should involve some consideration of its possible effects in terms of alcohol misuse.

In addition, some thought could be given to the quality of supervision and the training of staff in students' bars. These are licensed premises and the staff in all such premises should be trained in the law and about the kinds of problems which alcohol misuse can cause. A visitor to any students' bar, especially on a Saturday night, will find drunken students being served, which is illegal (see chapter 5). In addition to some training in their legal and social responsibilities, pastoral workers might find it useful to ensure that bar staff are fully aware of the range of services available on campus for students with an alcohol-related problem. Many students are well known to union bar staff who are in a position to recognize developing problems and to remind the student, or the friends of the student, where help can be obtained.

Workers in a student counselling service will usually be members of the British Association for Counselling and its specialist division, the Association for Student Counselling (see chapter 2). However, membership of this organization may be equally valuable for other pastoral workers with any kind of responsibility for, or interest in, student welfare. Some 90–95 per cent of all Association for Student Counselling members are professionals such as social workers, psychologists, and teachers. Since its inception the Association for Student Counselling has become the recognized professional body for workers in this area and most institutions now require any new student counsellor to have attended one of the nationally available accredited courses.

Local action: the example of schools

A wide variety of local workers concerned with young people's welfare and development can introduce alcohol education into their activities. However, although such initiatives are welcome, a comprehensive local prevention strategy cannot rely solely on the efforts of committed individuals. The aim must be to make regular well-developed alcohol education policy in as many appropriate organizations as possible.

Those seeking to promote a local prevention strategy should identify, persuade, and recruit the policy-makers whose knowledge, interest, and support will help to develop alcohol education initiatives in the important settings described in this chapter. Some of these policy-makers, such as health education officers, local authority education committees, major employers, and youth leaders have been mentioned, but there are many more. It is impossible to map out every contact point in every possible setting. However, schools provide an example of the variety of contact points offered by just one area in which alcohol education can be promoted. An analysis of other major settings will reveal a similar diversity.

Much of the information about the organizations, groups, and activities described below can be obtained from local education offices and from the *Education Year Book* published by Longmans and available in larger public libraries.

Education advisers

Every LEA employs a team of education advisers to advise education committees on such matters as curriculum development, staffing, and equipment. LEAs decide upon the number and the specialisms of advisers who are thus an important reflection of an LEA's education policy and priorities.

Traditionally, the home economics or physical education adviser has been responsible for health education but many LEAs now have an adviser with specific responsibilities for personal and social education which will usually include health education. Advisers may take responsibility for more than one topic. An adviser for in-service training will link with the local teachers' centres, professional centres, the youth services, and community education. 'Phase' advisers are responsible for specific parts of the educational process; early years, middle years, secondary schooling, and post-compulsory education.

Contact with the local adviser with responsibility for personal and social education is clearly important. They will be able to provide information on what is currently being done and where and how initiatives could be encouraged. Such advisers are potentially key figures in a local prevention effort.

The education inspectorate

All schools in England and Wales are regularly visited by Her Majesty's Inspectors (HMIs). England and Wales is divided into seven divisions each with a divisional office and smaller local offices. Every inspector has both general and specific responsibilities. Each has a list of schools which they visit, from time to time, in a non-specialist capacity. These schools will usually be located in a relatively restricted area, often within the boundaries of a single LEA. Each inspector will also have responsibility for a specialism, such as modern languages, and in relation to this the area covered by one inspector will usually be much larger. Inspectors will have links with other LEA advisers in their specialism where they exist.

HMIs do not have executive authority 'to make things happen'. It would be inappropriate for a local HMI with responsibility for personal and social education to tell schools what they should be including in their curriculum. Nevertheless, HMI views on priorities have an important influence on school curricula.

There is one aspect of HMIs' work which may be of specific interest to those designing and promoting a prevention strategy. The inspectorate is responsible for devising and mounting a national programme of short courses. Ideas for courses are submitted to the DES by groups of HMIs in particular specialisms. If agreement is obtained the HMIs are responsible for finding the venue for a course at a university, or perhaps, a teachers' centre (see below). The HMIs will organize publicity and, where necessary, obtain appropriate speakers. Most courses last for 3–5 days. Although course organizing is not a major part of inspectors' responsibilities it is an important one. Some inspectors may be interested in mounting short alcohol education courses as part of the annual programme of events.

Teachers' and professional centres

Every LEA has a number of teachers' centres where teachers meet to exchange information, discuss course development, maintain their skills, or acquire new ones. Centres also hold a wide range of education materials which teachers can view or borrow. Each centre is run by a warden helped by a steering or management committee made up largely of teachers. A centre's programme of activities will be regularly advertised in a newsletter or diary circulated to all schools within the LEA. The courses held by TACADE to introduce teachers to their materials usually take place in these centres.

Centres can mount activities on their own, but they often come together to offer an integrated programme to teachers within their LEA. Pressure for programmes will come from a variety of directions. The education committee may feel there is a need to mount a particular course. If so, an adviser for in-service training will bring this to the attention of the centre. Alternatively, suggestions might come from the warden's management committee or from individual teachers. The wardens themselves will have knowledge of training needs and can initiate specific events. Centres provide a flexible means of meeting teachers' training needs. Courses and training events can vary from a few hours to regular study days spread over a number of weeks. One additional advantage is that teachers tend to see centres as their 'own' training resource.

It would be helpful if every teachers' centre in a locality had examples of alcohol education materials which could also be publicized in any newsletter or diary.

Many LEAs will have a professional centre located in the college of higher education. These centres are part of the in-service training system and have two functions. The first is to make available college courses to local teachers. The second is to act as a 'short courses for teachers' unit, organizing in-service training courses, conferences, and seminars. For these courses a professional centre will draw heavily on the college's training resources. Courses are funded by the LEA and devised and developed in close liaison with their local adviser for in-service training.

A professional centre offers an important point of entry to teachers' in-service training and hence an opportunity to publicize the importance of alcohol education as part of young people's personal and social development.

The School Curriculum Development Committee

Every LEA has a nominated local 'associate' of the School Curriculum Development Committee (SCDC). The SCDC was established in December 1983 and together with the Secondary Examination Council (SEC) has replaced the Schools Council. The SCDC and the SEC are both based at:

SCDC/SEC
Newcombe House
45 Notting Hill Gate
London W11 3JB
(Tel: 01-229-1234)

The SCDC has an annual budget of approximately £2m provided equally by LEAs and the DES. Its role is to support curriculum development in schools in England and Wales and its main tasks are:

- To inform itself of curriculum development work being undertaken;
- To view and evaluate such work with particular reference to the likely future needs of the school education system and thereby to identify what further curriculum development work is, in the committee's judgement, essential;
- To undertake, and to assist others to undertake, such essential curriculum development work;
- To disseminate, and to promote the dissemination of, the results of curriculum development work whether undertaken by itself or others.

The SCDC has invited all LEAs and teacher training institutions to designate a senior member of staff as an SCDC associate to liaise and assist the Committee. The SCDC also hopes to work closely with teachers' associations and national bodies and has set aside modest funds to support specific work by local teachers groups. Further details of SCDC work and information about the continuation of certain Schools Council projects, new activities, and project dissemination are available from the SCDC Information Centre at Newcombe House.

School governors and PTAs

Every school has a board of governors whose powers and membership have been widened in recent years. The Education Act 1981 introduced parents and teachers onto governing bodies and, in addition, every LEA has the discretion to enlist pupil and non-teaching staff representatives. Where possible, a separate governing body for each school is established as a way of ensuring governors' maximum interest and concern with the life and development of that school.

Schools' governing bodies are becoming increasingly important. They are expected to develop an 'overview' of the schools' activities and to be consulted on its aims. They have a growing influence on the curriculum and on LEA policies. Each governing body must have a nominated governor with responsibility for overseeing the 'special needs' requirement of children in the school. This includes not only the physically and mentally handicapped but any children with problems or special requirements.

Parental interest and concern has a part to play in promoting alcohol education in schools. Boards of governors contain parent representatives, but Parent Teacher Associations (PTAs) could also be involved. Discussion of the best way to introduce young people to alcohol would be of interest to many parents. The increase in alcohol poisoning among children is another issue that could be raised. Questionnaires and discussions designed to lead to a review of the school's alcohol education activities would be useful.

Another way of interesting governors and PTAs in alcohol education might be through road safety education. School governors could be encouraged to enquire about the amount of road safety education being provided. It could be pointed out that individual schools and individual teachers can subscribe to RoSPA's Safety Education Department materials. The annual subscription for a school is £23.70 + VAT while the annual subscription for an individual is £7.00 + VAT. Parents might feel that a subscription to the RoSPA Safety Education Department would be an appropriate use of school or Parent Teacher Association funds.

This is intended to be a *living* 'guide to action'. Therefore, it needs to be revised and added to in the light of local needs and local experience.

The following two pages are for jotting down examples of good practice, and addresses relevant to the issues covered by this chapter.

We hope to update the guide, and would be delighted to receive any advice about corrections, new material or any other information which should go into the next edition. Please send all suggestions, before 31 December, 1987, to:

Philip Tether and David Robinson
Addiction Research Centre
University of Hull
Hull HU6 7RX

Examples of Good Practice

Useful Addresses and Telephone Numbers

Further reading

Cowley, J., David, K., and Williams, T. (eds), *Health Education in Schools*, Harper and Row, London, 1981

Department of Education and Science, *Health Education in Schools*, DES, London, 1977

Dorn, N., *Alcohol, Youth and the State: Drinking Practices, Controls and Health Education*, Croom Helm, London, 1983

Dorn, N. and Nortoft, B., *Health Careers: Teachers Manual*, ISDD, London, 1982

Finn, T. and O'Gorman, P.A., *Teaching About Alcohol: Concepts, Methods and Classroom Activities*, Allyn and Bacon, London, 1981

Health Education Council, *Alcohol Education: Publications and Teaching Aids*, a source list, Health Education Council, London, 1982

Hunt, J., *Notes for Youth Workers*, National Association of Youth Clubs Alcohol Education Project, 1978, PO Box 1, Blackburn House, Nuneaton, CV11 4DB

Jeanneret, D. (ed.), *Alcohol and Youth*, Karger, Basel, 1983

Keeley Robinson, Y., *Adult Education Issues for Health Education: A Review and Annotated Bibliography*, occasional paper, Institute for Health Studies, Hull University, 1984. Available from Health Education Council

Mills, K.C., Neal, E.M., and Peed-Neal, I., *Handbook for Alcohol Education: The Community Approach*, Ballinger Publishing Co., Cambridge, Massachusetts, 1983

Scottish Health Education Group, *Drinking and Your Child: Some Sobering Thoughts for Parents*, HMSO, 1983. Available from SHEG, Woodburn House, Canaan Lane, Edinburgh EH10

Sutherland, I. (ed.), *Health Education: Perspectives and Choices*, Allen and Unwin, London, 1979

What Every Teenager Should Know about Alcohol, Scriptographic Publications, 1981. Available from 92/104 Carnwath, London, SW6 3HW

Young People and Alcohol: Guidelines for Parents, 1977. TACADE, 2 Mount Street, Manchester, M2 5NG

CHAPTER 8

Alcohol and the helping professions

CHAPTER 8

Alcohol and the helping professions

'professional . . . staff who come into contact with people who regularly misuse alcohol would find it easier to understand the part they can play if it was generally accepted that misuse is a problem for everyone to be concerned with.' (*Drinking Sensibly*, HMSO 1981: 62)

The emphasis of this guide is that there are many alcohol problems which do not always require professional help. A wide range of non-professional groups and organizations can make a major contribution to the prevention of alcohol problems. Nevertheless, medical practitioners, nurses, social workers, and other helping professionals clearly have an important role to play in any local prevention strategy.

Helping professionals are employed in a variety of complex organizations and services. Similarly, they are involved in a wide range of therapeutic and supportive activities. It is not the aim of this chapter, however, to discuss either service structures or therapeutic strategies. The 1978 DHSS advisory committee report on *The Pattern and Range of Services for Problem Drinkers* still provides the broad framework for discussion about service development, while there are many books and articles setting out how to respond to alcohol problems (see 'Further reading').

This chapter considers the local opportunities for medical practitioners, nurses, and social workers to receive alcohol education, and focuses on two elements of good practice relevant to all helping professionals: doing 'research' and pressing for prevention.

219

Alcohol education for helping professionals

Since alcohol can be a component of every kind of health and social problem, it is becoming increasingly widely recognized that education about alcohol, its impact, its interaction with other substances, and the identification, management, and prevention of alcohol problems is relevant at all stages of professional training.

The DHSS Advisory Committee on Alcoholism reported in 1979 on *Education and Training* for those working in the alcohol field. As well as noting the extent and range of alcohol problems and the heavy demands which these already make on the statutory services, the committee drew attention to the fact that many professionals who come into contact with problem drinkers consider themselves unable to help. They tend:

- To consider that they lack both knowledge of alcohol and its related problems and the facility to translate whatever knowledge they do possess into practical action;
- To be pessimistic about being able to influence drinkers or their families;
- To lack confidence in their own effectiveness in this field;
- To be anxious at the thought of continuing contact with problem drinkers.

To those professionals who say that they have no time to help problem drinkers or to further their own knowledge and skills and build up their confidence, the advisory committee commented that '[for] all professional staff, time is of great importance, but many are already dealing with problem drinkers and unless they recognise this considerable time will continue to be taken up without avail' (p. 2).

A profession tends to educate itself – or at least to control those who educate its members. This is one aspect of being a professional. The governing bodies responsible for the education of professional helpers – such as the Central Council for Education and Training in Social Work, the National Boards for Nursing, Midwifery, and Health Visiting, the medical colleges and faculties, and others – all, to a greater or lesser extent, determine who is eligible to enter training, what the syllabus will be, who should be involved with teaching and examining, and at what standard a student should be judged to be capable of practising professionally. Given this, it is neither usual nor easy for outsiders to contribute to or greatly influence the content of professional education. Nevertheless, there is scope for local action.

It should be possible to draw on resources both within and outside professional disciplines not only to contribute to the individual training programmes of specific professional groups but also to mount multi-disciplinary alcohol educational activities. These would not merely serve to satisfy common professional needs but would enhance inter-professional understanding between those who are called upon to co-operate at the local level.

Those concerned with the prevention of alcohol problems at the local level should probably begin by giving attention to *current* training structures and opportunities for alcohol education. The task is to acquaint those who have responsibility for education and training with the materials and resources that are available to contribute to the alcohol education of helping professionals.

Features of professional training and goals of alcohol education

The structure of training varies both across and within professions. But whatever its precise structure, the training of any particular profession will contain certain basic features. Terry Lawrence in *Teaching about Alcohol Problems* (see 'Further reading') summarizes these as:

- The development of *understanding* of the complexity of problems: their bases – social, psychological, and physical; the context in which they occur and their interrelationship with other problems.
- The ability to *recognize* and *identify* specific problems within the whole gamut of those presented by the patient or client, which may not always be overt and obvious.
- A realistic acknowledgement of the professionals' *role* and *responsibility* and the limits of their professional expertise; how far it is appropriate for them to go; when to refer; where to look for support.
- The development of *management skills*, professional–patient and professional–client interaction and the application of these skills to case-work.
- An overview, or global perspective of the machinery of *service provision*, so that the relevance of specific professional skills can be seen within the comprehensive framework of what is available and what is possible.

Within this structure, the aim of any alcohol education for any professional group would be to achieve certain goals, again succinctly summarized by Terry Lawrence:

- Increased *awareness* of the nature and extent of alcohol problems.
- An ability to *detect* the alcohol component of the problems presented by patients and clients.
- *Conviction of the worth of intervention*, acknowledging and indicating to the patient or client the professional's awareness of the role of alcohol in presenting problems.
- *Confidence* in managing the alcohol problem.
- *Encouragement and support* for other members of the staff team to identify and respond to alcohol problems and cease to avoid or evade them.
- *Pressure for improved service facilities* and provision for problem drinkers at the local and national levels.

Medical practitioners

The medical education system is complex but there are fairly clear pathways from medical student to general practitioner or to a career post in a medical specialty such as surgery or psychiatry. The existence of key contact points of relevance to medical education will vary from locality to locality. Within every local area there will always be, for example, a postgraduate medical centre but, clearly, only in some areas will there be a medical school.

Given this variability, there is no standard pattern of contacts which it is desirable to make, nor is there a prescribed procedure for making those contacts. Any local prevention group must draw on its own resources – which would, one hopes, include lively medical representation – to decide who best to contact, in what way, for what educational purpose. Those, among others, who might be contacted are briefly indicted below.

Contacts in medical education   In a medical school the dean has overall responsibility for all aspects of the programme of medical education. In addition:

- The clinical sub-dean is concerned with undergraduate education;
- The postgraduate sub-dean is concerned with the immediate

postgraduate pre-registration year when all students undertake house jobs in particular specialties.

Once medical practitioners are registered, they will spend a number of years in further training posts as senior house officers and then as trainees for general practice or, for those who seek a career in hospital or community medicine, registrars and senior registrars in relevant specialties. During this period the regional postgraduate dean has overall responsibility for training posts and for co-ordination of rotational schemes. In addition:

- Clinical tutors oversee the training in community medicine and in each hospital specialty – such as anaesthetics, psychiatry, and surgery.
- General practice tutors in each locality co-ordinate the training provided by general practices approved by the Joint Committee in Postgraduate Training in General Practice and organize refresher courses.
- The postgraduate tutor, in each district, has the task of running, supervising, and co-ordinating the work of the local postgraduate medical centre.
- The postgraduate medical centre not only provides educational programmes for those in training posts but also seminars, lectures, courses, and training events for the continuing education of all medical practitioners in the locality.

The programme for the postgraduate medical centre is drawn up by the Postgraduate Medical Committee chaired by the postgraduate tutor, on which sit the clinical tutors and the general practice tutor.

Contacts in postgraduate education   The key person to approach in any locality in order to discuss the place of alcohol education in formal postgraduate training would be the postgraduate tutor, although local knowledge about the clinical interests and experience of specific consultants may indicate that a particular clinical tutor may be the one to bring the issue to the attention of the postgraduate tutor and the postgraduate medical committee. Particular attention needs to be paid to the question of how best to involve general practitioners in any programme of alcohol education since they are no longer required to undertake in-service training.

In addition to those who have direct responsibility for medical education and training others who could be approached in any locality about alcohol education for medical practitioners include:

- Regional advisers nominated by each of the Royal Colleges and faculties who oversee local postgraduate training and to whom both trainers and trainees can turn.
- Divisions of consultants in each specialty who meet to discuss matters of common professional and clinical interest.
- The Medical Executive Committee which contains representatives of each division and, among other things, presents their views to the district health authority.
- The Local Medical Committee which represents general practitioners and others who hold contracts under the Family Practitioner Committee.
- The Family Practitioner Committee itself, which holds the contracts of general practitioners and others such as dentists, pharmacists, and dispensing opticians.

The District Health Authority   This has responsibility for the overall planning of local health services. Approaches to the district health authority might also be made via the appointed consultant or university members of the authority itself or through any other member who is thought to have some interest in or concern for alcohol problems. In addition to stressing the need for alcohol education and drawing attention to the materials and local resources that are available, it might be appropriate to press for the District Health Authority to appoint consultant psychiatrists and physicians with special interest in alcohol problems. The other main channel for raising issues with the District Health Authority is:

- The Community Health Council which acts as a focal point for local comment on the local services and a body to be consulted by the District Health Authority over its future plans and intentions.

Other local organizations   Finally, medical practitioners come together for a variety of purposes in other settings such as in the local branch meetings of the British Medical Association, where members meet to discuss BMA business and other professional matters. The local Medical Society will have, among its activities, a programme of scientific meetings which could well include sessions on alcohol problems and associated clinical, service, organizational, and educational issues.

Nurses

Unlike the education of medical students, the basic education of nurses is not confined to a small number of university-based schools. The great majority of nurses in England and Wales receive their basic training in one of approximately 190 schools of nursing based in District Health Authorities. In addition, however, there are twenty or so institutions of higher education running courses in conjunction with local schools of nursing. Most of these courses lead to admission to the register for general nurses together with a bachelor degree in nursing, nursing studies, or nursing sciences. A small number lead to a degree together with admission to the register for mental nurses or to the part of the register for nurses of the mentally abnormal. Information about 'degrees with nursing' can be obtained from:

Nursing and Health Service Careers Centre
26 Margaret Street
London W1N 7LB
(Tel: 01-631-0979)

Information about the basic nursing training offered by a local school of nursing can be obtained from the school itself.

Basic nurse education All basic training courses in nursing must be approved by the appropriate National Board for Nursing, Midwifery, and Health Visiting. The address of the English National Board is:

English National Board for Nursing, Midwifery, and Health Visiting
Victory House
170 Tottenham Court Road
London W1P 0HA
(Tel: 01-388-3131)

Although the National Boards draw up the syllabus for pre-registration training the curriculum of each course is devised by the institution which has the responsibility for teaching it. The National Board will approve the detailed curriculum, but it is being proposed that the school of nursing or other responsible institution should set and mark the examinations. This will not lessen the scope for the introduction of alcohol education at the local level, drawing on specialist materials and local resources and, most importantly, for alcohol-related topics to be included in examination papers.

Nursing auxiliaries who are in-service trained to perform limited duties under the direction of qualified nurses, make up approximately one third of the nurse labour force in the United Kingdom. Clearly, the training which these nurses receive should include alcohol education. Nurse auxiliaries, who do not have any nurse management role, are often well placed to be confided in by patients and their families. An awareness by nurse auxiliaries of the possible alcohol component of health and social problems might contribute to the identification of otherwise unrecognized alcohol problems.

Post-registration courses   These allow for further training in specific aspects of nursing and enable entry to specialist nursing careers. Courses leading to professional qualifications in midwifery, district nursing, health visiting, community psychiatric nursing, and occupational nursing all have the potential to include alcohol education, linked to the particular nursing tasks being learned and to the particular patient groups and situations which the qualified nurse will encounter. Details of outline syllabuses for these courses and where they are run can be obtained from the English National Board – with the exception of details of occupational nursing courses which can be obtained from:

Royal College of Nursing
20 Cavendish Square
London W1M 0AB
(Tel: 01-409-3333)

Responsibility for setting the examinations for midwifery rests with the English National Board and for occupational nursing with the Royal College of Nurses. Responsibility for examinations in district nursing, health visiting, and community psychiatric nursing rests with the local teaching institution, so any local alcohol education initiatives can be immediately reflected in a local examination paper. But wherever the responsibility lies, the exam papers have to be approved by the English National Board which appoints external examiners to ensure that local performance is in line with national standards.

Specialist alcohol courses   In addition to basic pre-registration training and career training – such as for health visiting or occupational nursing – there is a wide range of specialist courses available which enable registered nurses to develop a particular area of knowledge, skill, and interest. The English National Board offers three courses which relate specifically to alcohol problems: course 612 – 'Drug and Alcohol Dependency Nursing'; course 620 – 'Alcohol Dependency Nursing'; and course 693 – 'Recognition of and Nursing Responses to the Problem Drinker'.

Courses 612 and 620 last 32–35 and 20–22 weeks respectively and lead to a certificate. Course 693 lasts 20–30 days spread over a period of not more than fifteen weeks and leads to a statement of attendance. The two certificate courses must be based in hospital units or departments which specialize in the treatment of dependent patients and the courses emphasize nursing care and the management of dependence. To date, these three ENB courses have been mounted in very few centres. Clearly, one role for a local group concerned with prevention – on which, one hopes, there would be vigorous nursing representation – would be to ensure that these courses were known about and put on by appropriate trainers in appropriate settings for appropriate trainees.

Given the wide variety of basic and post-registration courses available and the wide range of institutions involved there is no single contact point for raising local alcohol education issues in relation to nurse education. The National Boards have overall responsibility for nurse education with special advisers for each area of nursing activity such as midwifery or psychiatric nursing. Those, among others, who might be contacted at the local level are briefly indicated below.

Contacts with the district health authority At the district health authority level the person with overall responsibility for the school of nursing will be the director of nurse education. There will also be:

- Senior tutors in charge of each specialty for which there is an educational programme – such as general nursing, paediatric nursing, or mental illness nursing;
- Tutors for each nursing specialty providing classroom, community, and on-ward teaching;
- Clinical tutors for each specialty providing teaching and support on the ward.

Within the district, education and in-service training needs will be identified in conjunction with the director of nurse education and:

- The director of nursing services for each unit of management – which might be a hospital or a set of services for a particular client group such as the mentally ill or the mentally handicapped;
- The senior tutor for in-service training will have a district-wide responsibility for mounting training programmes and refresher courses;

- In-service trainers in each unit will support the senior tutor.

Approaches to the District Health Authority might, in addition, be made via the appointed nurse, consultant, or university member of the authority itself or through any other member who is known to have some knowledge or interest in the prevention of alcohol problems. As with medical practitioners, the District Health Authority could be pressed to appoint a senior nurse or tutor for in-service training with special interest in alcohol problems.

Other local contacts   The Royal College of Nursing (RCN) is a professional body with union affiliation which has national advisory groups covering each major area of nursing except midwifery, which is the responsibility of the Royal College of Midwives (RCM). In addition there are:

- Regional RCN and RCM professional officers and RCN and RCM stewards in each locality to advise local trainers and trainees about professional matters.

At the local level there will also be:

- Royal College of Nursing Centres and Royal College of Midwifery Centres at which nurses will meet to discuss professional business, hear lectures, and take part in seminars and other activities;
- Local representatives of trade unions such as COHSE, NUPE, NALGO, and T&GMWU which have nurse members will also have a concern for training and training opportunities.

In 1983 a Nurses' Interest Group for Drug, Alcohol, and Solvent Misuse was established. It changed its name in 1985 to the Association of Nurses in Substance Abuse. This Association is independent of any professional association or trade union and is seeking to initiate activities at the local level. It has a network of Key Regional Contacts. Information about the Association and its Key Regional Contacts can be obtained from:

Association of Nurses in Substance Abuse
National Temperance Hospital
Hampstead Road
London NW1 2LT
(Tel: 01-387-9300)

Social workers

The education of workers in the personal social services is complex, with several routes to the two basic qualifications: the Certificate of Qualification in Social Work (CQSW) and the Certificate in Social Service (CSS). Discussions are taking place about the merging of the CQSW and CSS into a single professional qualification.

CQSW Courses leading to the CQSW, the basic professional qualification for social workers in day, field, and residential services, are provided by a number of universities, polytechnics, and colleges throughout the United Kingdom. Any institution which wishes to mount a course must submit its proposals to the Central Council for Education and Training in Social Work (CCETSW).

There are procedures and skills of social work practice which need to be acquired by students before they can be considered qualified. As set out in CCETSW Paper No. 10, *Education and Training for Social Work*, these skills relate to:

- Observing and collecting information;
- Assessing client needs and resources with a view to intervention;
- Formulating objectives and planning intervention;
- Creating a structure for intervention;
- Intervention;
- Recording, reporting, and disseminating information;
- Monitoring and evaluating outcomes of intervention.

The core features of social work practice developed by CQSW training ensure that trained social workers already possess the skills relevant to the early identification and management of clients' problems. What needs to be grafted on is specific knowledge about the nature and range of alcohol-related problems, an understanding of the role which alcohol can play in the cases with which social workers are routinely called upon to deal and the confidence to identify and respond to the alcohol component of those cases.

CSS CCETSW also approves schemes jointly managed by local colleges and social services departments leading to the Certificate in Social Services (CSS). Based on a modular structure, the CSS is designed to meet the needs of a range of occupational groups – excepting social workers – already employed by statutory social services, educational and probation authorities, voluntary agencies, and some private bodies. These include management and supervisory staff in residential and day centres, instructors on adult training courses, home help organizers, volunteer organizers, social work assistants, and specialist workers with the physically handicapped – all of whom may come across alcohol problems in their routine social services work.

Making contact with trainers   Within the wide range of institutions and organizations involved in the training leading to CQSW and CSS there is no single key contact point for those who want to draw attention to the importance of alcohol education for social workers and social services staff or to the alcohol educational materials and local resources which are available. Those, among others, who might be contacted are briefly indicted below.

The Central Council for Education and Training in Social Work is the government-financed independent body which has statutory authority throughout the United Kingdom to promote education and training in the personal social services, to recognize courses, and to award qualifications. The Committee on Professional Studies and Qualification is responsible for the recognition of courses leading to the CQSW. Below national level, much of the work is conducted by:

- CCETSW principal regional advisers and their staff who have contact with employing authorities in order to keep abreast of training needs in the region, and who have a responsibility to run short courses on various topics in order to develop skills acquired during basic training and to adapt or to transfer them to other areas of work;
- Social work educational advisers will also have responsibility for particular aspects of social work education such as CQSW, CSS, post-qualifying or short courses and will act as the direct CCETSW link with particular educational institutions which put on social work courses.

Students undertake CQSW training in universities and other institutions of higher education where:

- The CQSW course tutor will have responsibility for the overall curriculum, course content, and for liaison with the local authority social services department, probation service, and voluntary organizations over practice placements.

In colleges of further and higher education, responsibility for the course component of the in-service training leading to the CSS will rest with:

• The head of CSS studies who will also liaise over placements.

Contacts in social services The Director of Social Services of the local authority has overall responsibility for all aspects of the personal social services including the education and training of staff. Detailed responsibility for such matters as the practice placements of students in training and the continuing education of serving workers rests in many authorities with a training section with a team of:

• Training officers who will supervise the placement of CSS students and oversee arrangements between educational institutions;
• Practice teachers within the social services department with whom CQSW students are placed for their practice experience. In a social services department with several courses being mounted in the vicinity it would not be unusual for half of all qualified social workers to be on the department's Register of Practice Teachers.

Other local contacts Since 1971 the British Association of Social Workers has been the professional association of field social workers. BASW makes representations to CCETSW and DHSS over all professional matters including those concerned with education and training. The business of BASW is conducted via the council and a staff of professional officers, while the main organization at the local level consists of:

• The branch office where members meet to discuss BASW business and issues of professional interest. Some branches arrange study days, seminar programmes, and other activities.
• Special interest groups dealing with, among other things, specific problems or illnesses. There is a specialist group concerned with alcohol problems which has representatives in each region who stimulate action at the local level.

Clearly a local group concerned with prevention – on which there would, one hopes, be vigorous social work representation – could contribute to both the work of a local special interest group on alcohol problems and to the programme of the local BASW branch.

Personal social services provision is the responsibility of the Social Services Committee of each County Council or metropolitan district. The committee is composed of elected councillors who have responsibility for broad and general policy. Nevertheless, there is the opportunity for approaches to be made to the chairperson of the Social Services

Committee or to any other member known to be interested in or sympathetic to alcohol education for social workers.

Materials and resources

Many basic alcohol education materials are described in other parts of this guide. In chapter 2, general materials and information together with materials for trainers and materials and information for helpers and self-helpers are outlined. Chapter 7 describes, among other things, material and information for schoolchildren, youths, and those in colleges and universities. In addition, the question of alcohol education in the workplace is dealt with in chapter 6. All materials in these three chapters could be used in the education of helping professionals.

Throughout the guide it has been stressed that in any locality there are a number of resources which can be mobilized for alcohol prevention activities. One of the tasks for those involved in local prevention will be to know about these resources, stress the need for them to be available, and press for their contribution to the alcohol education of helping professionals.

Part of the alcohol education of helping professionals will be a familiarization with etiological theories, epidemiological data, therapeutic strategies, and the organization of helping services. Much of this basic information is available in a number of well-regarded books which are listed under 'Further reading' at the end of this chapter. These books could be used by any alcohol educator as background material for the preparation of specific courses or exercises and as course reading for those undergoing training.

Teaching about Alcohol Problems   In addition to these books and the general alcohol education materials outlined in other chapters there are some materials which are specific to the task of educating helping professionals. For instance, Terry Lawrence's manual entitled *Teaching about Alcohol Problems* was written in the light of her experience of teaching medical students, CQSW students, and student nurses.

The manual sets out the principles of professional education, discusses the problems associated with gaining access to overcrowded curricula and indicates certain contextual questions in the light of which any particular course or module will be designed. Specific sections deal with the introductory session; early indicators of an alcohol problem; what constitutes an alcohol problem; at risk groups; alcohol and the family; client-worker relationships; referral; and concludes with a list of useful addresses.

The manual contains information, supporting materials, class exercises and case studies. The development work and field testing of the manual was supported by DHSS. Further information can be obtained from:

Alcohol Concern
305 Gray's Inn Road
London WC1X 8QF
(Tel: 01-833-3471)

Any member of the local prevention group with time and experience could negotiate access to the basic curriculum of a helping professional training course to introduce an alcohol education module based on *Teaching about Alcohol Problems*. Similarly, the manual could be brought to the attention of clinical sub-deans, directors of nurse education, CQSW course tutors, and others responsible for the basic education of helping professionals.

In any university or college there is likely to be someone with an interest in alcohol problems. In spite of the crowded curriculum, anyone offering a specific, well-thought-out teaching package dealing with a well-recognized and important aspect of professional practice – such as how to deal with alcohol problems – is unlikely to be refused.

The Medical Council on Alcoholism (MCA) The MCA has published *Alcohol and Health: A Handbook for Medical Students* which is distributed free of charge to all fourth-year medical students, and *Alcohol and Health: A Handbook for Nurses, Midwives and Health Visitors* which is distributed free of charge to all schools of nursing. These two guides, however, would be useful to any helping professional at any stage of basic or in-service training.

The MCA will also mount, at the request of any medical school, a one-day symposium on alcohol and health. In addition, the council encourages medical students to seek secondment, in their elective year, to general practices in which the principals are known to have an interest in alcohol problems. Students studying psychiatry will also be assisted by the MCA to obtain training placements in alcohol treatment units or in departments of psychiatry where there is a particular interest in alcohol problems. The address is:

Medical Council on Alcoholism
31 Bedford Square
London WC1B 3JS
(Tel: 01-580-3893)

A series of films have been produced by the MCA for professional audiences. The five films deal with:

- *The Web of Support*;
- *Clinical Aspects*;
- *The Drunken Offender*;
- *Differing Alcoholics – Differing Treatments*;
- *The Clinical Approach*.

Each film lasts approximately thirty minutes and can be obtained for hire or purchase from:

Concord Films Council
Necton
Ipswich
Suffolk
(Tel: 0473-76012)

Alcoholics Anonymous   Anyone responsible for running a course on alcohol problems could also contact the regional public information officer of Alcoholics Anonymous who will be able to arrange for speakers to attend and for a showing of the AA video-tape *AA Works One Day at a Time*. Contact with AA can be made via a local telephone directory listing or through:

General Service Office
Alcoholics Anonymous
11 Redcliffe Gardens
London SW10 9BQ
(Tel: 01-352-9779)

Alcohol Concern   This is another focus for discussion about the alcohol component of basic professional training. It has a responsibility for liaising with professional training bodies, for discussing the place of alcohol education within professional education, and for bringing appropriate alcohol education materials to the attention of training bodies. There is a sub-committee of Alcohol Concern examining ways in which alcohol education can be incorporated into undergraduate and postgraduate medical education. The sub-committee contains representatives from most of the medical colleges and faculties and from the national training boards. Any interested individual or organization which wants to contribute to national debate or seek advice about alcohol education should contact their regional Alcohol Concern representative or write to the educational division director at Alcohol Concern in London.

Drinking Choices This training manual for alcohol educators, produced jointly by HEC and TACADE, was introduced in chapter 2 and is referred to in other parts of the guide. It is particularly suitable for use with professionals who come into contact with people with drinking problems or who have any training or educational responsibilities. Every local prevention group, which will contain many of the key alcohol educators for its locality, should consider making arrangements for a 'Drinking Choices' course to be run for its members.

The manual originated in the north east, partly in response to the sudden rise in demand for alcohol education as a result of the HEC's north east campaign. The basic philosophy of the *Drinking Choices* manual and the associated 'Drinking Choices' course is that everyone is a potential alcohol educator and that all alcohol education resources within the community should be utilized. The course uses a participatory group-work approach with structured activity which helps people to learn effectively using, among other things, the following rules: voluntary participation in all activities; equality of all group members; learning through co-operation and sharing; maintaining open communication; learning may mean taking risks; and learning is fun.

The course provides:

- Education for the educator: it is a training programme for anyone acting as an educator related to alcohol and drinking;
- A client-treatment programme: the course can also be seen as an educational programme for treatment of clients, i.e. as the educational component of treatment.

In answer to the question 'Is the prospective educator being educated, trained, or treated?' the manual states that 'The answer is all three. S/he is being educated about alcohol and drinking, trained in the skills necessary to handle drinking situations and to act as an educator' (p. 7).

The *Drinking Choices* training manual includes an outline teaching plan for a five-day course. The five days would not run consecutively since there are practical and other tasks to undertake between each session. The manual ends with students' material, both factual and for use in connection with the training task, and trainer material, on how to teach facts, encourage value clarification, facilitate role-playing and listening skills, and other issues.

Those who have successfully completed a 'Drinking Choices' course can then act as a key tutor for a subsequent course. Every locality should build up a number of people who are able to act as key tutors for local 'Drinking Choices' courses. These courses might be held in a educational establishment in association with a specific training course, as part of some in-service professional training, or as an independent exercise in which members of a variety of professions and organizations come together to take part. Information on key tutors and the availability of local 'Drinking Choices' courses can be obtained from:

Health Education Council
78 New Oxford Street
London WC1A 1AH
(Tel: 01-631-0930)

Counselling   This is one component of the routine response to most alcohol problems. Many books deal with counselling in general and some contain specific chapters dealing with alcohol counselling in particular. The National Council on Alcoholism, which was superseded by Alcohol Concern in 1984, brought out, in 1981, a *Counsellor's Guide on Problem Drinking* which, in addition to setting the background scene about the development and nature of alcohol problems, discusses assessment, setting goals, counselling and psychotherapy, counselling for abstinence, and counselling for controlled drinking.

More recently, Stephen Marshall and Richard Velleman have produced *Training Volunteers to Counsel Problem Drinkers and Their Families – A Handbook*. This gives information on a variety of issues which should be of help to anyone involved with training alcoholism counsellors. The handbook deals in some detail with the questions of acceptable *minimum standards*, the *organization* of counsellor training, and the *management* of volunteer counsellors once trained. The development work for the handbook was financed by the DHSS. Information about the handbook can be obtained from Alcohol Concern, which has as one of its tasks to encourge the training of volunteer counsellors. Alcohol Concern also recognizes the need to make the most of the volunteers' abilities, and a working party is considering the possibility of a national scheme for the accreditation of counsellors.

A diploma course in alcohol counselling and consultation has been run at the University of Kent since 1982. The timetable is arranged on five modules of block teaching in order to enable practitioners who do not live in the south east of England to attend. The course is designed for those in the helping professions who want to develop or enhance their existing skills in work with problem drinkers. It emphasizes an integrated use of different approaches to assessment and intervention. Enquiries should be made to:

Alcohol Counselling and Consultation Course
Keynes College
University of Kent
Canterbury CT2 7NP
(Tel: 0227-66822)

The Alcohol Intervention Training Unit at the University of Kent also runs a number of short courses aimed at developing skills and knowledge relevant to working with alcohol problems. These courses focus on, among other things, prevention, assessment and intervention, group-work with problem drinkers, teaching alcohol intervention skills, and working in general practice settings. Information can be obtained from:

The Organizing Secretary
School of Continuing Education
Rutherford College
University of Kent
Canterbury CT2 7NY
(Tel: 0227-66822)

In several parts of the country there are other initiatives geared to stimulating interest and developing the education of professionals in relation to alcohol problems. In Leeds, for example, the Addiction Unit runs courses for people who wish to acquire the knowledge and skills to consolidate their own practice and advise and support their colleagues. Further information can be obtained from:

Tutor in Addiction
The Leeds Addiction Unit
40 Clarendon Road
Leeds LS2 9PJ
(Tel: 0532-456617)

Other local resources In some regions, multi-disciplinary alcohol action groups have been established with support from the regional medical officer and the regional postgraduate dean. These provide speakers for local courses and encourage curriculum and service development. At the local level some of the already available specialist resources will be based on an alcohol treatment unit or a community alcohol team where medical practitioners, nurses, social workers, clinical psychologists, and other professionals will be working together to identify, manage, and prevent alcohol problems. These professionals are a key resource and, one hopes, will be well represented on any local prevention group. Similarly, where there is a Local Council on Alcoholism there will in most cases be some training expertise, in particular in relation to counselling.

Aspects of good professional practice

Most good professional practice is, of course, geared to helping specific people with their problems. Although this guide is concerned with prevention rather than with the content of case-work, the difficulties associated with helping problem drinkers are well known and have implications for preventative action at the local level.

Many helping professionals are reluctant to approach their patients and clients about what they consider to be a sensitive issue while others are unconvinced that anything worthwhile can be done once a 'case' has been identified. Furthermore, the range of possible interventions is enormous and difficulties over the definition of what an alcohol problem is make it hard for many professionals to know precisely what to do about any particular problem.

Among the questions which are frequently raised are: Should the person be directly confronted about the drinking problem or approached indirectly? What information is really relevant to distinguishing the alcohol component of the problem and is that in any way different from the information required to deal with the problem overall? Is the alcohol component the real problem anyway? Is specialist help or some specialist technique required for this particular case? What should be the goal of intervention for people with alcohol problems? Should the goal be the same for all problem drinkers or should it vary according to the particulars of each case? If it varies, how is the decision to be made about which goal is relevant for which client? Whose problem is the problem anyway – the drinker's, the spouse's, the family's, the workmates', the friend's, everyone's? What implications does this have for the way the case is handled? The list of day-to-day practice questions is endless.

The task for the professional is to develop a body of good practice in relation to these questions. But although good professional practice is an easy phrase to say, it is a difficult phrase to define. Fortunately, however, there have been a large number of publications over recent years which have distilled the experience of clinicians and other professional helpers working in the alcohol field. Griffith Edwards, for example, has produced *The Treatment of Drinking Problems – a Guide for the Helping Professions*, based on over twenty years' experience of research and clinical practice in relation to alcohol problems. It is specifically written for multi-professional audiences who as part of their work are called upon to respond to alcohol problems. It provides clear guidelines for handling the encounter and for the overall management of the problem drinker. This and other guides are listed under 'Further reading' at the end of the chapter.

On the basis of pre-qualification training and continuing education, all professionals will have a set of theories and practices which form their day-to-day work. These together with additional alcohol education, knowledge and experience, will enable them to deal with the alcohol component of their routine case loads. The remainder of this section is concerned with two specific aspects of good professional practice which deserve emphasis: the need for professionals to 'do research' and 'to press for prevention'.

Doing 'research'

There is a view – widespread in many organizations, including government departments, the professions, local authorities, health and social services, voluntary organizations, and private companies – that research is something that only certain people can do, because only they have the skill, the time, the money, or the opportunity. It is stressed throughout this guide, however, that everyone involved with the prevention of alcohol problems should be concerned to monitor their activities and place them within the broader local context. It follows from this that 'research' is not for other people but, like prevention, is *everybody's* business. For helping professionals research is essential:

- To assess the extent of problems in the local community or in the case-load;
- To form one part of routine case identification;
- To assist with case management and case monitoring;

- To accumulate evidence for judging the success of treatment or intervention;
- To assess the impact of local prevention activity.

Being sceptical   In essence, to do research is to be sceptical. It is to be sceptical of established practice and procedure. It is also to be sceptical of anyone who claims that there is nothing more that we could or should know about our work, our discipline, our area of interest, our sphere of expertise, our organization, our locality, or whatever. Feeling good about the way things are – or are claimed to be – is just *not good enough.* In particular, it is not good enough for professionals who have the task of delivering care to those who need it.

Anyone who says that research into their organization is unnecessary is really saying 'I know everything about my own organization,' 'I know how to describe it completely; its structure, activity, personnel, its history, and relationships,' 'I know how it is going, how it is changing and developing,' 'I know how it compares with other organizations, agencies, and ways of working,' 'I know in what ways it is successfully doing what it is supposed to do and whether it would or would not be improved by specific change or changes.' Anyone who can say those things with complete honesty is very fortunate. Few people say it openly about their own organization but many people – including professionals – imply it by their attitude to research.

Basic research skills are not magical or mystical but can be learnt by anyone. Research need not be time-consuming nor need it be expensive. Everyone who breathes has the opportunity to do some research, while in all areas of contemporary life there is pressure on participants to be their own researchers, whether they like it or not. Everyone is being called upon to account for themselves, their skills, their activities, their impact, and the organizations in which they work, whether those organizations are industries, universities, or public services.

What is research?   At base it is merely diligent and careful study. Popular desk-top dictionaries define research in terms of 'the endeavour to discover new facts', 'the seeking of information' or 'finding out'. Clearly, this is nothing special, nor does it require great expertise. There is nothing in this simple definition about science, or methodology, or sophisticated technology, or mathematical models, or complex theory.

In fact, studying carefully, trying to discover new facts and seeking information is something which everyone does all the time. Everyone, whether professional or not, has ideas and theories about the way in which their everyday world works; about what matters to people around them and what makes them do what they do. Undertaking any work – whether professional or not – depends upon the participants understanding, interpreting, learning from, and theorizing about the causes and consequences of their own actions and the actions of those around them. *Everyone*, therefore, is constantly doing their own 'everyday' research.

The only difference between everyday research and research with a capital 'R' is that 'researchers' claims about the world are open to public inspection, debate, and questioning. Text books on research methods are all about the processes of collecting, manipulating, and displaying materials in such a way as to stand up to public scrutiny (see 'Further reading' for some guides to research and evaluation). Research which is made public is conducted *for* some public – some audience, interest, or group. Any alcohol research undertaken by helping professionals will have any number of interested audiences; funders, policy-makers, management teams, colleagues, the general public, clients, the DHSS, related organizations plus, of course, the professionals themselves.

Keeping records At the heart of any research is record-keeping. Unfortunately, there is a reluctance among many professionals to keep systematic records. There is a reluctance by some to keep records at all in the belief that it is an affront to the rights of the client. We do not share that view. This guide is based on the principle that systematic record-keeping by all helping professionals is essential for at least three main reasons:

- *For good case-work*: From the beginning of assessment, in order to identify 'caseness' and the profile of potential or actual problems, history-taking and the recording of systematic sets of information is essential. This material can be kept in the professional's head but, of course, any monitoring of the client's progress must be based on the comparison of data at different times and this can only be done by recording information systematically, where 'systematic' means ensuring that comparable and reliable pieces of information are routinely collected.
- *For intra-organizational efficiency*: Systematic recording of the nature of cases and their progress, and the range of resources brought to bear upon them, are necessary in any organization if it is to plan effectively the workload of team members, to have

meaningful case conferences, and to provide a basis for resource allocation, for service planning and for monitoring education and training.

- *For inter-organizational contact and collaboration*: Professionals have a variety of responsibilities in relation to other organizations such as, for example, in relation to court reports. These require accurate record-keeping in order that reliable information can be presented.

Information to put practice into context   The work of all professionals concerned with the prevention and management of alcohol-related problems must be informed by an understanding of the broader context within which they work. All professionals can contribute to that overall context by systematically recording and making available their judgements and accounts of their own activities. In any locality there are at least five major sets of alcohol-related information which ought to be available. Each set of information could contain five, ten, thirty, or a thousand individual strands. How much local information is routinely available will depend upon workers in many organizations – but particularly professional helpers – agreeing priorities and ensuring that information is produced. The five basic sets of local information relate to:

- *Alcohol use*: details of who drinks, how much, costing what, when, where, with whom, of which alcoholic drinks, etc.
- *Alcohol-related activities*: details of who is involved, in what capacities, in relation to alcoholic drinks, from production to distribution and sale, together with advertising, sponsorship and promotion, etc.
- *Alcohol-related attitudes*: details of who holds what views about alcohol and its use, about alcohol problems, and about who can or should do what to alleviate or prevent them, etc.
- *Alcohol-related problems*: details of who gets into what difficulties with alcohol, when and where, etc.
- *Responses to alcohol-related problems*: details of who is responding, in what ways, in what organizations, to which alcohol-related problems, and who is doing what to educate people about how to prevent or control the development of alcohol-related problems, etc.

The systematic collection and dissemination of these data would do much to focus the attention of professionals and others on important local issues. It would provide the factual background against which discussions of prevention activities and service developments could take place. No overall planning of services or even of the activities of particular professionals can be adequate unless it is informed by these background facts.

Evaluation There are frequent calls for services to be evaluated and those involved in any service should be regularly evaluating themselves. Evaluation research is, quite simply, research designed to assess whether something that was expected to happen has in fact happened, to judge the quality of something, or to see whether something matches up to something that was desired. It is the success question. In order to answer the question 'Has X been a success?' there are a number of subordinate questions that any researcher-cum-professional should be clear about:

- In *what ways* is X a success? There might be one or ten or fifty that are of interest.
- To *what extent* is X a success in any or all of these ways.
- In terms of *what criteria*? What is to stand for X being a success in this way and to this degree?
- *Judged how?* What has to happen for some criterion of success to be achieved?
- *Says who?* Who is judging anyway? Is it some outside evaluator, or some person involved in the situation which is being evaluated? The number of people who can make evaluative judgements is limitless.

Evaluating professional practice is all about making these issues explicit. There is no single answer to the question 'Is this treatment programme or organization a success?' The question has to be refined. Once it is refined into its – almost limitless constituent parts then the question will elicit an almost limitless series of answers.

It might be decided to let one particular answer to one particular question stand for an overall evaluation. But this has to be made explicit. If, for example, some organization decides to judge the effectiveness of its treatment programme by the criterion of a fall-off in new cases coming to the service – on the grounds that people are being 'cured' and therefore there are fewer people in need of help – then that is fine. There may be other explanations for a fall-off in people coming to the programme which, no doubt, someone assessing the service's evaluation might draw attention to. But at least there has been a judgement about the success of the programme and the grounds upon which that judgement has been made have been made clear.

Research tools   Any judgement about – evaluation of – a programme of prevention or treatment must be supportable. The supporting data must be public. Only when professionals systematically record their own activities and the progress of their patients and clients will their judgements about their own organizations, their work, and its value be taken seriously.

There are a number of research 'tools' which enable professionals to record details about their patients and clients, and about their own professional involvement. These tools are relevant for assessing the extent of the problem, for case identification and for repeated measurement in order to monitor the progress of particular cases and evaluate the service.

These research tools range from short self-completion questionnaires which patients and clients can fill in either for their own information or as one part of a broader professional assessment to specific laboratory tests – such as the measurement of the serum concentration of the enzyme gammaglutamyl transpeptidase (GGT) – which can be called for only by medical practitioners. But at the heart of all professional helping is the knowledge and experience of the practitioners themselves which enables them to identify signs of particular problems, judge the appropriateness of any particular tools, and assess the implications of the information they elicit.

There are thousands of text books and articles in professional journals which describe the development of particular research instruments, argue their importance, and describe their use in research and professional practice. A short, clear guide to 'what the non-specialist needs to know about understanding and managing alcohol problems' was presented in the series of articles entitled *ABC of Alcohol* published in the British Medical Journal in 1981. Four of these articles, by Dr Paton and his colleagues, were concerned with 'detection':

- 'Asking the Right Questions', including using two screening questionnaires 'which have withstood the test of time', the short Michigan Alcoholism Screening Test (MAST) and the 'CAGE' questionnaire.
- 'Tools of Detection', including breathalyzers and a range of laboratory tests – such as for GGT, red cell mean corpuscular volume (MCV), urinary alcohol concentration, and aminotrans-

ferase activity – where abnormal values should alert the practitioner to the possibility of an alcohol problem.

- 'Detection in Hospital', including reference to the patient's manner, social situation, overt physical signs, and illness conditions which are known to be the possible consequence of excessive alcohol consumption.
- 'Detection in General Practice' (or in any other helping professional setting), including physical signs, non-verbal signs during the case interview, social indicators, and the possible indications of an alcohol problem shown by members of the patient's family – such as developmental delay or non-accidental injury in a child.

Since the *ABC of Alcohol* articles were published, a number of other instruments have become available. Two of them could be incorporated into routine practice by any professional. The short-form 'Alcohol Dependence Data' (ADD) questionnaire provides an 'easy to complete, practical, self-report measure of alcohol dependence containing cognitive, behavioural and physiological questions'. The questionnaire (see Raistrick *et al*. in 'Further reading') is designed to be sensitive across the full range of dependence, sensitive to change over time, and relatively free of socio-cultural influence.

In addition to questionnaires such as MAST, CAGE, and ADD, there is the need to be systematic about the collection of information about patients' and clients' drinking. A large number of research reports have shown that the accuracy of self-reported drinking behaviour is sufficiently high over a retrospective period of one week for case identification and case monitoring purposes. The value, in any regime of professional help, of patients and clients keeping a prospective diary record of their drinking behaviour has also been recognized.

The DRAMS – 'Drinking Reasonably And Moderately with Self-control' – scheme is designed to assist general practitioners to help their patients to cope with problem drinking. The DRAMS kit was developed out of the *So You Want to Cut Down on Your Drinking* self-help manual (see chapter 2) designed by Ian Robertson and Nick Heather, and contains:

- A DRAMS medical record card for the GP to use;
- An initial two-week diary card for the patient to use;
- A follow-up self-help book containing details on drinking and health, how to cut down on drinking, the effects of alcohol, and further diaries for the patient to monitor progress.

Although DRAMS was designed for general practitioners and their patients there is no reason why it could not be used by any other helping professional as part of the case management of any client whose problem is alcohol-related. Information about DRAMS can be obtained from:

Scottish Health Education Group
Woodburn House
Canaan Lane
Edinburgh EH10 4SG
(Tel: 031-447-8044)

The DHSS Advisory Committee report on *The Pattern and Range of Services for Problem Drinkers* was based on the core assumption that the nation's alcohol problems could never be handled by relying solely upon specialist helpers. All professionals and other workers who give help were charged by the committee with responsibility for recognizing and dealing with the alcohol component of any problems with which they are faced. But in order for helping professionals to respond positively in this way they must be *willing* to do so. Unfortunately, many professionals reject the idea of giving anything other than the minimum of attention to alcohol problems even though an accumulation of research evidence has shown that a sizable proportion of the cases of every helping professional will have an alcohol component.

The development of alcohol education as part of pre-qualification education and in-service training will go some way toward increasing professional willingness to deal with alcohol problems. Any professional group or organization would also benefit from using the well-developed AAPPQ – 'Alcohol and Alcohol Problems Perception Questionnaire' – designed by Alan Cartwright as a tool for measuring:

- *Therapeutic attitudes* – motivation or willingness to work with drinkers; expectations of work satisfaction with these clients; feelings about the adequacy of knowledge and skills in working with these clients; extent of the right to work with drinkers; and esteem in this specific task;
- *Role support* in the professional or helping setting;
- *Self-esteem* as a helper.

Further information on the AAPPQ can be obtained from:

Alan Cartwright
Mount Zeehan Unit

St Martin's Hospital
Littlebourne Road
Canterbury
Kent

Pressing for prevention

This guide is based on the assumption that, at the local level, prevention is everybody's business. Nevertheless, helping professionals – because of their education and training, experience, organizational position, and involvement with a wide range of people with problems – are strategically placed to play a major part in the development of a local alcohol prevention strategy. Helping professionals are a key prevention resource. They:

- *Have legitimacy* to ask questions of individuals and groups and to raise alcohol prevention issues;
- *Have authority* as professionals to act and to require others to act in relation to the prevention of alcohol problems;
- *Have access* to resources through in-service training budgets or inter-organizational finance such as 'joint funding' arrangements, to support activities and organizations which have a part to play in the prevention of alcohol problems.

All professionals, therefore – in addition to providing help for their patients and clients and in addition to 'researching' the extent of the alcohol problem and the impact of prevention and other responses – have the task of *pressing for prevention*. Pressing for prevention is not just a good thing in itself and good for those who would otherwise develop a drinking problem but, given the extent of the alcohol component of routine professional case-work, it is good professional-organizational strategy.

Opportunities for prevention are almost limitless. This guide identifies some of them in relation to several major topic areas such as alcohol and work (chapter 6), alcohol and safety (chapter 4), and alcohol and the media (chapter 3). Opportunities for any professional to press for prevention will fall into five main categories: intra-organizational, multi-professional, supporting other groups, public education, and monitoring.

Intra-organizational pressure Professionals can press for recognition of the alcohol problem within the routine work of their own organizations.

They can press for special workers to be appointed to take responsibility for keeping the alcohol problem under review, collecting materials, and contributing to special in-service training. Professionals can press for alcohol and work policies to be implemented in their own organization and also to ensure that the identification and management of problems is enhanced by systematic and routine record-keeping based upon up-to-date knowledge and the use of standardized and well-recognized procedures and instruments.

Multi-professional pressure   Professionals can join with colleagues in other organizations to press for the joint funding of relevant activities and organizations such as a local Council on Alcoholism or a local advisory or counselling centre. Multi-disciplinary training events, specifically geared to alcohol issues, can be arranged which would not otherwise be supported by one organization, profession, or group. Professionals can press for all professional organizations to discuss – and press for – the adoption of comparable data systems. In this instance, comparable data systems does not mean systems which exchange data between organizations, but merely that where data are collected on the alcohol component of patients' or clients' problems they are collected in a systematic and comparable way, so that comparisons can be made between types of alcohol problems and the ways in which they are identified and responded to in different settings. Only in this way can an adequate local 'pattern and range of services for problem drinkers' be developed.

Supporting other groups   Professionals of all kinds should be key participants in any local prevention group which itself will be pressing for prevention. In addition, professionals may well be associated with other organizations which they can encourage to press for prevention. These other organizations include local Councils on Alcoholism and any other multi-disciplinary groupings which come together for specific alcohol prevention purposes, such as a licensing forum (see chapter 5).

Public education   Because of their authority, education, and experience, professionals are ideally placed to take part in public education about the prevention of alcohol problems. Taking part in local radio and television programmes and producing informative material for the local press together with arranging and being involved with seminars, public meetings, and alcohol education in schools is all part of the professional task of pressing for prevention.

Monitoring Professionals are, again, particularly well placed to raise and press for the routine data collection and monitoring which is so essential to any local alcohol prevention strategy. In association with local staff members who have an interest in alcohol problems from, for example, institutions of higher education, professionals can press for community surveys, drinking surveys, surveys of case-loads, and other monitoring activities. The collection of routine official statistics from local organizations could be used in the monitoring of the impact of local prevention activities.

Over the past decade there has been a shift towards community care and a wider recognition of the alcohol component of many health and social problems. During this period, experience suggests that if a small group of professionals take a particular interest in alcohol issues then the whole locality's appreciation of the extent, nature, and need to prevent alcohol problems is rapidly enhanced. This can certainly be done without the involvement of helping professionals; but with their involvement – pressing for prevention – progress is so much quicker.

This is intended to be a *living* 'guide to action'. Therefore, it needs to be revised and added to in the light of local needs and local experience.

The following two pages are for jotting down examples of good practice, and addresses relevant to the issues covered by this chapter.

We hope to update the guide, and would be delighted to receive any advice about corrections, new material or any other information which should go into the next edition. Please send all suggestions, before 31 December, 1987, to:

Philip Tether and David Robinson
Addiction Research Centre
University of Hull
Hull HU6 7RX

Examples of Good Practice

Useful Addresses and Telephone Numbers

Further reading

Abramson, J.H., *Survey Methods in Community Medicine*, 2nd edn, Churchill Livingston, Edinburgh, 1979

Advisory Committee on Alcoholism, *The Pattern and Range of Services for Problem Drinkers*, DHSS, London, 1978

Advisory Committee on Alcoholism, *Education and Training*, DHSS, London, 1979

Asbury, A.J., *ABC of Computing*, articles from the *British Medical Journal*, British Medical Association, London, 1983

Bailey, M.B., *Alcoholism and Family Casework: Theory and Practice*, the Community Council of Greater New York, New York, 1968

Bean, M.H. and Zindberg, N.E. (eds), *Dynamic Approaches to the Understanding and Treatment of Alcoholism*, Free Press, New York, 1981

Bennett, P. and Lupton, S., *Social Work and Alcohol Dependence*, 1983. Available from Editorial Office, Social Work Monographs, SOC, University of East Anglia, Norwich NR4 7TJ

Bernadt, M.W., Munford, J., Taylor, C., Smith, B., and Murray, R.M., 'Comparison of Questionnaire and Laboratory Tests in the Detection of Excessive Drinking and Alcoholism', *Lancet*, 6 February, 1982

Carley, M., *Social Measurement and Social Indicators*, Allen and Unwin, London, 1981

Coates, M. and Paech, G., *Alcohol and Your Patient: A Nurse's Handbook*, Addiction Research Foundation, Toronto, 1979

Davies, I. and Raistrick, D., *Dealing with Drink: Helping Problem Drinkers – A Handbook*, BBC Publications, London, 1981

Donaldson, R.J. and Donaldson, L.J., *Essential Community Medicine: Including Relevant Social Services*, MTP Press, Lancaster, 1983

Edwards, G., *The Treatment of Drinking Problems: A Guide for Helping Professions*, Grant MacIntyre, London, 1982

Edwards, G. and Grant, M. (eds), *Alcoholism: New Knowledge and New Responses*, Croom Helm, London, 1977

Edwards, G., Gross, M.N. Keller, M., *et al.* (eds), *Alcohol Related Disabilities*, World Health Organization, Geneva, 1977

Gore, S.M. and Altman, D.G., *Statistics in Practice*, articles from the *British Medical Journal*, British Medical Association, London, 1982

Harwin, J., Leckit, J., and Hebblethwaite, D., articles in *Social Work Today*, 10, 41, June 1979

Hedley, R., *Measuring Success: A Guide to Evaluation for Voluntary and Community Groups*, ADVANCE, 14 Bloomsbury Square, London, 1985

Hore, B.D. and Ritson, E.B., *Alcohol and Health: A Handbook for Medical Students*, Medical Council on Alcoholism, undated

House, E.R., *Evaluating with Validity*, Sage Publications, Beverly Hills, 1980

Hunt, L., *Alcohol Related Problems*, Heineman Educational Books, London, 1982

Kendell, R.E., 'Alcoholism: A Medical or a Political Problem?', *British Medical Journal*, 1, 367–71, 1979

Knox, E.G., (ed.), *Epidemiology in Health Planning*, Oxford University Press, Oxford, 1979

Lawrence, T., *Teaching About Alcohol Problems*, Alcohol Concern, London, 1986

Manson, L. and Ritson, B., *Alcohol and Health: A Handbook for Nurses, Health Visitors and Midwives*, Medical Council on Alcoholism, London, 1984

Marshall, S. and Velleman, R., *Training Volunteers to Counsel Problem Drinkers and Their Families: A Handbook*, Addiction Research Centre, University of Hull, 1985. Available from Alcohol Concern

Morris, L.L. and Fitz-gibbon, C.T., *The Program Evaluation Kit*, Sage Publications, Beverly Hills, 1978

Orford, J. and Edwards, G., *Alcoholism*, Maudsley Monograph No. 26, Oxford University Press, Oxford, 1977

Paton, A. *et al.*, *ABC of Alcohol*, British Medical Association, London, 1982

Raistrick, D., Dunbar, G., and Davidson, R., 'Development of a Questionnaire to Measure Alcohol Dependence', *Brit. J. Addict.*, 78, 89–95, 1983

Rathod, N. (ed.), *Counsellor's Guide on Problem Drinking*, National Council on Alcoholism, London, 1981. Now available from Alcohol Concern

Richards, P., *Learning Medicine*, British Medical Association, London, 1983

Rossi, P.H., Freeman, H.E., and Wright, S.R., *Evaluation: A Systematic Approach*, Sage Publications, Beverly Hills, 1979

Scottish Home and Health Department, *SLAINTE MHATH? (Good Health): Medical Problems of Excessive Drinking*, memorandum of guidance for doctors in clinical practice prepared by a working party of the National Medical Consultative Committee (undated)

Simnett, I., Wright, L., and Evans, M., *Drinking Choices: A Training Manual for Alcohol Educators*, Health Education Council/ TACADE, London, 1983

Wilkins, R., *The Hidden Alcoholic in General Practice*, Elek Science, London, 1974

Wiseman, S.M., Tomson, P.V., Barratt, J.M., Jenns, M., and Wilton, J., 'Practice Research: Use of an Alcometer', *British Medical Journal*, vol. 285, 1982

Alcohol and non-statutory workers

CHAPTER 9

Alcohol and non-statutory workers

'many groups such as personnel and welfare officers, magistrates, police officers, teachers *and many voluntary workers* [emphasis added] . . . are well placed to identify signs of alcohol misuse . . . and to . . . help.' (*Drinking Sensibly*, HMSO 1981: 61)

In every locality a variety of non-statutory workers offer help, assistance, and advice to people with problems. Although there is a growing awareness of alcohol-related problems, few workers in non-statutory organizations receive any alcohol education in their training. Consequently, they have little understanding of the nature and extent of the alcohol component of the problems with which they deal. And even when they do, they often feel ill-equipped to offer advice and help.

Four organizations which are well placed to play a role

The first part of this chapter describes four organizations working at the local level which are well placed to play a role in an alcohol prevention strategy: Citizens Advice Bureaux; the Samaritans; Marriage Guidance Councils; and the Churches.

Citizens Advice Bureaux

CAB staff provide help and advice on a wide range of problems in relation to housing, employment, social security, family, money, and consumer matters. In recent years the emphasis in CAB work has begun to shift from just providing clients with advice and information to mediating on their behalf with other organizations. Most cities and large towns will have a CAB walk-in office. The address of the National Association of Citizens Advice Bureaux (NACAB) is:

National Association of Citizens Advice Bureaux
115–123 Pentonville Road
London N1 9LZ
(Tel: 01-833-2181)

Training   With the changing role of CAB the importance of training has increased. Training is now based on a careful analysis of the skills and knowledge that workers will need to advise and mediate successfully on their clients' behalf. The NACAB provides a national training service through its seventeen areas in England and Wales. In each area the training is managed by area training officers with the help of CAB workers who act as tutors.

Each CAB is guided by an organizer who arranges induction and training programmes. New staff receive a pre-training pack which is provided by the NACAB Training Department. This pack deals with the scope, style and implications of CAB work. Bureaux tutors supervise the progress of trainees and arrange training events, case discussions, and practice exercises.

After the initial induction, the trainees attend a basic training course. This is normally provided for trainees from a cluster of neighbouring bureaux. They are then expected to make use of self-study material and to continue their tuition within the bureau or on special courses dealing with particular issues.

Alcohol education   The training department of NACAB recognizes the importance of raising the bureaux workers' awareness that some of their clients will have alcohol-related problems. However, CAB workers cannot be expected to act as alcohol counsellors. The nature and volume of their work precludes any extended and intensive involvement with their clients. Any alcohol education for CAB workers would have to concentrate upon increasing their awareness that alcohol can be an aspect of many problems, developing confidence to offer sensible advice to clients, and gaining a knowledge of materials (see chapter 2) that clients might find useful. A Local Council on Alcoholism or other group concerned with prevention could offer this kind of alcohol education to

CAB workers at two levels – through the basic training programme for new workers and as part of the continuing training programme for experienced workers.

It is difficult, at present, for outside agencies to make a contribution to CAB workers' basic training. The range of subjects on which workers need training far exceeds the amount of training time available. Nevertheless, anyone interested in contributing to the education of CAB trainees could approach area training officers with a view to looking at how knowledge of alcohol-related problems could be integrated into the basic training course. A full list of names and addresses of areas training officers can be obtained by writing to the NACAB. Post-basic level training for CAB workers offers more scope for alcohol education by outside organizations. This could be either through a workers' meeting at an individual bureau or through the courses for experienced workers run by training officers.

NACAB produces a monthly Training Newsletter which is circulated to bureaux and to training staff. This newsletter reaches large numbers of CAB staff and could be a useful vehicle for increasing awareness of the training needs of CAB workers and of the alcohol-related problems of their clients.

The Samaritans

The Samaritans was founded in 1953 by Prebendary Doctor Chad Varah OBE to help the suicidal and despairing. Samaritans' volunteers are in a position to offer some counselling to clients with alcohol problems although this is limited by the shift system in which they work and the fact that the great majority of their helping is done over the telephone.

There are 180 local branches covering the Republic of Ireland, Northern Ireland, Scotland, Wales, England, and the Channel Islands. The address of the general office, which organizes national training events and which undertakes the administration is:

The Samaritans
17 Uxbridge Road
Slough
Bucks SL1 1SN
(Tel: 0753-32713/4)

Training   One of three vice-chairmen of the Samaritans is responsible for training. In addition, the Samaritans have recently appointed a national training co-ordinator to develop training at all levels and to act as a resource and facilitor. Each of the ten Samaritan regions in England and Wales has a training officer and there is a training officer in each of the local branches. At the national level, a working party has recently been established to review training policy.

The training of new volunteers is carried out at branch level. Each branch has a relatively free hand concerning the structuring of this training and there is no detailed control over content and method although central guidelines are laid down and the national organization monitors local training developments. Typically new volunteers meet for six evenings for two to three hours and sometimes for a weekend or part of a weekend, but the pattern varies between branches.

Continuing in-service training is now mandatory for all Samaritan volunteers but branches differ in the amount of training they provide. There will, usually, be several training events provided in each year.

Alcohol education   Alcohol-related problems feature prominently in the Samaritans' work. Not infrequently, they are the presenting problem. Suicidal and para-suicidal episodes often involve drug overdoses accompanied by alcohol. The Samaritans recognize the importance of the topic and they are always ready to include alcohol education contributions in national, regional, and local training.

Although alcohol education does appear quite regularly in the Samaritans' training events at all levels it often concentrates upon 'alcoholics' and 'alcoholism'. An appreciation of the full range of alcohol problems and of materials that clients might find useful (see chapter 2) would be helpful. Anyone wishing to contribute to national training events should write to the vice-chairman (training) at the general office. The general office can also provide a list of the names and addresses of the training officers in the Samaritan regions. Approaches at the local level should be made to the trainer in the local branch.

Marriage Guidance Councils

Marriage Guidance Councils help both married and unmarried people with their relationship problems. The first council was established in 1937. There are currently 170 councils offering counselling in five hundred centres throughout England and Wales, Northern Ireland, the

Channel Islands, and the Isle of Man. These councils are organized in six regions under the National Marriage Guidance Council (NMGC) at:

National Marriage Guidance Council
Herbert Gray College
Little Church Street
Rugby CV21 3AP
(Tel: 0788-73241)

There is an independent Scottish Marriage Guidance Council. The Roman Catholic Church has its own Catholic Marriage Advisory Council which has 82 branches (see below).

Training All marriage guidance counsellors are part-time trained volunteers who undertake counselling either to complement their professional work as, for example, teachers or social workers or just to gain satisfaction from personal service. Aspiring counsellors go through a rigorous selection procedure which leads to a training programme consisting of three modules. Each module involves two residential events at NMGC in Rugby and a regional component. The full curriculum is detailed in the *Basic Counsellor Training Prospectus* which can be obtained from the NMGC in Rugby.

Alcohol education The curriculum does not contain any specific sessions on alcohol problems but it is an issue frequently referred to in case material and in discussion of contemporary stresses in marriage. Anyone wishing to offer an alcohol input into marriage guidance counsellor training should contact their nearest NMGC tutor consultant. A list of names and addresses can be obtained from Rugby. Alternatively, an approach could be made to any local Marriage Guidance Council which would almost certainly welcome a contribution to their training programme.

In addition to their counselling work, marriage guidance counsellors meet with groups of youngsters in schools and colleges, with parents in ante-natal clinics, with prisoners, with engaged couples, and with small groups to discuss growing up, parenthood, and other aspects of family life.

A growing aspect of this MGC work has been the provision of marriage guidance training for people in other agencies and professions. Multi-discipline residential courses are run at NMGC in Rugby, dealing with counselling, personal relationships, and group-work. Non-residential in-service training, staffed by NMGC tutors, is provided in the regions for workers in a variety of voluntary and statutory organizations. The links with other groups of workers are not just educational. The NMGC plays a complementary role to the medical and social work professions and in some places marriage guidance counsellors are working with social work teams, in GP surgeries, and in health centres. All these aspects of their work mean that marriage guidance counsellors are in a strong position to provide counselling for individuals with alcohol problems. A counsellor with specialist alcohol counselling skills would be an important asset in any local Marriage Guidance Council.

The Churches

Clergy of all denominations have an important role to play in the early identification of problems and in the provision of helpful advice and support. Although they have a crucial role to play, their contribution in relation to alcohol problems is, as yet, under-developed – especially at the local level. A local co-ordinated prevention strategy should aim to develop an awareness of alcohol-related problems among the local clergy of all denominations, promote the confidence needed to identify and respond, in their pastoral role, to problems in their congregations, and draw local Churches fully into local prevention activities.

Another important reason for fostering an awareness of alcohol-related problems among the clergy and for developing their local role in relation to such problems is that the clergy themselves are an 'at risk' group. Their working days are long and unsupervised. They often work alone and they may be subject to stress. All these are well-recognized hall-marks of an occupational group which may be particularly susceptible to alcohol-related problems. A prerequisite of helping others would be the introduction of 'alcohol and work' policies by Churches for their own clergy (see chapter 6).

National organizations Most Christian denominations in the UK have a national department concerned with social issues. There may also be a specific, standing committee or working party on alcohol and drug abuse. For instance, the General Synod of the Church of England has a Board for Social Responsibility with a Social Policy Committee which can be contacted at:

Board for Social Responsibility
Church House
Dean's Yard
London SW1P 3NZ
(Tel: 01-222-9011)

The board has produced for Synod a report on *The Use of Alcohol* and has put together an 'Alcohol Pack' containing background information and guides to local church action.

The Roman Catholic Church has a Social Welfare Committee and an Alcohol and Drugs Working Party. The address is:

Social Welfare Committee
1A Stert Street
Abingdon
Oxfordshire
(Tel: 0235-21812)

These boards, committees, and working parties act as a focus for social policy concerns. Some take the lead in sponsoring practical projects and developments within their own denomination while others act more as 'clearing houses' for information, ideas, and issues. But whatever their particular orientation these departments are linked, at the national level, by two inter-denominational organizations which highlight the Churches' collective concern for social issues in general and alcohol and drug abuse in particular.

The British Council of Churches (BCC) has a Division of Community Affairs which provides an opportunity for the various Churches to discuss social issues and problems and to develop joint approaches. The Division of Community Affairs has looked at a number of areas of concern such as race relations, opportunities for volunteers, the implications of communications technology for the work of the Churches, and marriage and alcohol problems. The address of the BCC is:

British Council of Churches
2 Eaton Gate
London SW1W 9BL
(Tel: 01-730-9611)

The other major inter-denominational organization is the Churches Council on Alcohol and Drugs (CCOAD). It is an 'enabling' organization acting as a clearing house for information and as a forum for the consideration of local and national policy and practice. It acts for the Churches nationally, linking with other alcohol and drug agencies to press for more attention by governments and the public to the alcohol and drug issue. The address of CCOAD is:

Churches Council on Alcohol and Drugs
4 Southampton Row
London WC1B 4AA
(Tel: 01-242-6511)

Local networks   At the local level, there are a number of Church networks – some linked to the national organizations outlined above – which could be used to develop an awareness of alcohol problems, promote education and debate, and draw the Churches into an integrated local prevention strategy.

The British Council of Churches has a local dimension which provides one local Church network of concern and influence. There are approximately seven hundred local Councils of Churches. Local prevention workers could contact any of the local Christian denominations through these councils. Although the Churches Council on Alcohol and Drugs does not have any regional or local organization, individual members do link their membership of CCOAD into their local church.

The Church of England   Nearly all the forty-three dioceses in the Church of England now have their own Board for Social Responsibility with a full or part-time adviser or officer. Many of them have organized themselves into regional groups. Some produce newsletters which could be used to initiate and develop local concern over alcohol-related problems. Other useful resources which exist in each diocese are diocesan education officers who have contacts with schools and youth groups and diocesan communication officers who are a channel for information generally. The Church of England Social Services Directory which can be obtained from Church House (see above) and most libraries contain the names and addresses of the diocesan Boards of Social Responsibily and of the education and communication officers. The cost is currently 65p – including postage.

The Roman Catholic Church   The Roman Catholic Church has a number of organizations specifically devoted to alcohol problems such as KALIX which seeks 'to interest Roman Catholic men and women with alcohol problems in the virtue of total abstinence and to promote their spiritual development'. The organization works with problem drinkers and contact addresses in London, Newcastle, and Leicester can be obtained from the annual national Catholic Directory, which lists all the Church's many organizations and can be obtained from most libraries.

The Roman Catholic Church also runs the Westminster Council on Alcohol Addiction and several orders have residential rehabilitative establishments for laity and clery. The Roman Catholic experience has been that problems among clergy are very difficult to uncover because of the collusion of colleagues and the fierce loyalty of the laity.

There is no local Roman Catholic Church structure similar to the diocesan Boards of Social Responsibility in the Church of England. However, the Roman Catholic Social Welfare Committee's Alcohol and Drugs Working Party has examined the problem of how to direct attention and resources to alcohol problems and the equivalent of a Board for Social Responsibility officer might be introduced, perhaps at Deanery level, with further aid and help being provided from the parishes.

In the Roman Catholic Church the Society of St Vincent de Paul has traditionally concerned itself with helping the old, the housebound, and hospital patients but, in some localities, has been extending its concern to the field of alcohol-related problems. Other parish-based Roman Catholic organizations which could have a role to play are the Knights of St Columba, the Catholic Women's League, and the Union of Catholic Mothers.

Local prevention workers might find that the best way to draw the local Roman Catholic Church into a local prevention strategy would be to stimulate the interest and concern of any of these organizations – particularly the Society of St Vincent de Paul. Each diocese produces a local version of the national Catholic Directory which lists all the local clergy and organizations together with contact addresses. A copy should be available from any local priest.

The local Roman Catholic Marriage Advisory Service could provide another useful, local contact point. Its eighty-two branches are found across the UK but their spread tends to reflect the density of the Catholic population. Like the NMGC, the Roman Catholic service provides not only counselling for clients but also undertakes educational work with various groups such as the young and engaged couples. The address of the national organization is:

Roman Catholic Marriage Advisory Service
15 Lansdowne Road
Holland Park
London W11
(Tel: 01-727-0141)

Local clergy training   Local prevention workers could contribute to the training of the clergy. In all denominations there is a growing emphasis on pastoral studies, and tutors in pastoral studies usually have close links with their local social services department, the probation service, and other organizations. The examination of alcohol problems is usually included in most courses.

The opportunity may exist for students to undertake placements in hospitals or hostels. At one Roman Catholic Seminary, for example, students opt for a placement in a rehabilitative establishment and all final year students spend a half-day with members of Alcoholics Anonymous whilst students are encouraged to attend local AA meetings (see below). Anyone wanting to make a contribution to the alcohol education of the clergy should be able to obtain a list of the nearest training establishment from a local church.

The training of most clergy now includes elements of counselling and has largely moved from lectures cataloguing social problems to a more person-centred and experiential approach. Clergy can be encouraged to develop specific alcohol counselling skills. Clergy interested in acquiring and developing alcohol counselling skills may find membership of the British Association for Counselling and, in particular, its specialist division, the Association of Pastoral Care and Counselling, particularly useful (see chapter 2).

Two organizations concerned specifically with alcohol problems

There are two non-statutory organizations which are specifically concerned with alcohol problems: local Councils on Alcoholism and Alcoholics Anonymous.

Councils on Alcoholism

There are approximately thirty-five local Councils on Alcoholism in

England and Wales which contribute to the community response to alcohol problems. Due to their varying histories, funding structures, and uneven amounts of local support and interest, the councils differ greatly in the scope and range of their prevention activities. But a well-established Council on Alcoholism is one obvious base from which to disseminate this guide.

Most local councils were, until 1984, affiliated to the now defunct National Council on Alcoholism. Alcohol Concern, the new national agency, has taken over the role of encouraging the development and growth of local Councils on Alcoholism. The address is:

Alcohol Concern
305 Grays Inn Road
London WC1X 8QF
(Tel: 01-833-3471)

The aims of the councils   Local Councils on Alcoholism can provide not only counselling, advice, and support for problem drinkers but also be a recognized 'place' where local alcohol activities and services can be discussed, developed, and co-ordinated. The need, in any locality, for such a 'place' was stressed in the DHSS Advisory Committee's report on the *Pattern and Range of Services for Problem Drinkers*.

It is widely accepted that, ideally, councils should:

- Provide counselling help and support, by trained volunteer counsellors, for those with a drink problem and extend that support to the drinker's family.
- Play a part in the education and training of primary care workers such as probation officers, social workers, and nurses.
- Contribute to local public education and prevention activities.
- Undertake some of the co-ordination of a local response to drinking problems.

Staff, finance, and training   A Council on Alcoholism requires, at the very least, an experienced, full-time director, a secretary, and an office with a counselling room. These minimum resources will not enable the council to undertake a wide range of activities. The duties of a council director are, among other things:

- To recruit, train, manage, and support a team of volunteer counsellors.
- To take part in information, education, and prevention activities.

- To act as a full-time knowledgeable link between the various statutory and non-statutory agencies which have a part to play in the overall community response to drinking problems.

The DHSS currently provides 'pump-priming' support for four years, after which the council has to find other funds. This can be done through 'joint funding' – made available in the NHS budget to stimulate co-operative NHS-local government ventures in areas of mutual concern – inner-city funding, contributions from local industry, and so on. Those councils with the firmest financial base have secured this by drawing on a wide range of public and private funds.

The DHSS 'pump-priming' is negotiated by Alcohol Concern on behalf of any locality seeking to establish a council. Initial support is currently on the following scale:

Year 1	*Year 2*	*Year 3*	*Year 4*
50% of costs	40% of costs	40% of costs	30% of costs

where 'costs' are £22,000 per annum maximum.

Training in alcohol counselling is provided by some local Councils on Alcoholism. There are approximately 250 voluntary counsellors currently working for local Councils on Alcoholism, most of whom have been trained by the councils themselves, some as part of DHSS-funded experimental training schemes. The task of developing the training of voluntary alcohol counsellors has been taken over by Alcohol Concern which is reviewing possible structures for national, regional, and local schemes. Anyone who is interested should contact Alcohol Concern from where a handbook on *Training Volunteers to Counsel Problem Drinkers and Their Families* by Stephen Marshall and Richard Velleman can be obtained.

A focus on local prevention activities   Although it would be difficult for a council to take on the full range of activities which go to make up a comprehensive local prevention strategy, a local Council on Alcoholism is one ready-made focus for the dissemination and promotion of this guide.

Councils can, at the very least, act as a *catalyst*, spreading information about the existence of this guide and promoting debate about the need for the kind of prevention strategy which is outlined. Part of this role would be to *convene* the nucleus of a local prevention group with membership drawn from a wide range of the local organizations identified in the guide. A Council on Alcoholism could also have an important *enabling and supporting* role, providing other local prevention workers with a meeting place, expertise, contacts, and educational materials. For example, RoSPA has produced a series of pamphlets on *Drinking and Driving* for a range of different audiences, including one for voluntary workers. A Council on Alcoholism could ensure that all local voluntary organizations have the appropriate pamphlet. RoSPA's address is:

Royal Society for the Prevention of Accidents
Cannon House
The Priory
Queensway
Birmingham B4 6BS
(Tel: 021-233-2461)

The precise role of a local Council on Alcoholism is something to be decided in each locality. But, one hopes, with the ideas and suggestions contained in this guide, many local councils will be better equipped to fulfil their role in relation to the prevention of alcohol problems.

Alcoholics Anonymous

Alcoholics Anonymous, which originated in Akron, Ohio, in 1935, is a 'fellowship' of men and women who believe that the only way to cope with their alcohol problem is to give up drinking completely. There are now over two thousand AA groups meeting every week in the United Kingdom and there are over one million members of AA world-wide.

Activities and information   The activities of Alcoholics Anonymous are concentrated at the local group level. In the United Kingdom, the groups themselves are organized in a broad regional structure and there is a General Service Board which co-ordinates the business of AA at the national level in accordance with the wishes of the General Service Conference to which group members go as delegates.

AA produce a great deal of well-designed and informative literature about themselves and their activities. The 'big book' *Alcoholics Anonymous* explains the AA philosophy and contains the case histories of thirty early members. The book also contains the now well-known 'Twelve Steps of Recovery', the first of which contains the core of the fellowship's ideas about the nature of their shared problem: 'We admitted we were powerless over alcohol – that our lives had become unmanageable.'

The dozens of different pamphlets produced by AA cover specific aspects of 'recovery', often for specific categories of people, such as *AA for the Woman, Memo for an Inmate, What Is AA?, AA and the Alcoholic Employee, AA in Your Community*, and many more. In addition, AA has its own film '*AA: an Inside View*', and its public information video-tape 'AA Works: One day at a Time'. The AA General Service Office, from where literature and other materials can be obtained together with information on where to find AA in the United Kingdom – and world-wide – is at:

AA General Service Office
11 Redcliffe Gardens
London SW10 9BQ
(Tel: 01-352-9779)

In most localities, however, AA contacts and the times and places of AA meetings can be found by ringing the local AA number which will be listed in the telephone directory. As well as the regular weekly group meetings throughout the country there are Alcoholics Anonymous groups in almost every prison and in almost every hospital in which there is a specialist alcohol treatment unit.

The AA self-help process   AA is now a well-known, widely respected, rapidly spreading network engaged in a wide variety of educational and other activities. But all these activities are geared to the AA 'primary purpose', which is 'helping the still suffering alcoholic'. This is the heart of the AA self-help process and the root of all activity is the local AA group.

An AA group will be composed of, on average, fifteen or sixteen people who meet regularly to help each other to help themselves to stay sober. The only requirement for membership is a desire to stop drinking and a determination to stay stopped. There are no membership fees and no contributions are accepted from non-members. All funds to support the activities of local groups, such as the rent of meeting rooms and the purchase of AA literature, are collected from members at the end of AA meetings.

At a routine AA meeting members will talk about their alcohol problem, how it affected them, how they came to AA, and how they have been helped to cope with their problem by being 'in the fellowship'. Newcomers to the group are drawn in by identifying with these 'stories' from long-standing members.

The mutual aid process of Alcoholics Anonymous demands *openness* in several crucial ways. First, members have to be open with each other about their past, their activities, their relationships, and their emotions in order to create the necessary common bond of shared experience and understanding. Second, AA operates an open membership policy in which the characteristics which are normally used to distinguish people such as age, sex, occupation, religion, and race are ignored while the one thing which members share, their alcohol problem, is emphasized. Third, members of AA have to be open to the possibility of change. It is an essential part of the mutual aid process that members help each other to modify their self-perception, their network of friends and relationships, and even the style and content of their everyday life.

The fact that so many new groups are being set up, an increase of approximately 10 per cent per year, shows that, for many people, the AA approach to the handling of alcohol problems is acceptable and successful. For other people, however, AA is not 'the answer'. The only way for someone with a problem to find out if AA is for them is to go to an AA meeting. Similarly, those who wish to offer help and advice to someone else with an alcohol problem would also benefit from going to AA and talking to its members and finding out what is involved. Only then can any professional or concerned helper offer realistic advice to a patient or client, friend of relative.

Al-Anon and Al-Ateen   In addition to Alcoholics Anonymous there are two other organizations which are quite independent of AA but which operate on similar self-help principles; Al-Anon for the families of Alcoholics:

Al-Anon
61 Great Dover Street
London SE1 4YF
(Tel: 01-403-0888)

and Al-Ateen, for the children of alcoholics, which can be reached through Al-Anon.

This is intended to be a *living* 'guide to action'. Therefore, it needs to be revised and added to in the light of local needs and local experience.

The following two pages are for jotting down examples of good practice, and addresses relevant to the issues covered by this chapter.

We hope to update the guide, and would be delighted to receive any advice about corrections, new material or any other information which should go into the next edition. Please send all suggestions, before 31 December, 1987, to:

> Philip Tether and David Robinson
> Addiction Research Centre
> University of Hull
> Hull HU6 7RX

Examples of Good Practice

Useful Addresses and Telephone Numbers

Further reading

Alcoholics Anonymous, *Alcoholics Anonymous*, 1st edn, Works Publishing Co., New York, 1939; 2nd edn, World Services, New York, 1955

Alcoholics Anonymous, *Alcoholics Anonymous Comes of Age: A Brief History of AA*, World Services, New York, 1957

Clinebell, J.J., *Understanding and Counselling the Alcoholic*, Abingdon Press, New York, 1968

Hackney, H. and Cormier, L.S., *Counselling Strategies and Objectives*, 2nd edn, Prentice-Hall, Englewood Cliffs, New Jersey, 1979

King, B.L., LeClair, B., and O'Brien, P., 'Alcoholics Anonymous, Alcoholism Counselling, and Social Work Treatment', *Health and Social Work*, 4. 4, November 1979

Levitt, R., *The People's Voice in the NHS: Community Health Councils after Five Years*, King Edward's Hospital Fund for London, London, 1980

Marshall, S. and Velleman, R., *Training Volunteers to Counsel Problem Drinkers and their Families: A Handbook*, Addiction Research Centre, University of Hull, 1985. Now available from Alcohol Concern, 305 Gray's Inn Road, London WC1X 8QF

Maxwell, M.A., *The AA Experience: A Close-up View for Professionals*, McGraw Hill, New York, 1984

Orford, J. and Harwin, J. (eds), *Alcohol and the Family*, Croom Helm, London, 1982

Proctor, B., *Counselling Shop: An Introduction to the Theories and Techniques of Ten Approaches to Counselling*, Burnett Books, London, 1978

Rathod, N. (ed.), *Counsellor's Guide on Problem Drinking*, report of the Working Party on Treatment Goals, National Council on Alcoholism, 1981. Now available from Alcohol Concern, 305 Gray's Inn Road, London WC1X 8QF

Robinson, D., *Talking Out of Alcoholism: The Self-Help Process of Alcoholics Anonymous*, Croom Helm, London, 1979

Simnett, I., Wright, L., and Evans, M., *Drinking Choices, A Training Manual for Alcohol Educators*, Health Education Council/ TACADE, London, 1983

Tyler, L., *Work of the Counsellor*, 3rd edn, Prentice-Hall, New York, 1969

CHAPTER 10

Alcohol and the offender

277

CHAPTER 10

Alcohol and the offender

'As alcohol lessens inhibitions and to an extent weakens people's self-control it may in some individuals and in some situations lead directly to violence and crime. Links between drinking and acts of vandalism and hooliganism have been shown, particularly by young people in groups, as at football matches. . . . Other studies have shown that varying and sometimes substantial proportions of violent offenders have been drinking at the time they committed the offence.' (*Drinking Sensibly*, HMSO 1981: 14–15)

Alcohol is implicated in many kinds of offence. A survey in Torquay revealed that two-thirds of all persons arrested had been drinking in the previous four hours and that between 10 pm and 2 am – a period in which nearly half of all arrests occurred – over 90 per cent of those arrested were intoxicated. In certain offences, such as pedestrian drunkenness and drunken-driving, alcohol misuse is the offence. In others, there appears to be a strong association between drinking and criminal activity which suggests that drinking may be a significant contributory factor.

Those in close contact with offenders, such as magistrates, the police, prison officers, probation workers, and social workers have little doubt that alcohol is a major factor in a large proportion of the cases with which they deal. As the Justices' Clerks' Society has said:

'We are concerned deeply . . . as we see the effect of alcohol consumption on our daily court lists. There can be few, if any, courts which do not see as a daily occurrence the effect of excessive consumption of alcohol manifest itself in drunkenness, drunken driving and all those offences connected with public disorder, assault

279

and criminal damage. Many offences of dishonesty including burglary and theft are committed whilst in drink.'

(Licensing Law in the Eighties, 1983: 9)

This chapter discusses the many local opportunities for identifying the alcohol component of offences and the strategies which can be developed in response to them. A number of 'good practices' have been developed in several parts of the country. The task for every locality is to ensure that these good practices are promoted, to develop and extend them, and to link them with other aspects of the local prevention programme.

Magistrates' training

Magistrates administer justice at the local level. Unlike the stipendiary magistrates, they are unpaid and undertake their duties on a part-time basis. Because of the complexity of their work, magistrates must undergo prescribed training.

The training programme

Magistrates' basic training occurs in two stages, both of which must be completed within a year of their appointment. The first stage includes attendance at court as an observer and a course of instruction in:

- The magistrate's office;
- Court practice and procedure;
- The sentencing of offenders;
- The court's civil jurisdiction.

The second stage consists of visits to penal institutions and other places to which offenders may be committed, further observation in domestic and other courts, and a course of instruction in:

- Practice and procedure of magistrates' courts;
- Road traffic offences;
- Punishment and treatment;
- Probation supervision;
- Domestic proceeding;
- Miscellaneous matters.

The syllabus for these two stages of training lays down minimum requirements. Training officers can build on this foundation (see below).

All magistrates appointed since January 1980 have been required to undergo further training over and above their two-stage basic training programme. The aim of this further training is to provide a broadly based programme to widen experience and knowledge, to increase understanding and, thus, to increase confidence. Following the third anniversary of their appointment, each magistrate must undertake at least twelve hours of further training in each three-year period. There are only two prescribed further training topics:

- Training in chairmanship. As a general rule a magistrate should have substantial experience of regular court attendances before taking the chair.
- Training for the Crown Court.

The syllabus for further training is unspecific so that local programmes can meet the particular needs and interests of magistrates. Further training takes the form of evening meetings, seminars, weekend conferences, and other regular meetings to which lawyers, probation officers, and social workers are invited.

Most universities now offer facilities for stage two basic training and for further training. Full details of the structure and organization of magistrates' training can be found in *The Training of Magistrates* and *Further Training for Magistrates*, both of which are available from:

Lord Chancellor's Office
House of Lords
London SW1A 0PW
(Tel: 01-219-3000)

Training committees and training officers

There are eighty-nine Magistrates' Courts Committees in England and Wales with responsibility under the Justices of the Peace Act 1979 for administering magistrates' courts. There is one committee for each non-metropolitan country, metropolitan district, and various London areas. Committee membership is made up of magistrates elected annually by their colleagues.

Each Magistrates' Court Committee is required by the Lord

Chancellor to appoint from among its members a training committee. A training committee reviews, develops, and promotes training programmes for magistrates. Training committees can co-opt non-magistrates to help in their work but there should never be more than three co-opted members and they do not have the right to vote.

Neighbouring training committees liaise closely to avoid unnecessary duplication. The Lord Chancellor urges committees to take full advantage of the facilities offered by the Magistrates' Association and its branches, academic institutions, and any organization or group which can contribute to the education programme.

Each training committee has one or more training officers who should have knowledge and practical experience of the duties and needs of lay magistrates, their courts and committees. The vast majority of training officers are clerks to the justices or their deputies.

Schemes of Instruction

Training committees and training officers submit an outline of their proposed training programme in a 'Scheme of Instruction' to the Lord Chancellor's Office for approval. A scheme must include:

- The basic training for newly appointed magistrates;
- The basic training for magistrates following appointment to Juvenile Court Panels;
- The further training for magistrates as prescribed by the Lord Chancellor;
- Periodic visits by magistrates to penal institutions and other places to which they may commit;
- The categories of persons whose services will be utilized as tutors.

A list of topics which can be included in a scheme of instruction without further approval being obtained is issued by the Lord Chancellor's Office. The list includes 'Betting, Gaming, and Liquor Licensing' and 'Alcoholism and Crime'. If a training committee wishes to include any other topic in its scheme it must obtain specific approval from the Lord Chancellor's Office.

Local action

The requirement for magistrates to undergo local basic and further training offers excellent opportunities to develop their alcohol education. Unlike the education of some other professional groups (see especially chapter 8) there is no rigid or overcrowded training programme, while the basic programme already contains two relevant 'approved' training topics – 'liquor licensing' and 'alcoholism and crime' – and the further training syllabus is deliberately left 'open' for local development.

Both magistrates and their clerks report that alcohol education is seldom included in the training programme because of a lack of local expertise. However, they recognize the importance of the topic, so an offer of training is likely to be welcomed. The key contacts in any locality are the training officers.

Other useful contacts might be developed through a local licensing forum of the kind described in chapter 5 which would, of course, have licensing justices among its members. A discussion of liquor licensing raises many important alcohol issues and a licensing forum could help develop training in this 'approved topic' area.

The development of alcohol education for magistrates might include the production, by the local prevention group, of a small handbook which *outlines* the many ways in which alcohol misuse impinges upon a magistrate's work, *advertises* the existence and aims of the local prevention strategy, and *underlines* the presence of local educational expertise and training resources.

Cautioning schemes for drunken pedestrians

The figure for the combined finding of guilt and cautions for drunkenness offences rose sharply in 1979 but has since declined to its 1977 level. However, the figures for recent years are still higher than those of a decade ago.

Year	Total findings of guilt and cautions
1973	99,820
1975	104,990
1977	109,461
1979	118,423
1981	109,356
1983	109,724

Home Office, Statistical Bulletin Issue 16/84, *Offences of Drunkenness in England and Wales*.

The fluctuation in numbers may be due in part to changes in police practice. However, in 1981/82 per capita consumption of alcohol fell for the first time in post-war Britain from 10.4 litres of pure alcohol per adult to 9.2 litres.

Public drunkenness: a problem for policy-makers

Drunkenness itself is not an offence. Apart from certain specific offences such as being drunk in charge of a child under the age of seven and being drunk in charge of a firearm, the two main categories of drunkenness offences are:

- Simple drunkenness ('drunk and incapable') – being found drunk on a highway or other public place or unlicensed premises;
- 'Drunk and disorderly' – displaying any kind of disorderly behaviour whilst drunk in a public place.

The police exercise considerable discretion in their approach to simple drunkenness. In general, inebriates in the company of sober friends or who are not a danger to themselves or to others will not usually attract police attention. The association of disorderly behaviour with public drunkenness considerably reduces the scope for police discretion but even 'disorderliness' is open to interpretation.

Public drunkenness tends to be a nuisance and many people find it offensive. However, a major problem is posed by the habitual drunken offenders. They regularly appear in the courts and many have an alcohol problem. The constant cycling of such offenders through the courts and prisons show that fines and prison sentences have little, if any, deterrent or rehabilitative effect.

Attempts to divert habitual drunkenness offenders from the penal system go back to the nineteenth century. The Habitual Drunkards Act of 1879 enabled local authorities to license retreats for their reception, control, care, and treatment. These retreats, with a qualified medical superintendent, were private and entry to them was entirely voluntary. They were primarily a means of diverting middle-class offenders away from the penal revolving door. The Treatment of Habitual Inebriates Act of 1898 empowered a local council or private individuals to establish 'inebriate reformatories' which had a much harsher regime than the 'retreats'. Inmates could be held for a maximum of three years and the Act did not require a medical practitioner to be in attendance. Reformatories were special 'prisons for drunkards' which in effect extended the range of penalties for drunkenness laid down in the Intoxicating Liquor Licensing Act of 1872.

Fresh attempts in the UK to find alternatives to punishment for the habitual drunken offender gained momentum during the 1960s and 1970s. The aims of these efforts were to keep the habitual public drunk out of prison and to establish alternative facilities for treating and helping them. Changing penalties for drunkenness, a Home Office report, and changes in departmental responsibility for the habitual drunken offender all reflect these aims. The major landmarks were:

- Section 91(1) of the Criminal Justice Act 1967 which provided for the abolition of the short period of imprisonment which could be imposed for the offence of being drunk and disorderly. At the same time, the fine was increased to £50. However, the Act stated that imprisonment for this offence would not be abolished until sufficient, suitable accommodation became available for the care and treatment of persons being convicted of being drunk and disorderly.
- The 1971 Home Office report of the Working Party on Habitual Drunken Offenders which recommended the establishment of 'detoxification centres' to which drunks could be taken for care, assessment, and advice and from where, if necessary, further help and assistance could be arranged. The working party defined 'habitual' as more than three convictions in a year and calculated that about 16 per cent of drunken offenders fell into this category. The report also recommended the development of other local facilities such as hostels and advice centres.
- Section 34 of the Criminal Justice Act 1972 which allows the police to take public drunks to a place approved by the Secretary of State as a 'treatment centre for alcoholics'.
- In 1973 responsibility for habitual drunken offenders' rehabilitation was vested in the DHSS although, of course, the police retain responsibility for enforcing the law. DHSS Circular 21/73 urged local government and health authorities to collaborate in the provision of hostels and other services for the habitual drunken offender. 'Pump-priming' funds were made available for a limited period to encourage this development.
- The Criminal Law Act 1977 activated the provisions of the Criminal Justice Act of 1967 regarding the abolition of imprisonment for drunk and disorderly offenders. Commencement Order (No. 4) came into force on 1 February, 1978. It was argued that

'suitable accommodation' had become available. Circular 21/73 had led to over seventy hostels being established. In addition, two detoxification centres had been set up under section 34 of the Criminal Justice Act of 1972 and a third centre was planned.

Despite these initiatives, most public drunks who come to the attention of the police sober up in police cells, or in A and E departments. The range of facilities envisaged by Circular 21/73 either failed to materialize or, where they did, often failed to survive the expiry of pump-priming funding.

The attempt to keep drunkenness offenders out of prison has also largely failed. Although the Criminal Law Act of 1977 abolished imprisonment for being 'drunk and disorderly' it also increased the fines for drunkenness offences. In 1977, 2,270 people went to prison for non-payment of fines. This figure had risen to 2,698 by 1982. In the following year the figure fell to 2,467 but the trend is once again upward.

Cautioning schemes – a local solution

In 1973 a total of 540 cautions for drunken offenders were made in England and Wales. In 1983 the figure had risen to 2,099. They are likely to show a further, substantial increase due to the spread of 'cautioning schemes'.

A caution is not a substitute for an arrest but an alternative to subsequent charging and court appearance. An individual might still be arrested by a police officer for being publicly drunk but the station officer can decide to caution rather than charge. Only if a decision is made to charge will an offender appear in court.

Cautioning schemes offer potential savings in time and money if offenders can be diverted from the courts. The cost of bringing a drunken offender to court has been estimated at £115 and one study revealed that drunkenness offences occupied approximately a quarter of some London court lists. However, the potential saving of court and police time was not the only reason for introducing the pioneering cautioning scheme in 'F' District of the Metropolitan Police. It was felt that such a scheme could help to identify individuals in need of assistance which would, it was hoped, be the starting point for the development of local helping and rehabilitative services. Screening out the occasional 'one-off' offender would mean that resources would be directed where they were most needed.

The scheme which was adopted incorporated a 'cautioning threshold' fixed at three cautions within any four-week period. Individuals exceeding this threshold are charged and appear before the court where consideration is given to how to help them (see below). The establishment of a cautioning threshold results in savings for the police and the courts and provides a safety net for those in difficulty.

In outline, the operation of the scheme is simple. When a drunk is brought in, the station officer evaluates both the evidence for the arrest and the medical condition of the individual. If there is no other charge involved the station officer will check the records to ensure that the offender has not accumulated three cautions during the four preceding weeks. During detention, the offender's medical condition is checked regularly to ensure there is no deterioration. When a detainee is sufficiently sober to understand the circumstances, then the caution will be given.

Cautioning schemes are spreading. In a national survey of police forces carried out at the end of 1983, six had introduced schemes. Three of these have the same cautioning threshold as 'F' District while the other three have no cautioning threshold at all. A further five forces indicated that cautioning schemes were being seriously considered.

Local action

Cautioning schemes for drunkenness offenders are an important development. At best, they offer an opportunity for saving police and court time, screening out the occasional offender and identifying a core of problem drinkers. However, their introduction, content, and implementation needs to be developed in conjunction with other local agencies who have a responsibility to respond to the alcohol problem. Unfortunately, it seems that some of the cautioning schemes have not had the benefit of full local debate.

A key issue for local discussion must be the cautioning threshold. It has been argued that three cautions in four weeks filters out most of those with a severe drinking problem. However, 'F' District's experience reveals that some habitual offenders, already known to the police, escape a court appearance because of this threshold. A locality considering the introduction of a scheme or reviewing an existing one could pay close attention to the threshold which it feels would identify the core of individuals needing help. The 1971 Home Office report of the Working Party on Habitual Drunken Offenders defined 'habitual' as more than three convictions in a year. This definition could form a starting point for local debate about cautioning thresholds. There is, of course, nothing to prevent a cautioning threshold being changed in the light of local debate, research, and experience. But whatever the cautioning threshold adopted, localities could make some alcohol education material available for all those who are cautioned. A cautioning scheme offers an excellent opportunity for providing basic education to a group of individuals who have, by legal definition, been misusing alcohol. This opportunity should not be ignored. None of the current schemes supply such material to offenders, although it is being discussed in 'F' District.

The new Criminal Evidence Bill proposes that police stations should have a custody officer on duty at all times. This may well tend to further establish the local police station as an informal detoxification centre. Another development which might affect the public drunkenness issue concerns official records. In the past drunkenness cautions have been recorded nationally and incorporated into the Home Office statistics – for instance, Home Office Statistical Bulletin Issue 16/84 has a table headed 'Total Findings of Guilt and Cautions'. This may not be so in the future. It has been suggested that cautioning records should only be collected locally and not aggregated into national figures.

The spread of cautioning schemes combined with the lack in some of those schemes of a threshold, the increasing use of police stations as 'sobering up' centres and no national record of cautionings could result in the public drunkenness problem becoming much less visible.

The introduction of any police cautioning scheme clearly has major implications for local services. There is little point in identifying people in need of help or assistance if, at the end of the day, there are no facilities available. Any locality which hopes to turn a police cautioning scheme for drunken offenders into something more than a means of removing a difficult problem from view must decide what kind of a scheme they want, why, and what complementary community provision is needed. The introduction of a scheme should involve not only alcohol agencies, but also housing departments, the social services and the health authority.

The participants in a local prevention strategy, involved in debates about the development of a police cautioning scheme and the provision of facilities for drunkenness offenders might find it useful to contact Out of Court, an umbrella body for organizations working to keep drunken offenders out of prison. Out of Court is serviced by, but separate from, Action on Alcohol Abuse and can be contacted via 'Triple A' at:

Livingstone House
11 Cartaret Street
London SW1H 9DL
(Tel: 01-222-3454/5)

The probation service

The probation service has its roots in the work of the Police Court
Missionaries who in the late nineteenth century were sponsored by the
Church of England Temperance Society to 'rescue' habitual drunks
from the courts. Concern for offenders' alcohol problems diminished as
the service developed and its responsibilities grew. However, it is now
increasingly recognized that many clients have an alcohol problem and
that this must be tackled if the probation service is to meet its
obligations to offenders.

The aims and structure of the service

Probation officers are court social workers charged with the care of
offenders who are the subject of probation and supervision orders, the
welfare of prisoners in custody, and their resettlement after discharge.
A probation officer's task is to befriend offenders and to provide the
counselling, advice, guidance, and support necessary to encourage the
development of a stable and responsible style of life.

Any offender aged seventeen or over can be placed on probation
provided that the law does not require a fixed sentence for the offence.
A probation order can be made for any period between six months and
three years. An offender *must* consent to a probation order being made.
A probation order is not a sentence but an alternative to a sentence.
This alternative requires an offender to be supervised and to abide by
the conditions of the order. The basic conditions are printed on the
order itself and usually require the probationer to:

- Be of good behaviour and lead an industrious life;
- Inform the supervising probation officer immedi ely of any
  change of address or employment;
- Keep in touch with the supervising probation officer in accordance
  with instructions and receive visits at home.

A wide range of other conditions can be added to an order requiring an offender to participate in, or refrain from, certain activities. If probationers do not abide by these conditions they may reappear in court.

Juveniles between the ages of ten and sixteen can be made the subject of a supervision order. These orders can be roughly described as the junior equivalent of probation orders, but an offender's consent to the order is not required and greater emphasis is placed on supervisory contact with parents, schools, and other individuals and organizations in a position to influence and guide the offender. In many localities the social service and probation service share responsibility for these young people with, for example, social workers supervising the 10–14-year age group and probation officers the 14–16-year age group.

Following the Children and Young Persons Act of 1969, as amended by the Criminal Justice Act of 1982, juveniles on supervision orders can be required, as a condition of the order, to participate in local programmes of activity known collectively as Intermediate Treatment (IT). A requirement to participate in IT can be made under section 12 of the Children and Young Persons Act 1969 or section 12.3(c) of the Criminal Justice Act 1982. IT programmes are funded by local authorities, which are required to draw up an official IT scheme. In drawing up this scheme, authorities consult probation committees, which can contribute to the cost of the programme.

The service is responsible for preparing social enquiry reports (SERs) for the courts, although local authority social workers will usually complete SERs for very young offenders. An SER is an investigation into an offender's background, circumstances, character and personality, in order to assist the court to determine the best way of dealing with the case.

SERs are not standardized and in general services resist the notion of a common format. Although the SER format will vary from area to area, they will usually consist of a minimum proforma front sheet where basic personal details can be recorded, followed by a series of blank pages. SERs will usually include the officer's conclusion as to the best way of dealing with the offender.

The organization of each local probation service is coterminous with non-metropolitan County Councils, metropolitan County Councils, and London boroughs. There are fifty-six probation areas in England and Wales. Each service is headed by a chief probation officer (CPO) who is assisted, in the large metropolitan area, by a deputy chief probation officer (DCPO). Elsewhere, CPOs are supported by assistant chief probation officers (ACPOs). These senior officers have their own organization, the Association of Chief Officers of Probation (ACOP). At the time of writing ACOP is seeking premises for its new Secretariat, which will be established in April 1986. Every probation service will have this address.

Each local probation service is divided into a number of districts for each of which a team of probation officers is responsible. Each team is headed by a senior probation officer (SPO). Whilst the majority of teams are geographically based there will be some involved with the organization and running of specific functions such as bail hostels or probation day centres.

Central government makes a grant of 80 per cent toward the running of each local probation service. Each service is administered by a probation committee which is composed of magistrates. The CPO is the professional adviser to the probation committee which has power to co-opt members to help them in their work.

Probation teams are assisted by voluntary helpers as a result of an attempt made in the late 1960s to draw upon community resources. Voluntary helpers are accredited and assist the service in many different ways. In Birmingham probation officers are assisted by a Court Alcohol Service which has been developed by the alcohol agency Aquarius. It works closely with the probation service and its purpose is to help people recognize and deal with the reasons for their offending when it is through drink. Magistrates can recommend that a defendant visit the court service, both for a named drink offence and when the offence is drink-related – be it assault, criminal damage, debt, or theft. The service assists magistrates with verbal and written opinions and probation officers are invited to discuss clients' drinking problems with the service. They can ask for a written opinion on an SER (see above) whenever they feel it might be of assistance. Further details can be obtained from:

Court Alcohol Service
3rd Floor, The White House
111 New Street
Birmingham B2 4EU

Every probation service has a wide range of resources, activities, and programmes for offenders under its supervision. Third parties can assist the service in its work with offenders. Schemes and any premises involved must be approved by the local probation committee (see below) under Schedule 11 of the Criminal Justice Act 1982.

Alcohol initiatives

A growing number of local services are developing alcohol initiatives. These include attendance at an alcohol education group as a condition of probation order, training programmes for probation staff, and links with other organizations. A survey of the fifty-six probation services in England and Wales revealed that very few had no activities in this area. The initiatives from four services described below indicate the wide range of activities that are possible in relation to alcohol problems.

Northamptonshire   In its work with problem drinkers this service has developed alcohol education groups for probationers and links with the many local organizations and services which offer help and support. Its activities include:

- Promoting alcohol education with clients who attend a group as a condition of their probation order. Groups meet twice weekly over six or eight weeks.
- Representation on the local authority – health authority, Joint Care Planning Team for Adult Mental Health – Alcoholism.
- Producing, with the police, a video-tape 'C2H5OH' which deals with alcohol-related crime among juveniles. It has received extensive publicity in the local press and on radio and television and is shown in schools and youth clubs.

All these activities, initiatives, and links are supplementing individual counselling provided by Northamptonshire probation officers.

Lancashire   This service has promoted alcohol education groups in various parts of the county and in different settings and has developed an interesting computer initiative. Its activities include:

- Developing an alcohol education group in a probation day centre for both probationers subject to day centre orders and others who attend voluntarily. The programme of meetings is short and the mixed clientele appears to present no problems.
- An alcohol education group has been established in Lancaster prison led by members of Alcoholics Anonymous. Prisoners are informed of the group's existence on reception and although problem drinkers are actively encouraged to attend, individuals do so voluntarily. Probation officers in the prison work actively with AA members.

- A computer learning program has been devised to enable clients to explore their own problems and difficulties. Clients can work on their own and information can be stored so that they can check their progress. A print-out of drinking patterns and progress is given to the client for discussion with family members. This method is very useful with clients who do not readily respond to normal interview or group techniques.

Cheshire A senior probation officer in this service has devised several computer packages for problem drinkers. They are written for the Sinclair Spectrum 48k and used extensively by clients. The three programs are:

- 'You Know All About Drink Do You?', which is a twenty-question quiz where participants are asked to select one of four options designed to identify knowledge about alcohol, its effects, and the problems it can cause. Incorrect answers trigger an immediate on-screen explanation of the correct response.
- 'What's Your Poison?' is another questionnaire taken directly from the BBC publication of the same name with a graphic on-screen analysis of the results and description of vulnerability to problem drinking.
- 'mg' is a simple questionnaire that produces a print-out of levels of blood/alcohol taking account of sex, weight, amount drunk, and time of drinking.

Essex In addition to developing alcohol education groups this service has sought to promote an organizational commitment in the problem drinking area. Its measures include the following:

- Each of the service's districts has two or three officers designated as an information resource who act as consciousness-raisers. These officers meet as a Problem Drinking Resource Group three or four times a year.
- Seminars are held from time to time for probation officers *and* voluntary workers.
- A strategy document entitled *You Can Work with Drinkers Can't You?* produced by the ACOP in the training region (see below) has encouraged the Essex service to prepare a statement of intent as a basis for incorporating work with problem drinkers more explicitly within its annual Statement of Objectives and Priorities.

Local action

The probation service's many duties and responsibilities toward offenders of all kinds makes it well-placed to identify and respond to clients' alcohol problems. In many localities the probation service is developing initiatives to identify and help probationers with alcohol-related problems. Every probation service should be encouraged to develop a comprehensive set of activities and strategies based upon the good practices and models already available.

An alcohol education group for probationers is likely to be the most visible part of any programme and those involved in other areas of a local prevention programme could offer support and help, possibly by organizing a probationers' group as an approved local resource under Schedule 11 of the Criminal Justice Act 1982.

Any education initiatives in relation to alcohol and the offender need not be restricted to probationer's groups. Intermediate Treatment programmes offer an opportunity for developing basic alcohol education with a group of at risk young people. Social services will have designated staff with specific IT responsibilities and their attention could be drawn to the wide range of alcohol education materials for young people which could be used in IT work.

The development of alcohol education initiatives for probationers or young people on IT programmes must be built on the workers' awareness and knowledge of alcohol-related problems and confidence in their ability to respond. There are opportunities in every locality for contributing to the basic and continuing training of both social workers and probation officers.

Like social workers, probation officers take the CQSW as a basic qualification. The structure and content of the CQSW is outlined in chapter 8 which also gives information on the in-service training undertaken by social workers. The in-service training of probation officers is organized in conjunction with the regional staff development service located in four regions in England and Wales. Each local service will also have an officer with specific responsibility for in-service training. These will usually be assistant chief probation officers, who combine this responsibility with other duties. The regional staff development service is funded by local probation committees – whose representatives sit on the regional staff development committee.

Regional service development officers help to identify local training needs and to develop appropriate responses. They, along with local officers with a responsibility for in-service training, are key contacts for anyone who can make a contribution to the further training of probation officers.

Training provided for probation and social workers could usefully raise the issue of whether SER forms should be redesigned to incorporate automatically information on clients' drinking habits.

It would be helpful if each local service could be encouraged to appoint a specific officer with responsibility for developing the local service's response to offenders' alcohol-related problems. Such an officer would be an obvious candidate to attend a 'Drinking Choices' course, thus providing a local service with an information and education resource. An appointment of this kind would also increase the visibility of the 'alcohol and the offender' issue within the local probation service and underline its commitment to developing a comprehensive response. An eventual aim might be to incorporate this commitment into the annual statement of objectives and priorities which many services produce.

Together with local social services and health authorities, a probation service has an interest in the provision of accommodation for individuals with alcohol-related problems and an important role to play in local initiatives to develop such accommodation. The provision of hostel accommodation for problem drinkers is one important component of a local prevention strategy. A number of agencies including, of course, the probation and social services, will be involved in the negotiations that precede such initiatives. However, there are other forms of accommodation than hostels. A local probation service could seek to negotiate, with the housing department, for some public sector housing units, perhaps maisonettes, to be allocated to probationers with both drinking and housing problems whose chances of rehabilitation would be enhanced by such help.

The drunken-driving offender

Convictions in England and Wales for driving while unfit through drink or drugs, including convictions for failing to provide a specimen for analysis, have shown a steady increase in recent years (see table on page 296). In part, these figures reflect the high priority which many

Convictions for drunken-driving in England and Wales – driving whilst unfit through drink or drugs

Year	Number of offences
1973	61,000
1975	65,000
1977	53,000
1979	67,000
1981	71,000
1983	98,000

Home Office, *Statistical Bulletin*, 18/85

police forces now give to apprehending the drunken driver, recent streamlining of the testing procedure, and the closing of certain loopholes in the drunken-driving law. However, these changes have not created drunken drivers – they have merely uncovered them.

This section focuses on the offender. It should be read in conjunction with chapter 4 which examines alcohol and road safety from the point of view of prevention. Details of useful drinking and driving educational materials can be found in chapters 6 and 7.

The legal limit in the UK

In 1983 there were 20.2 million vehicles licensed for road use. The Road Traffic Act of 1967 made it an automatic offence to drive, attempt to drive, or be in charge of a motor vehicle in a public place if blood/alcohol content (BAL) exceeds 80 milligrammes in 100 millilitres of blood (80 mg/100 ml). This Act introduced the breathalyzer as a screening test which, if positive, was followed by an evidential blood or urine test taken at a police station and then sent away for analysis.

The Act had a dramatic initial effect in reducing alcohol-related accidents and driving offences but this beneficial result soon began to fade. By 1974 the problems associated with the Act had become so acute that a working party was set up 'to review the operation of the law and make recommendations'. The subsequent Blennerhassett Report advocated, among other things, that the government should look at new devices with a view to improving roadside screening and introducing evidential breath testing in police stations instead of taking blood and urine samples.

Following extensive investigations of many devices which showed that breath testing was a practical possibility, Parliament approved the Transport Act 1981 which allows such tests to be used in court proceedings. The legal breath/alcohol limit is 35 microgrammes of alcohol in 100 millilitres of breath 35 ug/100 ml).

Penalties comparable in scale to those for drunken-driving must be imposed for refusing a specimen. Despite the concentration on the 'legal limit' as the focus of our drinking and driving law it is still an offence to drive with less than the legal limit if the amount of alcohol consumed renders a driver 'unfit'. This is, of course, often a difficult charge to substantiate.

Eight European countries have the same alcohol limit as the UK. However, ten European countries, including Sweden, Norway, and Greece, have lower limits. In Bulgaria it is an offence to drive with any alcohol in the body.

The process of bringing an offender to court is important. All offenders are subject to roadside arrest, but, thereafter events may take one of two courses. In the first, arrest is followed by charge when the evidence has been presented to the appropriate station officer. The offender is then bailed or held in custody. The police are then responsible for arranging a court appearance which can be as soon as they wish. In the other procedure, the evidence is considered by the police and then laid before the magistrates who authorises a summons, which is an instruction to appear in court on a given date.

Summons were more appropriate when the drink-driving law contained a number of procedural complexities and loopholes and samples of blood and urine had to be sent away for analysis. Many of these loopholes have now been closed and the introduction of the evidential breath test provides immediate evidence of an offence, although motorists do have both a statutory and a non-statutory right to alternative tests (see below).

Appearance in court could be considerably speeded up if offenders were arrested, charged, and bailed instead of being brought to court by summons. Moreover, it might be thought that the arrest-charge-bail procedure more adequately reflects the gravity of the offence and might well have a salutory effect on the individuals involved. In most forces, arrest and charge for drink-driving offenders is unusual except where other offences are involved. But, in the final analysis, the choice of which procedure to follow lies entirely with the police. Here is an area of considerable interest and potential where local action could have a significant affect on the way drink-driving offenders are viewed and treated.

Safeguards for the motorist

The motorist has a number of safeguards:

- The 1981 Transport Act requires a motorist to provide two samples and court proceedings are taken on the lower of the two readings.
- When blood/alcohol (or urine/alcohol) measurements were the evidential test the Forensic Science Laboratories deducted 6 per cent from the mean result of the blood/urine analysis when reporting their findings. A similar allowance is now made for breath tests. Thus, in practice, readings between 36 ug and 40 ug per 100 ml breath do not lead to prosecution. In other words, the legal limit is not what it is commonly understood to be.
- If the lower reading is between 36 and 50 ug, i.e. equivalent to a blood/alcohol concentration of between 80 and 115 mg per 100 ml blood, the motorist has the right to ask for an alternative blood or urine sample be taken. The resultant analysis replaces the breath analysis in any court proceedings. Above 50 ug, the law does not allow alternative samples.

The new evidential breath testing machines became operative throughout the UK on 6 May, 1983. From the first, claims were made that the machines were defective. The popular press and motorists' defence organizations mounted a vigorous campaign around these allegations claiming that all motorists should have the option of a blood or urine test whatever their breath reading.

Following these claims the machines were re-evaluated over a period covering April–October 1984. Motorists with alcohol/breath readings of 51 ug and upwards were given the right to a blood or urine test. These tests did not substitute for the breath test but provided an additional check. In effect, motorists were volunteering to participate in an evaluation programme. This non-statutory option for motorists with breath readings of 51 ug plus is being retained whilst machines undergo the slight modifications needed. In the meantime motorists' defence organizations are continuing their campaign to have the temporary, non-statutory right to alternative tests made permanent.

Procedures for identifying drinking and driving offenders must be fair and be seen to be fair. However, a number of important safeguards do exist and anyone interested in the drunken-driving issue should be aware of their details. Not only are they interesting and raise many issues, but they have an important bearing on the often ill-informed debates that have surrounded evidential breath testing.

The powers of the police to test

It is claimed that the powers of the police to stop and test suspected offenders are too limited. Police officers currently have the power to breath test a motorist who commits a moving traffic offence, is involved in an accident, or they have 'reasonable cause' to believe that the motorist has alcohol in their body. The first two grounds for testing are unproblematic and, of course, a 'moving traffic offence' can cover everything including the slightest infringements of the traffic law. The problem is held to occur with the third ground when the officer has to have 'reasonable cause'. Driving too slowly and with excessive care could provide an officer who is so minded with the justification for administering a test. Smelling alcohol on the breath of a driver stopped for a routine check of any kind (not necessarily for a traffic infringement) would also be sufficient justification. In other words, the form of words in the legislation which confers upon police officers the right to require a breath test is elastic and open to interpretation.

Random testing is a term which is often used interchangeably with discretionary testing but it is clearly quite different. The introduction of 'discretionary' testing would remove completely any restrictions upon police officers to request a breath test, but testing would still be guided by a suspicion of guilt. By contrast, 'random' testing is exactly what it says – the testing of motorists on a purely random basis such as, say, every tenth car. Calls for 'random testing' usually really mean 'discretionary' testing.

It is argued that a widening of police powers would have considerable deterrent effect. Since the introduction of the breathalyzer in 1967 the number of roadside tests has increased by over 300 per cent and, overall, convictions appear to have had a fairly direct relationship with the number of tests. Thus, if drinking patterns remain stable an increased number of breath tests is likely to increase the number of convictions.

The possible enhancement of police powers is something which all those concerned with drinking and driving will want to debate. Of more immediate local importance will be how the police interpret the considerable powers which current legislation confers on them. The overall rise in breath tests administered conceals wide variations across the country, and these in turn yield very different positive and negative results. Juxtaposing neighbouring forces' breath test figures and convictions will give an interesting insight into the importance and effectiveness of local drink-driving policy.

A survey of the drinking and driving behaviour of over 3,000 drivers in England and Wales was recently commissioned by the Home Office as part of the 1982 British Crime Survey. The survey sought to identify not only drinking and driving habits, but also drivers' knowledge of the penalties that could be incurred and their beliefs about how much they could drink before failing a roadside test. The survey assumed that five units of alcohol would take most drivers up the 'legal limit'. A 'unit' of alcohol is one half-pint of beer, a single measure of spirits, a glass of wine, or their equivalent.

When asked about drinking and driving, 24 per cent of men and 7 per cent of women in the sample reported having driven in the previous year after drinking five or more units of alcohol. There were also considerable differences between different age groups:

Survey of drinking and driving behaviour

Reported driving over the 'limit'	Men drivers			Women drivers		
	16–30	*31–60*	*61+*	*16–30*	*31–60*	*61+*
Never	63	75	94	88	95	100
1–9 times	23	18	5	10	4	0
10–40 times	9	4	1	2	1	0
More than 40 times	5	4	1	0	0	0
Average number of times	4.6	2.9	0.5	0.6	0.3	0

D Riley, Research Bulletin No. 17, *Drivers' Beliefs about Alcohol and The Law*, Home Office, 1984

Extrapolation of these rates indicate that during the survey year there were approximately 25 million drinking and driving occasions on which motorists were very likely to fail a test. When compared with the number of drink-driving convictions it appears that drinking drivers' chances of being apprehended and convicted are in the order of 1:250.

The most interesting feature of the survey was that many 'offenders' over-estimated the amount of alcohol which could take them over the legal driving limit. It has been argued that education about how much it is 'safe' to drink before driving may have the affect of encouraging drivers to drink up to the limit. However, the survey indicates that education and publicity about the quantity of alcohol that can be consumed before the limit is reached may have some affect in reducing drink-driving offences.

A study carried out by the Transport and Road Research Laboratory, entitled *The Male Drinking Driver: Characteristics of the Offender and His Offence*, collected data on 1,032 male drivers charged with drink-driving offences in Birmingham during an eighteen-month period from 1 January, 1976. It was found that:

> 'Overall, 1 in 7 offenders (14.9%) had a previous conviction or convictions for an alcohol-related motoring offence during the past ten years. One offender in 11 (9.1%) had at least one previous conviction for an alcohol-related non-motoring offence. Convictions for driving whilst disqualified were rare (3.1%) but a third of offenders (32.6%) had current endorsements for further motoring offences. Previous 'criminal' convictions were fairly common (23.3%).'

It is unusual for records of non-motoring offences to be produced in a traffic court. However, such records might be of great use to concerned magistrates seeking to use existing disability legislation to remove drunken drivers with an alcohol problem from the roads (see below).

The high-risk offender procedure

The Road Traffic Act 1972, as amended by the Road Traffic Act 1974, obliges applicants for, and holders of, a motor vehicle licence to notify the Secretary of State for Transport of any 'relevant or prospective disability' which may affect their competence to drive. Sections 5 and 6 of the current application for a driving licence asks questions about eyesight, general health, and any disabling conditions. Since January 1976 licences run to the holder's seventieth birthday. After that date licences can be granted up to a maximum of three years but their issue may be dependent upon a doctor's report.

In addition, the legislation requires courts and insurers to notify the Secretary of State of any disability which may come to their attention. Section 92 of the Road Traffic Act of 1972 requires courts to notify the Secretary of State of any disability which comes to their attention during proceedings for an offence committed in respect of a motor vehicle and the same section requires insurers to do the same if they refuse a motor insurance policy on the grounds of health.

However, the law places no legal obligation on medical practitioners to notify the licensing authority of patients' conditions which may impair their ability to drive safely. Doctors have a professional duty to warn their patients of the risks to themselves and others and they must do their best to persuade such patients to give up driving voluntarily. If the patient refuses to listen it is up to the doctor to decide whether to notify the authorities. N. L. Taylor in *Doctors and the Law* observed:

'As in the case of criminal revelations, it will be difficult to condemn the doctor if he decided that his duty as a citizen over-ruled his duty as a doctor.'

If there are reasonable grounds for believing that a person who is an applicant for, or the holder of, a licence may be suffering from a 'relevant or prospective disability' then the Secretary of State may:

- Require a registered medical practitioner to make available relevant medical facts on the applicant or holder;
- Require the applicant or holder to submit to a medical test by a practitioner nominated by the Secretary of State;
- Require the applicant or holder to submit to a 'test of competence' appropriate to the class of vehicle involved.

Notifications of disability are handled by:

Medical Advisory Branch of the Department of Transport
Oldway Centre
Orchard Street
Swansea SA1 1TU
(Tel: 0792-42091)

The Medical Advisory Branch receives approximately 600 notifications per day of possible cases of disability. The branch examines these notifications and recommends appropriate action. The notifications stem from a number of sources. The great majority are from families worried about the ability of a relation to drive safely. Some come from the police, when accident investigations have revealed a driver to be suffering from some disability. A few come from insurance companies although they usually deal with drivers who are health risks through loading the premium rather than refusing to insure.

In 1976 the Department of the Environment Departmental Committee Report, *Drinking and Driving* – the Blennerhassett Report – said in section 1.23:

'the present law allows a person with a drinking problem to have his licence returned to him automatically after a period of disqualification, not withstanding that his condition may be undiagnosed and untreated. . . . Analysis of convictions shows that of those who are disqualified, at least one in ten repeats the offence within ten years, and it is unlikely that mere recklessness is the only explanation. Repeat offenders also show on average a significantly higher BAC than first offenders. We are in no doubt that, as in other countries which have studied the characteristics of drinking drivers, alcoholism is a factor in the situation; and that special measures are needed in response to it.'

The Committee went on to recommend procedures to identify high-risk offenders who could be removed from the road until they had received appropriate treatment and help for their drinking problem. Although the committee's recommendations were not followed exactly, a high-risk offender (HRO) procedure was introduced in May 1983. The procedure is based on the 'disability' legislation.

The HRO procedure comes into effect when an offender has incurred two drink-driving convictions (or one conviction for drunken-driving and one for refusing to provide a specimen) within a ten-year period with a BAC of over 200 mg/100 ml – which is two and a half times the legal driving limit. A second drink-driving conviction at any BAC level automatically carries with it a three-year disqualification. At the start of this disqualification period all HROs receive a letter from the Driver Vehicle Licensing Centre (DVLC) advising them that they may have a problem, where to receive help, and informing them that they will be required to undergo an examination at the end of the disqualification period in order to establish their competence to drive. It is made clear to offenders that, if this test is 'positive', they will not get back their licence at the end of the disqualification period. The examinations are carried out at ten centres in the UK and are accompanied by blood tests which are carried out centrally.

The new HRO procedure is a welcome first step in removing dangerous drivers from the roads and ensuring that they obtain help. However, many would argue that the definition of an HRO is pitched much too high and secures only a proportion of repeat offenders who clearly cannot use alcohol responsibly and may well have a 'problem'. If magistrates and others concerned with drinking and driving are unhappy with the present definition, there is nothing, in principle, to prevent them notifying the DVLC of any offender who they suspect has a problem. They have been urged to do exactly that by the Blennerhassett Report which said in section 7.10:

> 'it will occasionally be apparent to the court trying an offender who is not within . . . the proposed high-risk category . . . that he may be dependent upon alcohol or some other drug. We would like to see use made in these cases, and in cases of other traffic offences, of the provision (Section 92 of the 1972 Road Traffic Act) that the court should notify the licensing authority, since addiction to alcohol or a drug is clearly a disease or a disability which will be likely to cause the driving by them of motor vehicles to be a source of danger to the public.'

The soundness of this advice is underlined by a recent study of 440 convicted drunken drivers in Tayside, which found evidence of chronic excessive drinking in a fifth of the sample and in one third of those aged over thirty. Drivers of heavy goods and public service vehicles arrested were more likely than the average to have the raised levels of a liver enzyme which point to regular excessive drinking. The report went on to say that present methods of identifying motorists with an alcohol problem do, on this evidence, seem inadequate.

The problem, of course, lies in obtaining evidence of a 'problem'. The most obvious approach would be to take the principle of the HRO procedure but amend it locally in terms of breath/blood alcohol content levels, or offences in a specific period, or both.

In practice, a magistrate would have difficulty in estabilishing his or her own HRO procedure based on the existing disability legislation because breath/blood alcohol levels are not recorded on an offender's licence, nor on the form DQ3 from the DVLC which can be applied for if there is any doubt that a licence cannot be produced in court. The only records of alcohol levels on past offences available to courts are found on their own copies of the D20 form which are used to inform the DVLC of motoring convictions which require an endorsement. Convicted motorists' licences and the accompanying D20s are sent by courts, in batches, daily to the DVLC for processing. The form D20 has space for recording the 'alcohol level' for motorists convicted of drunken-driving charges, but instructions to the courts require the section to be filled out only if the alcohol content is:

65 or more ug of alcohol in 100 ml of breath
150 or more mg of alcohol in 100 ml of blood
201 or more mg of alcohol in 100 ml of urine.

A court's copies of D20s would thus not be of any use if the local HRO procedure was pitched below the notifiable levels. Moreover, even if it was at or above the amounts recorded on D20s, considerable administrative effort would be involved in extracting and presenting the figures.

These difficulties would be eliminated if endorsed licences displayed blood/breath/alcohol levels for drunken-driving convictions, thus supplying important information about the offence and the offender. Pending this obvious reform, the difficulties could be circumvented if a court decided to record all levels above the legal limit for all convicted offenders. This would need only to be a very simple record system to fulfil its purpose – to provide the courts with the information they need to decide whether, under their own 'local HRO procedure', a drunken-driving offender appears to have an alcohol problem and should, therefore, be referred under the existing 'disability legislation' to the DVLC.

Non-traffic criminal records are another means of establishing whether an offender has a problem (see above). These could be called for automatically in all repeat cases or, indeed, in first offences where the level of alcohol in the breath or blood appears particularly high, or where there are other serious features to the case. Magistrates would need to devise guidelines for the police to ensure that, say, simple drunkenness and drunk and disorderly conviction records were available to the court in drunken-driving cases of a certain type or gravity. Given the spread of cautioning schemes (see above), cautioning records might also be needed. Of course, police records only 'say' so much. A series of offences of breach of the peace (section 5, Public Order Act 1936) may all involve drink but will not be recorded as such, although a reference to the offender's condition will appear on the charging documents held on police files. Nevertheless, important and relevant information can be obtained from police records. There will, inevitably, be great resistance to setting up additional court procedures and assembling appropriate information. It will take time and some trouble. However, given that the aim is to remove potential killers from the road, it would be a worthwhile exercise.

Finally, it has been suggested that GPs should be told of patients' drink-driving convictions – something which is done in many other countries. The Tayside study (see above), which surveyed 440 convicted drunken drivers, found that a substantial proportion displayed evidence of chronic excessive drinking. At present most GPs do not know which patients who drive have drink difficulties, and so cannot offer help. There is nothing to prevent a notification system being developed in a locality if this was thought desirable. Such a move would require negotiation with the courts and the Local Medical Committee (LMC) which represents GPs in an area. Issues of privacy and confidentiality would undoubtedly figure in discussions about such an initiative. However, the fact is that, ultimately, convictions obtained in an open court are a matter of 'public record'.

Sentencing offenders

The maximum penalty for a drunken driving or driving with excess alcohol conviction is £2,000, disqualification for at least twelve months (unless 'special reasons' apply), endorsement of the licence and/or six months' imprisonment. Disqualification must be for at least three years if there has been another conviction for drunken-driving in the previous ten years.

The Magistrates' Association offers 'suggestions' for courts' assessment of penalties for the main traffic offences. These are *not* a fixed tariff of penalties and courts *must* take into account the individual circumstances surrounding each offence and, crucially, the defendant's ability to pay the fines imposed. The current Magistrates Association's suggestions for the offence of drunken-driving or driving with excess alcohol are:

BAC (mg per 100ml)	Fine	Disqualification
80 mg-150 mg	£120	1 year
150 mg-200 mg	–	18 months
200 mg-250 mg	–	2 years
250 mg-	–	3 years

Whilst the Magistrates' Association indicates that £120 is an appropriate penalty for an 'average' offence committed by a first offender of average means it also says that:

'Experience has proved that drinking and driving offences account for very many accidents, injuries and deaths. The Court of Appeal has consistently upheld high penalties for offenders with higher blood/alcohol, and it is suggested that fines and especially periods of disqualification should reflect this.'

The notes emphasize that local variations will occur since, among other things, average rates of pay are much higher in some areas than in others. The 'suggestions' leave a column blank for each bench to insert its norm and the Association urges magistrates to complete this column for their area after considering the Association's 'suggestions' and consulting neighbouring benches.

Copies of *Suggestions for Traffic Offence Penalties* can be obtained from:

The Magistrates' Association
28 Fitzroy Square
London W1P 6DD
(Tel: 01-387-2301)

Some benches have taken a much tougher line with drink-driving offenders than is suggested by the Magistrates' Association. The Grays Bench of Magistrates in Essex has made headlines on a number of occasions with heavy fines, lengthy periods of disqualification, and custodial sentences even for first offenders. Offenders with twice the legal amount of blood/alcohol have been sentenced to short periods of imprisonment under section 134 of the Magistrates' Courts Act 1980, which empowers magistrates to sentence offenders to police cell custody up to a maximum of four days, although this strategy is dependent upon having cells approved by the Home Office for such a purpose. Participants in a local prevention strategy might wish to ascertain whether their area has any such cells and, if not, whether they would wish to see them introduced.

Despite the Association's 'suggestions', widely differing sentencing policies appear to exist across the country, and even within the same region. Sentencing is important since it has a major part to play in establishing the 'visibility' of drink-driving issues in a locality and shaping public attitudes toward the offence which, too often, is still seen as merely a misdemeanour.

A new group which is particularly interested in ensuring that drunken-driving penalties reflect the seriousness of the offence is the Campaign Against Drinking and Driving (CADD). Its press release states its purpose is to bring about the following changes:

- *Bail* to be allowed after a positive breath test only on condition that driving licence is surrendered prior to the case being heard;
- *Case* to be heard within weeks rather than months;
- *Working* towards a reduction in the allowed blood-alcohol level until it is zero rated;
- *Bringing* a charge of manslaughter against drunken drivers who kill innocent people;

- *Monitoring* court cases and protesting when sentence is only token or trivial;
- *Allowing* victims the same rights of appeal as are allowed to a criminal.

It also aims to provide help and support to victims and families in the following ways:

- *To prepare* a victim information pamphlet explaining their rights and what they are entitled to do and know;
- *To prepare* a victim pamphlet offering advice on how to cope with the unique grief of parents;
- *To prepare* a victim pamphlet offering advice on how to help children to cope with death in the family;
- *To give* supportive help and guidance to families who have suffered a tragedy at the hands of a drunken, reckless, or careless driver.

CADD can be contacted through Action on Alcohol Abuse – 'Triple A' – at:

Campaign Against Drinking and Driving
Livingstone House
11 Carteret Street
London SW1H 9DL
(Tel: 01-222-3454/5)

The encouragement and promotion of a high-profile sentencing policy is not incompatible with alcohol education for drink-driving offenders. Indeed, it may be argued that they are two options in any considered local response to drink-driving offenders. Alcohol education for offenders is unusual. Only a very small number of drivers are put on probation orders, and an even smaller number find their way, as a condition of the order, onto alcohol education groups (described above). Probation orders for drink-driving offenders are, in general, seen as inappropriate and unsuitable, since the offence is not 'criminal'. However, if drunken-driving is considered to be a serious offence then a probation order, particularly one which includes a condition of attendance at an alcohol education group, is surely an appropriate response.

Hampshire Probation Service has pioneered an alcohol education group specifically for drunken-driving offenders, and its scheme is being studied in Yorkshire, Warwickshire, Berkshire, and Kent. The Department of Transport has ruled that the course can help an HRO offender (see above) to get his licence back if the probation officer in charge gives a good report on the offender's progress on the course.

Offenders attend the course for two hours each week for eight weeks. A written project must be completed after each session. These cover:

Week 1: Getting to know the different strengths of drinks.

Week 2: How alcohol affects the body.

Week 3: An American police study, on film, is shown to display how even highly trained drivers lose their skill after drinking.

Week 4: In a mock court with real magistrates, police and lawyers, the probationers sit alongside magistrates to pass sentences.

Week 5: Health education.

Week 6: How to say 'No' to a drink.

Week 7: A drinker's diary, listing a week's consumption.

Week 8: Alcohol questionnaire, alcohol responsibility, your goal, and control.

This is intended to be a *living* 'guide to action'. Therefore, it needs to be revised and added to in the light of local needs and local experience.

The following two pages are for jotting down examples of good practice, and addresses relevant to the issues covered by this chapter.

We hope to update the guide, and would be delighted to receive any advice about corrections, new material or any other information which should go into the next edition. Please send all suggestions, before 31 December, 1987, to:

> Philip Tether and David Robinson
> Addiction Research Centre
> University of Hull
> Hull HU6 7RX

Examples of Good Practice

Useful Addresses and Telephone Numbers

Further reading

British Medical Association, *Alcohol, Drugs and Driving*, BMA, London, 1984

Christian Economic and Social Research Foundation, *Chief Constables' Reports: England and Wales; and Scotland: 1984 Drink Offences*, 32nd Annual Report, 1985. Available from the Christian Economic and Social Research Foundation, 19 Bethell Avenue, Ilford, Essex IG1 4UX

Clayton, A.B., Booth, A.C., and McCarthy, P.E., *A Controlled Study of the Role of Alcohol in Fatal Adult Pedestrian Accidents*, Transport and Road Research Laboratory, Supplementary Report 332, 1977. Available from Accident Investigation Division, Safety Department Transport and Road Research Laboratory, Crowthorne, Berks.

Clayton, A.B., McCarthy, P.E., and Breen, J.M., *The Male Drinking Driver, Characteristics of the Offender and His Offence*, TRRL, Supp. Report 600, 1980

Collins, J.J., *Drinking and Crime*, Tavistock, London, 1982

Cook, T., Gath, D., and Hensman, C. (eds), *The Drunkenness Offence*, Pergamon, London, 1969

Department of the Environment, *Drinking and Driving*, report of the Departmental (Blennerhassett) Committee, HMSO, London, 1976

Dunbar, J., Ogston, S., Ritchie, A., Devgun, M., Hagart, J., and Martin, B., 'Are Problem Drinkers Dangerous Drivers? The Tayside Safe Driving Project', *British Medical Journal*, vol. 290, March 1985

Heard, P.F., *Drunkenness Cautioning: A Way Forward for Whom?* unpublished dissertation submitted in part fulfilment of the degree of MSc in Health Administration, University of Hull, 1984

Hershon, H., Cook, T., and Foldes, P.A., 'What Shall We Do With the Drunken Offender?', *British Journal of Psychiatry*, vol. 124, 1974

Home Office Working Party Report, *Habitual Drunken Offenders*, HMSO, London, 1971

Jeffs, B.W. and Saunders, W.M., 'Minimizing Alcohol Related Offences by Enforcement of the Existing Licensing Legislation', *British Journal of Addiction*, 78, 1983

Priors, M., *Offenders, Deviants or Patients*, Tavistock Publications, London, 1979

Raffles, M., (ed.), *Medical Aspects of Fitness to Drive: A Guide for*

Medical Practitioners, Medical Commission on Accident Prevention, London, 1978

Riley, D., *Drivers' Beliefs about Alcohol and the Law*, Home Office Research and Planning Unit, 1984

Robertson, I.H. and Heather, N., 'An Alcohol Education Course for Young Offenders', *British Journal on Alcohol and Alcoholism*, 7, 1, 1982

Sabey, B.E. and Staughton, G.C., *The Drinking Road User in Great Britain*, TRRL, Supp. Report 616, 1980

Smith, R., *Prison Health Care*, British Medical Association, London, 1984

Taylor, N.L., *Doctors and the Law*, Oyez Publishing, London, 1976

West, L.H.T. and Hore, T. (eds), *An Analysis of Drink Driving Research*, Higher Education Advisory and Research Unit, Monash, 1980

Index

315

research: being sceptical 240; by
professionals 239–47; evaluation 243–
44; for good casework 241; for inter-
organizational contact 242; for intra-
organizational efficiency 241–42;
information about practice context 242;
keeping records 241; tools for 244–47;
what is it? 240–41
Retail Fruit Trade Federation 176
Riley, D. 300
Road Accidents – Great Britain 102
Road Safety Advisory Committee 104, 105
road safety and alcohol: and community
initiatives 107–09; and work 106–07; car
design 104–05; driving schools 105–06;
local action 104–09; pedestrian safety
105; problem size 103–04
Road Safety Education Unit, University of
Reading 163, 201
Road Safety Officers 105
Road Traffic Act, 1967 102–03, 296
Road Traffic Act, 1972 301, 304
Road Traffic Act, 1974 301
Robertson, Ian 35, 245
Roman Catholic Church 261, 263, 264,
265; Alcohol and Drugs Working Party
(of The Social Welfare Committee)
263, 265; Social Welfare Committee
263, 265
RoSPA 97, 98, 99, 100, 101, 106, 128, 163,
164, 173, 174, 200, 201, 202, 211, 269;
Drinking and Driving Booklets for
Various Groups 106, 128, 164, 202, 269;
Home and Leisure Safety Division 92,
98, 99, 100; National Occupational
Health and Safety Committee 174;
National Water Safety Committee 98;
Occupational Health Safety Groups
Advisory Committee (OHSGAC) 174;
Occupational Safety Division 174;
Road Safety Division 106, 164, 202;
Safety Education Department 97, 211;
Water Safety Department 100, 101
Rounds 200
Royal Colleges, The 224
Royal College of Midwifery Centres 228
Royal College of Midwives 228
Royal College of Nursing (RCN) 38, 173,
226, 228
Royal College of Nursing Centres 228
Royal College of Psychiatrists 28
Royal Life Saving Society (RLSS) 99
Rules of the Game 200

'safe' limits 28–9
Safety Education Journal 97
Sallon, J. 14
Samaritans 257–60; alcohol education for
260; structure 259; training 259–60
Savile, J., OBE 203
School Curriculum Development
Committee (SCDC) 210
School Traffic Education Programme
(STEP) 202

schools: alcohol education in 190–91, 207–
11; curriculum development 210;
education advisors 207–08; education
inspectorate 208; governors and PTAs
210–211; health education coordinators
191, 198; teachers' and professional
centres 209
Schools Council, The 198, 199, 210
Scottish Association for Counselling 37
Scottish Marriage Guidance Council 261
Scottish Health Education Group 35, 161,
246
Scriptographic Publications Ltd 32
Secondary Examination Council 210
Sensible Drinking 162
Shaw, M. 203
'shop-within-a-shop' policy 133–34
Simnett, I. 34
Smirnoff 59
Social Enquiry Reports (SERs) 290, 291,
295
Social Services Committees 231–32
social workers: alcohol education for 229–
38; contacts in social services 231;
contacts with trainers of 230–31; CQSW
229; CSS 229–30; counselling and 236;
materials and information for 232–36
Society of Health Education Officers 92
Society of St Vincent de Paul 265
So You Know All About Drink Do You?
293
*So You Want To Cut Down On Your
Drinking?* 35, 245
Sports Council 69, 74
sports sponsorship: Advisory Service 69,
72; and alcohol 72–4; a two way deal 69;
growth of 69, 72–3; guidelines for 70–1;
local action on 74; spending on 72;
television and 70–1
Star Rider 202
Stevens and Hall Ltd 107, 159
Strathclyde Firemaster 94
Suggestions For Traffic Offence Penalties
306–07

Tavistock Institute of Human Relations
102
Taylor, N.L. 302
Tayside Safe Driving Project 304, 305
Teaching About Alcohol Problems 34, 221,
232
Teachers' Advisory Council on Alcohol
and Drug Education (TACADE) 31,
32, 34, 162–63, 196, 197, 199, 209, 235
Teenagers and Traffic 163, 200, 201
television: and alcohol advertising 65–68;
and presentation of alcohol 75–78; and
sports sponsorship 70–71
Television Programme Gui ˈines 71, 76,
78
Tetley Bittermen 60
That's The Limit 34–5, 206
The Advertising Of Food and Drink 67, 68
The Big Book 269